The Downfall of Hitler

The Downfall of Hitler

His Personal, Military and Social Failures

Michael FitzGerald

AN IMPRINT OF PEN & SWORD BOOKS LTD.
YORKSHIRE – PHILADELPHIA

First published in Great Britain in 2024 by
Pen & Sword History
An imprint of
Pen & Sword Books Ltd
Yorkshire - Philadelphia

ISBN 978 1 39907 989 1

A CIP catalogue record for this book is available from the British Library

Typeset in INDIA by IMPEC eSolutions
Printed and bound in the UK by CPI Group (UK) Ltd, Croydon, CRO 4YY

Pen & Sword Books Ltd. incorporates the Imprints of Pen & Sword Archaeology, Atlas, Aviation, Battleground, Discovery, Family History, History, Maritime, Military, Naval, Politics, Railways, Select, Transport, True Crime, Fiction, Frontline Books, Leo Cooper, Praetorian Press, Seaforth Publishing, Wharncliffe, White Owl and After the Battle.

For a complete list of Pen & Sword titles please contact
PEN & SWORD BOOKS LIMITED
47 Church Street, Barnsley, South Yorkshire S70 2AS, United Kingdom
E-mail: enquiries@pen-and-sword.co.uk
Website: www.pen-and-sword.co.uk

or

PEN AND SWORD BOOKS
1950 Lawrence Rd, Havertown, PA 19083, USA
E-mail: Uspen-and-sword@casematepublishers.com
Website: www.penandswordbooks.com

Contents

Introduction

If Hitler had died in August 1939 he would have been regarded as a great if ruthless leader. The Second World War laid bare every one of his personal failings and demonstrated his unfitness for high office.

Even though he failed he remains one of the biggest and most extraordinary leaders in world history. The war brought to the forefront character defects that had been hidden during the years of peace. These personal faults were the primary reason for his failure.

His lack of vision made him unable to see the bigger picture. He remained obsessed with pet projects to the exclusion of more fundamental measures that would have improved matters and particularly have altered the course of the war for the better.

His narcissism prevented him from taking advice and particularly from listening to more cautious counsel or unwelcome news. His inability to listen robbed him of the chance to adopt better courses of action.

Hitler's megalomania made him believe that he was always right and he consistently refused to consider the possibility he might be in error. Any failures were never his fault but always the result of the mistakes or inadequacies of other people. He surrounded himself with yes-men and displayed misplaced loyalty towards old comrades who were completely unsuitable to hold public office. Hitler had no close friends with the courage to tell him unpalatable truths. His poor choice of advisers greatly handicapped both the everyday running of the country and the prosecution of the war.

His indecisiveness had a paralyzing effect on the direction of government which was a problem in peacetime but became a major handicap once his country was at war. By contrast he was often impatient and impulsive when a course of action was undertaken which meant that it was either rushed or instigated prematurely.

His laziness held up both the everyday business of the Reich and the planning of the war. At times important decisions were held up often for weeks while Hitler refused to be disturbed. This had particularly disastrous consequences in terms of Dunkirk and D-Day.

His cowardice made him unwilling to face the people of Germany when they were being bombed or to visit his troops who were suffering huge privations on the Russian Front. Instead he sent Goebbels and other Ministers to try to rouse the spirits of the people while remaining hidden away from public gaze.

His lack of attention to detail meant that crucial aspects of a situation or problems arising from a plan were overlooked or dismissed. He increasingly failed to recognize that the high casualties incurred in the course of the war meant that an intense focus on the smallest aspect of a problem or strategy needed to be pursued.

His inflexibility meant that lives were lost needlessly through his refusal to follow a different strategy in the light of events. He was incapable of seeing that sometimes a policy of retreat and retrenchment was necessary and insisted on attack at all costs regardless of the situation or the available resources.

His anti-intellectualism meant that he failed to grasp scientific and technical developments that could have changed the outcome of the war. This was particularly true in terms of the atomic bomb where at one stage Germany was ahead of the Allies in nuclear research and in terms of other scientific advances that would have greatly assisted his nation.

All these factors combined with a series of poor military, political and economic mistakes to make it impossible for him to achieve his aims. They were challenging but if he had acted differently could have come to fruition.

The seeds of Hitler's ultimate defeat were sown in his youth. He failed at school, failed to gain recognition as an artist and at one point in his life sank so low that he was reduced to sleeping on park benches. In spite of this – perhaps partly *because* of it – he indulged in increasingly fantastic delusions of grandeur. August Kubizek, one of his few close friends during his youth, recorded how excited he became both at performances of Wagner's operas and when watching the mass street demonstrations of the Social Democrats in Vienna.[1] Both Wagner and these processions exercised a decisive influence on Hitler's future development.

During his formative years Hitler's grandiose vision of himself was constantly contradicted by the reality of his existence. Instead of being recognised and admired he was ignored and despised. This contrast between his dreams and the world outside gnawed away at him and led to an increasingly bitter outlook on life.

When he eventually came to power these personal flaws proved disastrous. In spite of genuine achievements – ending unemployment, introducing 'green' policies, restoring the sense of national pride – his inflexibility, dogmatism, arrogance and inability to consider other points of view ultimately resulted in the catastrophic downfall of his country and his own suicide.

The question remains – was his failure inevitable? Were his fantasies of world domination capable of being realised? The standard answer is that they were not but if different decisions had been taken at crucial times it is by no means certain that Hitler's projects were doomed from the start. His plans were grandiose and ambitious but not incapable of realization. This book examines both his personal failings and the series of misjudgements and blunders that led to the destruction of his dreams.

The Dark Dreamer

Even in his youth Hitler displayed many negative aspects of his character. He seethed with a mixture of sullen resentment and a sense of entitlement that remained with him all his life. Much of this stems from his upbringing in a small provincial town with a strict – even brutal – father and a mother who indulged his every whim.[1] At his elementary school he did well and was one of the leading pupils but when he commenced his secondary education it was a different story. In almost every subject he performed poorly and twice had to retake examinations to continue at the school. Only in gymnastics was he regarded as exceptional and he struggled with both French and mathematics. He hated learning French and described it later as "a waste of time."[2]

Hitler spent much of his time playing Cowboys and Indians or drawing and painting. He was obsessed with Westerns and particularly enjoyed the novels of James Fenimore Cooper and Karl May, the leading German writer of Western fiction. During the First World War, on one occasion he had to deliver a message under heavy fire and successfully used a technique he had read about in his Western novels.

Hitler had genuine talent as an artist but his dilettante approach to life and lack of discipline meant he was unable to produce constructive results. His family tried to get him to follow a trade and an attempt was made to apprentice him as a baker but he flatly refused.[3]

In his primary school Hitler was fascinated by Catholic ritual. He became a choir boy and was said to have a fine singing voice. For a while he contemplated becoming a priest but this aspiration soon faded, particularly after he was caught smoking and reprimanded.[4]

Hitler may have abandoned thoughts of a clerical life but the effect of ritual on the observer was not lost on him. Later he consciously incorporated religious trappings into Nazi ceremonies. The Nuremberg rallies became like religious services.

Hitler's political thinking began in his youth. His father was a proud Austrian and a staunch supporter of the Habsburg monarchy. By contrast, most of Hitler's school friends were Pan-Germans who rejected the idea of a separate Austrian Empire and wished for all German speakers to be united in a great German Reich.[5] To the anger of his father, Hitler shared their convictions.

Further fuel for his nationalism was provided by Wagner's operas. At the age of 12 he attended a performance of *Lohengrin* at the Linz Opera House and became a lifelong devotee. Wagner's German nationalism inspired the young Hitler though at this stage in his life he did not share the composer's racism.[6]

His secondary schooling fluctuated with a string of poor results leading ultimately to a narrow pass but his school was so dissatisfied with his attitude and application that eventually they told him he would have to complete his studies elsewhere. This would have meant a considerable journey to and from his home and as he had already contracted a respiratory infection he used this as an excuse to abandon education altogether. His decision to leave without obtaining the *Abitur* – the school certificate – had serious consequences for him over the next few years.[7]

In the meantime he made one of the few close friendships in the course of his life. The young August Kubizek was the son of an upholsterer and his father intended him to follow the same trade. Having discovered Kubizek's musical talent Hitler urged him not to adopt that line of work but to concentrate on his music.

Kubizek describes how throughout their friendship Hitler was always the dominant force and he the passive one. Hitler would talk and Kubizek listened; Hitler would issue commands and Kubizek would obey. It was a one-sided relationship in which Hitler led and his friend followed.[8] Even at this early stage of his life Hitler's narcissism and self-centeredness were clearly apparent.

On the death of his father Hitler felt free at last. He threw himself into his art and general self-indulgence. After drifting for a while he told his mother that he planned to follow a career as an art student in Vienna. She was cool towards the idea but her son persuaded her to agree. The result was that Hitler and his friend Kubizek set off for Vienna, Hitler in hopes of studying art and Kubizek of becoming a music student.[9]

They made a preparatory visit to the city and Hitler fell in love with the architecture and the museums. He was highly critical of some of the buildings and told Kubizek endlessly of how he could 'improve' the city. Hitler even drew detailed diagrams of his proposed town planning for Vienna. Then, having decided that they liked the idea of moving to Vienna, they returned to Linz.

It was at this time that Hitler formed his first romantic attachment. This turned out to be a dismal failure where Hitler did not even have the confidence to initiate contact with the woman who had caught his eye. The girl in question was Stefanie Isak, a young woman who has been mistakenly called Stefanie Jansten. Stefanie was not Jewish by faith although Hitler may have assumed she was on the basis of her name. He used to watch her walking out with her mother from a safe distance without ever approaching her directly.

She had no idea that Hitler was besotted with her until many years later and in spite of his friend Kubizek's suggestion that he should introduce himself to her Hitler never summoned up the courage to do so. One of his last acts in Linz was to send Stefanie an unsigned love letter. She never knew the identity of its writer and was astonished when, years later, she discovered that her secret admirer had been Adolf Hitler. Stefanie married an officer in the Austrian army and Hitler never saw her again.[10]

In the light of Hitler's other relationships with women she might be considered to have had a fortunate escape. Six of the women who became involved with Hitler tried to commit suicide and three of them succeeded in killing themselves.

Soon after, Hitler returned to Vienna and once more applied to be admitted to one of the art schools in the city. Yet again he was unsuccessful. On taking the entrance examination for the Academy of Fine Arts in Vienna he received a crushing verdict on his work. "Test drawing unsatisfactory." When Hitler queried their decision they told him that "my ability obviously lay in the field of architecture."[11]

Hitler then made enquiries about admission to the School of Architecture but was informed that to gain admission he needed a diploma from the School of Building and to enter that he needed his *Abitur*. Once more Hitler's failure to complete his education created problems.

Kubizek passed the entrance examination for the Academy of Music and was astonished by Hitler's reaction. Instead of congratulating his friend he became extremely moody. Kubizek wrote that "Adolf had become unbalanced" and "he would fly into a temper at the slightest thing. He was at odds with the world. Wherever he looked he saw injustice, hate and enmity."[12] Eventually Hitler told Kubizek about his rejection and his friend asked him what he would do now. Hitler smiled, sat in a chair and began reading. He assured his friend that things would turn out all right in the end.

Vienna made Hitler increasingly arrogant, bitter and moody. The young schoolboy who had been so popular – "we all liked him" was the memory of one of his fellow pupils[13] – was now a sullen, brooding, apathetic dilettante. As he sunk lower and lower in terms of his everyday life his grandiosity grew greater. From dreams of becoming a great artist he fantasised about writing operas, designing cities and, in a confused and unsystematic way, entering a career in politics.[14]

Hitler's failure to realise any of his dreams led to a growing awareness that he could not continue to live the carefree life he had enjoyed. Money problems were becoming acute in spite of his increasingly desperate attempts to economise. Kubizek describes how he frequently lived on bread and milk. Eventually it became obvious to Hitler that he had been living beyond his means and needed to retrench drastically.

It was at this point that Hitler abruptly terminated his friendship with Kubizek. He gave no explanation or even a farewell but simply vanished. Though Kubizek did not know what had happened, Hitler disappeared into the underbelly of Vienna.

Initially the weather was warm and he slept on park benches or in the doorways of shops. As the nights grew cold he recognised that he needed to find shelter. His solution to his economic problems was to live on charity. He booked into a men's hostel where he mixed primarily with down-and-outs. Here he continued to draw and paint but with no outlet for his productions became increasingly frustrated. Some of the inmates at the hostel describe how he sat in a corner quietly and exploded suddenly into furious bursts of anger.

There is no doubt that his time in Vienna had a decisive influence on Hitler's thinking and in some respects laid the foundation for his future. In spite of the highly selective version of events that Hitler presents in *Mein Kampf*, on the whole his account of those formative years has been shown to be relatively accurate.

The first hostel in which he stayed was insalubrious and not congenial in any way to the young drifter with his unrealistic expectations of life. Hitler was furious that his clothes were removed for delousing, but this was standard practice at the hostel and in view of Hitler's own penurious existence for the last few months he could hardly object. He also found the regime at the first men's hostel to be uncongenial to his Bohemian preferences.

During his stay at the hostel he was at least fed and sheltered. He also struck up a friendship with another hostel dweller, an enterprising inmate by the name of Reinhold Hanisch.[15] At first Hitler cleared snow from the streets or carried luggage but his health was so poor that he was forced to abandon those activities. When jobs for ditch digging were offered Hitler thought about applying but Hanisch told him he was incapable of any arduous physical labour.

When Hanisch discovered that Hitler was an artist he suggested that he should paint some pictures which he would sell on his behalf. Hitler responded with the gloomy news that he had not only been forced to sell all his good clothes but also his paints and brushes. Hanisch suggested writing to his family for money and Hitler contacted his Aunt Johanna who sent him a fifty kronen note. (The krone was the currency of Austria until 1925 when it was replaced by the schilling.) The exultant Hitler held it aloft as he stood in line waiting to be readmitted to the hostel. Hanisch immediately warned him to hide the note or he would be robbed.

Hitler used his aunt's money to buy a winter coat. He also moved to a superior men's hostel. This was cleaner, more modern and more welcoming to the inhabitants. Four days later Hanisch joined him and persuaded Hitler to produce postcard-size pictures. He was successful in selling Hitler's work but knew that larger scale pictures would make more money so encouraged Hitler to paint water-colours. Hitler was soon producing a painting every day.

In this hostel Hitler made two new friends, both Jewish. One was a locksmith called Robinson and the other a part-time art dealer called Josef Neumann. Neumann and Hitler became particularly close and he gave Hitler a long frock coat. Hitler described Neumann as "a very decent man."[16]

Hitler's love of art was beginning to take second place to a growing interest in politics. His views were neither systematic nor consistent. Hitler hated the monarchy, aristocracy and landlords but in spite of his admiration for the Social Democratic massed processions he was contemptuous of the party. His Pan-Germanism also angered some of the other inmates and his mixture of left and right wing views confused them.

In many ways this lack of consistency persisted throughout his life. Hitler was never an ideological politician and this lack of a fixed viewpoint came to be both a strength and a weakness in the course of his rule.

It was at this time that he discovered the racist ideas of Adolf Lanz. Hitler read his magazine *Ostara* which introduced him to the notion that the Jews were responsible for all the evils of the world and that Aryans were a noble race of supermen born to rule over "inferior races." This dark vision excited Hitler who began to think that he might be a failure on an individual level but at least he belonged to the "Master Race."[17]

The consequences of this fantasy were unimportant until Hitler became Chancellor of Germany. From that point on he relentlessly persecuted the Jews and ultimately sought their annihilation.

In spite of his exposure to Lanz's views Hitler showed no signs of anti-Semitism before 1919. Most of his favourite singers and actors were Jewish and as well as Wagner and Beethoven he enjoyed the music of Mendelssohn and Mahler. He and Neumann became so friendly that they left the hostel and planned to relocate to Germany. This scheme never got off the ground and instead they spent a few days self-indulging in Vienna before returning to the hostel considerably poorer.[18] This was a typical example both of Hitler's impulsiveness and his frequent habit of starting a project but failing to follow it through to completion.

In spite of this abortive attempt, Hitler was growing tired of hostel life and dreamed of a new start in Germany. He had become popular with the other inmates and they were sorry to see him go. Karl Honisch (another hostel inmate who in spite of the similarity of their names is not to be confused with Hanisch) described him as "a friendly and charming person" and as "goodhearted and helpful." After his departure Honisch remarked "we lost a good comrade with him; he understood everyone and helped whenever he could,"[19]

Hitler was growing tired of Vienna, of Hanisch's pressure to produce his art and of the men's hostel. He decided to pursue his dream of living in Germany. By now he had enough funds to leave the hostel and travelled to Munich with an unnamed friend, probably Neumann.[20]

His time in Munich laid the foundations for his subsequent career although at the time – 1913 – there seemed no realistic prospect of a future in politics.

Munich in 1913 was second only to Paris as a cultural centre. He took lodgings with the Popp family which he vastly preferred to the men's hostel. Hitler lived in Schwabing, the "artist's quarter" of the city. He hoped to be more successful in selling his art in Munich but with no contacts he found it harder than in Vienna. He was often reduced to hawking his work in bars or even knocking door to door.

Gradually Hitler found acceptance among the artistic community of Schwabing but continued to struggle financially. He was a frequent visitor to cafes where he talked endlessly about art and politics. He also visited libraries where for the first time he studied Marxism. His landlady described how Hitler "camped in his room like a hermit with his nose stuck in those thick, heavy books and worked and studied from morning to night."[21]

In spite of his new interest in Marxism Hitler remained a Pan-Germanist. He saw no contradiction between the two positions and in many ways this period of his life saw him begin to evolve the philosophy of "National Socialism." What he objected to in the Social Democrat and Communist Parties, at least at this time, was their internationalism. All his life Hitler hated monarchy and aristocracy and the 'socialist' side of National Socialism asserted itself throughout his career.

Even at this stage of his life he still found it difficult to listen. Again and again Hitler argued with his acquaintances and refused even to consider the possibility that he might be wrong. This trait manifested itself throughout his life and had disastrous consequences once he became Chancellor of Germany. This insistence that he was always right and that dissenting opinions were wrong robbed him of many opportunities to take a wiser course of action.

When the First World War broke out Hitler volunteered with a Bavarian regiment and served in Belgium and France. This showed yet another of Hitler's personal defects – his lack of empathy. When war was declared Hitler was exultant and though his reaction at the time was typical of many others, he showed no signs of war weariness. Men like Owen, Rosenberg and Sassoon were moved to write poems full of anger and compassion whereas Hitler remained unmoved by the squalor and slaughter around him. His letters to his landlord and landlady show no sense of the horror of the war, still less any desire for the fighting to end. As the campaign dragged on, casualties rose and new recruits arrived at the front. Hitler became involved in angry exchanges with them, on one occasion having a fight where both men took tremendous punishment but Hitler emerged on top.[22] He saw their lack of enthusiasm for the war as signs of cowardice and defeatism.

Only twice during the war did Hitler express sorrow and in both cases it was because of a personal loss. The first occasion was when a railway worker stole his dog Fuchsl and the second was when his paints and brushes were stolen by another soldier. Throughout the war Hitler showed not a trace of pity or even regret at the human suffering. Only when he experienced a personal loss did he become gloomy. This is one of many examples of his narcissism and lack of empathy.

As a soldier Hitler was brave though at times his conduct was reckless and impulsive. He was one of the few NCOs awarded the Iron Cross First Class during the war. For all his bravery he was one of those who in the words of Wilfred Owen:

> "By choice they made themselves immune
> To pity and whatever moans in man."[23]

1918 saw the last German offensive. Russia had pulled out of the war and Ludendorff threw everything against the Allies on the Western Front. Their lines buckled and bent but did not break. Soon they counter-attacked and the Germans began to retreat.

At this crucial moment in the war Hitler was gassed. Transported to a hospital in Germany, he was unaware of the growing collapse of the German army. He was however aware of the growing anti-war sentiment in Germany and the beginning of strikes that ultimately led to a revolution later that year.

This period of his life has been the subject of much speculation. There is no doubt that Hitler's account in *Mein Kampf* is almost entirely fictitious. It has not helped that some historians have either taken Hitler's version of events more or less at face value while others have too readily accepted the gloss put on that period of Hitler's life by Marxists. The truth is more complex and perhaps more disturbing.

One theory is that he was not gassed at all which is demonstrably false as six other members of his group were gassed at the same time. Hitler's account in *Mein Kampf* is highly dubious, not so much in terms of his description of his illness but because he pretended that it led him to "realize" that the Jews were responsible for all the troubles of the world and that it marked the beginning of his sense of "mission."[24] His claims are false on both points. He showed no signs of anti-Semitism until 1919 and was an active and enthusiastic supporter of Soviet Bavaria and its overwhelmingly Jewish leadership. Far from having any sense of "mission" or "destiny" Hitler drifted until the fall of the Soviet republic.

It has been suggested – and that was the verdict of the doctor who examined him initially – that his temporary blindness was hysterical rather than the result of his gassing when in fact it is a common symptom of exposure to mustard gas.[25] Hitler may well have been hysterical – in 1918 there was hardly any recognition of shell shock or similar battle traumas – but his temporary blindness certainly had an organic rather than psychological origin.

Another claim has been made that Hitler was hypnotized into becoming a German nationalist, an anti-Semite and anti-Communist. There is no doubt that the psychiatrist treating him used hypnosis – among other forms of treatment – but Hitler was already an ardent Pan-German and needed no hypnotist to push him in that direction. As for the claims that the doctor hypnotized him into anti-Semitism and anti-Communism, they are totally at variance with the facts. The doctor was Jewish and so hardly likely to encourage anti-Semitism. If he tried to inculcate anti-Communism in Hitler his attempt was spectacularly unsuccessful as events showed during the Soviet Bavaria period.

It has been suggested by an American psychoanalyst that Hitler's anti-Semitism dated from this period. His theory is that Hitler associated his gassing with the iodoform treatment given to his mother by her Jewish doctor. Hitler therefore blamed him for his mother's death and projected an image of Germany as representing his mother and being brought down by Jews.[26]

This is contradicted by all the available evidence. Hitler always spoke warmly of Dr. Bloch, the physician who treated his mother, and described him as "a noble Jew." Not only did he not persecute Bloch once he became Chancellor but – entirely untypical of the fate of other Jews – allowed him to leave with all his money.[27]

It cannot be stressed too much that there is *no* evidence of anti-Semitic utterances or behaviour by Hitler before 1919, long after his release from hospital.

Hitler allegedly had a vision while he was hospitalized in which he "saw" that the Jews were the secret rulers of the world and had conspired to destroy Germany. There are various versions of this vision, the best known being in *Mein Kampf.* All need to be treated with suspicion as attempts to project Hitler's anti-Semitism further back in time than was the case. Whether or not Hitler genuinely had a "vision" it certainly did *not* influence his thinking or behaviour for the next few months.

Hitler's account of what happened next is blatantly false. Germany was in chaos and revolution broke out in Berlin, Saxony and even Bavaria. The abdication of the Kaiser saw the last Imperial Chancellor hand over power to the Social Democrat leader Fritz Ebert. Ebert was stunned at the catastrophe and incapable of taking decisive action.

In Munich the Jewish radical Kurt Eisner seized power. This event marked the beginning of what became known as Soviet Bavaria.[28] Hitler, who had been irresolute and depressed following his discharge from hospital, suddenly found a cause. Nor was it, as he dishonestly pretended in *Mein Kampf*, to overthrow the new regime. Hitler became an active supporter of Eisner and Soviet Bavaria.

The whole affair demonstrated clearly how – for all his wartime bravery – there was a part of Hitler that remained cowardly. Technically he was still a soldier and though army discipline was breaking down and thousands of soldiers were joining the revolutionaries, if Hitler truly *had* been against Soviet Bavaria he could have laid low or even joined counter-revolutionary organizations like the Thule Group. Hitler did neither of those things and was elected to a Soldiers' Council and actively supported the rebellion.

Eisner introduced a number of social reforms which Hitler approved. Then elections were held and centrist parties won a majority. Eisner decided to quit but while he was travelling to the *Landtag* to deliver his letter of resignation he was assassinated.

Hitler admired Eisner greatly and his admiration for the fallen leader probably dated back to his first year in Munich. Eisner had been the editor of the Social Democratic newspaper but was considered insufficiently fanatical by his editorial board. He moved to Schwabing, the same part of Munich where Hitler lived. More earnest comrades described Eisner contemptuously as a "Schwabing Bolshevik." In their eyes he was a dilettante and art lover rather than a serious revolutionary.[29] Hitler was still serving on the Soldiers' Council and attended Eisner's funeral, an event that was captured both on film and in a still photograph. He wore a black mourning band and a red band indicating his support for the government.[30]

The result of Eisner's assassination was chaos which led to another revolution where the Socialists and Communists took supreme power. They elected the Socialist Johannes Hoffmann as Eisner's successor but it soon became apparent to the radicals that Hoffmann was a moderate. The result was yet another revolution in which Hoffmann fled to Bamberg in Northern Bavaria while the poet Ernst Toller became the new leader.

Toller was a dreamer full of romantic notions and proved completely incapable of holding the movement together. For all his vision and likeability he neglected practical politics.[31] After six days he was overthrown in turn by hard-line Bolsheviks led by the Russian Jew Eugen Leviné.[32]

Leviné was ruthless and crushed opposition by force. Summary executions and confiscation of property became the norm. Hoffman tried to break into the city with loyal troops but his attack was repulsed. Ironically it was Toller, riding on a horse, who commanded the Soviet forces and drove Hoffman's army back.

The result was more repression and executions in Munich. Hoffmann appealed to the national government for help. The Defence Minister, Gustav Noske, sent a mixture of regular troops and *Freikorps* units to suppress the revolution. The *Freikorps* – Free Corps – was a body consisting principally of former soldiers. They were utterly brutal in their methods and killed or beat numerous innocent people along with the revolutionaries.

In addition to Hitler himself Julius Schreck, his future chauffeur and the first leader of the SS, was an active and enthusiastic member of the "Red Army." Schreck signed up and served as a member of the Red Army in late April 1919.[33] Balthasar Brandmayer, one of Hitler's closest wartime friends, remarked "how he at first welcomed the end of the monarchies" and the establishment of the republic in Bavaria.[34] Once again the accounts of both Hitler and some of his political opponents are at variance with the available facts.

Hitler engaged in the defence of the "Red Republic" against the Freikorps and federal troops and was arrested for firing on them when they entered the city. Fortunately for him he was recognized by soldiers who had served with him during the war and was set free.

At this point Hitler demonstrated both his dishonesty and cowardice. He denied being involved with Soviet Bavaria and claimed that he had tried to infiltrate and subvert the revolutionaries. He proceeded to betray many former comrades and was rewarded by being sent on a training course by the army.

Hitler was subjected to a series of lectures and other methods of indoctrination designed to produce a nationalist and conservative orientation in German soldiers. One of the lectures turned out to be a decisive influence both on Hitler's ideology and his future political career. Gottfried Feder gave a lecture on economics that profoundly affected Hitler. It was an attack on capitalism and particularly what Feder called "interest slavery." Feder was anti-Jewish but not a fanatical anti-Semite. He believed that capitalism – which he tended to refer to as "high finance" – was run by the Jews and therefore he wanted to eliminate their influence.

Hitler's reaction to Feder's talk was curious. He rushed home and began re-reading Karl Marx, particularly *Das Kapital*. The fact that he saw no contradiction between Marx's anti-capitalism and the conservative attitudes of the German army is revealing. It shows how confused Hitler's thinking was and how he had still not adopted the fully-fledged version of anti-Semitism and anti-Communism that became his hallmarks. Feder's talk reinforced anti-Semitic attitudes but only to a degree.

Not long after Hitler heard Feder's talk blaming the Jews for capitalism he read a pamphlet by Dietrich Eckart. Eckart was a fanatical anti-Semite and blamed the Jews for everything – capitalism, Communism, socialism, liberalism and above all for Germany's defeat in the war. Hitler's views were still in transition at that time but Eckart's words had a powerful effect upon him and tilted him further towards a more extreme anti-Semitism.

During his courses Hitler found himself under the tutelage of Captain Karl Mayr. Before long he began speaking and one of his instructors, Alexander von Müller, told Mayr: "one of your men is a born orator."[35] Mayr then listened to Hitler speaking and agreed.[36]

The result was that Hitler was recruited as a V-man, an undercover agent for German military intelligence. His job was to investigate a number of political groups in Bavaria. One of these meetings turned out to be the decisive moment in his transformation from drifter to politician and world leader.

When Hitler attended a meeting of the DAP (German Workers' Party) he was deeply disappointed. There were only a handful of people present and the atmosphere was more like a private club than a political party. The main speaker at the meeting was Feder who again delivered a talk on capitalism and singled out the Jews as its prime movers.

What turned out to be a crucial moment in the meeting was in the discussion following the talk. A member of the audience stood up and demanded the independence of Bavaria and the restoration of its former monarchy. This incensed Hitler who launched into a rant that so impressed the party leader that he whispered to his colleague: "My God, he's got the gift of the gab. We could use him."

The two leaders of the party were Anton Drexler, a railway worker, and Karl Harrer, a sports writer. Most of the party's members were Drexler's fellow railwaymen. It was Drexler who chased after Hitler when the meeting finished and handed him a copy of his pamphlet *Meine Politisches Erwachene* – My Political Awakening. He also obtained Hitler's address and sent him a membership card in the post. In spite of his subsequent lies in *Mein Kampf* Hitler was *not* the seventh member of the party but the seventh member of its steering committee. He was actually party member 55.

Hitler read Drexler's pamphlet with interest and was impressed. He then agonized over whether or not to accept the invitation to join the party, yet another example of his indecisiveness. He reported back to Mayr who in turn asked Ludendorff for advice. Ludendorff urged him to persuade Hitler to join the fledgling party.

Once Hitler became a party member he soon met Eckart who until then he had only known from his pamphlet. The result was mutual admiration for each other. Eckart became a mentor to Hitler on numerous levels, giving him better clothes to wear, teaching him to use a knife and fork, making him less awkward in company and introducing him to people from a new social milieu as well as indoctrinating him in Eckart's own fanatical version of anti-Jewish prejudice.

Even at this stage Hitler's later political philosophy was not fully formed. Eckart and Feder were anti-Semites but also anti-capitalist and Hitler continued to display considerable signs of his former involvement with the "Red Republic." He actively sought out socialists and Communists, believing that they were the most likely group of people to embrace his evolving political philosophy. Eckart too, although he denounced what he called "Jewish Bolshevism", was so fiercely anti-capitalist that on one occasion when he was facing down some Communists they could not believe that a man so violently opposed to capitalism could be a political opponent and let him go.

This state of affairs was to change in the next few months. The Bolshevik Revolution led to a wholesale exodus of former conservatives from Russia many of whom brought with them a particularly vicious and extreme form of anti-Semitism and in particular the idea that Communism was a Jewish conspiracy. One of the most important and influential of these refugees was Alfred Rosenberg, a German exile from Estonia.

Like Eckart, Rosenberg exercised a decisive influence on Hitler's thinking and future political development. Both men were very different characters and even their ideology was not entirely the same. They were both fanatical anti-Semites and were largely responsible for inculcating in Hitler an extreme and paranoid hatred of Jews. On the other hand, while Eckart continued to be ferociously anti-capitalist Rosenberg was much more conservative. Both men subscribed to bizarre racial mythologies about lost Aryan civilizations and Rosenberg also introduced Hitler to the notion that Freemasonry was a Jewish conspiracy.

It is almost impossible to overstate the influence of both men on Hitler, particularly Rosenberg. For the first six or seven years of the Nazi Party Hitler could reasonably be described as Rosenberg's mouthpiece.[37]

Before long Hitler was asked to reply to enquiries from soldiers. One concerned the "Jewish question" and in his reply Hitler, for the first time, declared that the only "solution" was the "*entfernung*" – removal – of the Jewish people from Germany. This of course implied forcible deportation which remained the preferred Nazi policy until 1941 when the persecution of the Jews turned into their systematic extermination.[38]

The influence of men like Eckart and Rosenberg was yet another example of Hitler's poor judgement of other people. Throughout his career he showed a consistent and almost always misplaced loyalty to "old comrades" from "the era of struggle." Rosenberg and Eckart were the first but by no means the last of the numerous bad advisors Hitler chose.

Another dubious figure from the early years of the party was Herrmann Esser. Although he came from a middle class background Esser was a crude and brutal thug. Esser was already a member of the DAP before Hitler joined and Drexler and Harrer found him a constant embarrassment. He was a notorious womanizer and utterly lacking in charm. On the other hand he was one of the party's best speakers and always to the forefront when it came to physical confrontations. Hitler continued to favour and promote this man who was entirely unsuitable to hold any kind of position of responsibility.[39]

By contrast Hitler was extremely wary of the Strasser brothers. The younger brother Otto was a brilliant speaker and like his brother Gregor, Hitler, Goebbels and several other early members of the Nazi Party, was a former Communist. Otto and Gregor were fiercely left-wing but also fervent German nationalists. How they came to join the Nazi Party is an interesting story. The brothers were listening to an address – in what Otto described as "broken German" – by Zinoviev, an emissary from Russia who was trying to win over the deeply divided German left-wing and drag it into the Communist camp. Apparently his speech infuriated many members who walked out in disgust. It certainly had that effect on the Strasser brothers. They were soon invited by Hitler to join the new party and while Gregor was enthusiastic Otto was more cautious. Eventually they capitulated and became Nazis. Both men were for a time among the chief assets that Hitler possessed but eventually Otto was driven into disillusioned exile and Gregor was murdered.[40]

Another early Nazi who was if possible even more repulsive than Esser was Julius Streicher. He was the most vicious anti-Semite of all the Nazi leaders. Streicher was a brutal thug who always appeared in public with a whip that he brandished as a weapon. Even as a young man it was said that he "restlessly wandered from place to place with a rucksack full of anti-Semitic books and pamphlets."[41] Although he led a small group of his own called the German Socialist Party, as soon as he heard Hitler speak Streicher not only joined the Nazis but merged his party with Hitler's.[42]

Streicher became notorious for his vulgarity, his sexual appetite and his general bad character. Even most senior Nazis loathed him but Hitler continued to protect him and show him favour. His newspaper *Der Stürmer* enjoyed a wide circulation and was devoted to visceral demonization of the Jews. Hitler admired Streicher's unquestioning loyalty and in spite of his utter incapacity for high office continued to reward him. He remarked:

> "*More than once Dietrich Eckart told me that Streicher was a schoolteacher, and a lunatic to boot, from many points of view. He always added that one could not hope for a triumph of National Socialism without giving one's support to men like Streicher.*"[43]

Robert Ley was not one of the earliest Nazis but after he read Hitler's speech at his trial when the Munich putsch failed he was so impressed that he joined the Party. He soon became a loyal and devoted acolyte of Hitler and in return Hitler ignored numerous complaints about his incompetence, alcoholism, arrogance and corruption. Ley came from a working class background and always favoured the socialist wing of the party but remained totally loyal to Hitler in any conflict within the Nazis. When the Nazis came to power Ley was put in charge of the huge Labour Front organization and though at first he achieved some success he was gradually moved to the sidelines.[44] Again Hitler preferred to give vast powers to Ministers who were incapable of performing their duties simply because of their loyalty to him. This was a mistake Hitler repeated time and time again.

Hans Frank was a 20-year-old law student when he heard Hitler speak. He was addressing an audience of 2000 people which was the largest crowd he had spoken to up to that time. At this meeting Hitler first introduced the twenty-five points of the party programme to the public. He spoke for two and a half hours and Frank believed that "if anyone could master the fate of Germany, Hitler was that man."[45]

Frank was a weak and inconsistent man whose one constant was his hero worship of Hitler. He claimed at different times to be resurrecting German Common Law, creating a new National Socialist legal system and to regard force as superior to any law. His vacillating character, detachment from reality and inability to see the appalling brutality over which he presided as Governor-General of Poland made him, like most of Hitler's ministers, completely unsuitable to hold a position of power.

Another example of Hitler's misplaced loyalty was Rudolf Hess. He was one of the few Nazi leaders for whom Hitler felt genuine affection, addressing him by the pet names Rudi and Hessrl. Hess was an early disciple but never shared his leader's anti-Semitism. When he was promoted to the position of Deputy Führer he quickly revealed his incapacity. Hess was not simply cranky but severely mentally ill and soon found it almost impossible to take decisions. He was appalled at the *Kristallnacht* pogrom and slowly became disillusioned with Hitler. In a quixotic attempt to make peace he flew to Scotland in 1941 and was arrested. Hess pent the remainder of his life as a prisoner.

Martin Bormann came to prominence gradually. As Hess' deputy he carried out the duties of which his chief was incapable. Bormann was completely lacking in personality and had no interests. He was a machine-like bureaucrat who tidied up, organized, researched and kept control over every minute detail of Nazi Germany. Given the lack of attention to detail shown by most Nazi Ministers, this quickly brought him to the attention of Hitler.

Before long he was virtually in charge of the Nazi regime and became not simply indispensable as a gofer, a fixer and source of information and gossip but eventually the gatekeeper to those who wished to access Hitler. He saw off every one of his rivals except Speer and Eva Braun, both of whom enjoyed a unique relationship with Hitler. Goebbels tried to fight him and eventually collaborated with him instead. Goering,

Himmler, Rosenberg and Ley tried to fight him but were simply swept aside. A man whom every single Nazi leader hated – even more so than Streicher – became the "brown eminence" at the heart of Hitler's rule.[46]

The story of Hitler's promotion of incapable people into positions of power is legion. The only competent ministers he had were Speer and Goebbels. Goering was vain, pompous, vulgar, and incapable of attention to detail and fixated on an entirely false idea of how the war in the air could be won. Himmler was cranky and mentally ill. In spite of their failings Hitler was unable to see beyond their loyalty and seemed to believe that being surrounded by yes-men was the right way to govern.

This megalomania and his conviction that he was always right and any dissenting view must be mistaken cost him dearly throughout the war. With an absence of advisers willing to tell him unpleasant truths this inflexibility and dogmatism led to needless loss of lives and to wastage of resources and materials.

His indecisiveness was shown throughout his life. He agonized over whether or not to join the German Workers' Party, whether or not to launch the Munich putsch, whether or not to accept a coalition government when Hindenburg reluctantly offered him the Chancellor's position, what his course of action should be once Britain and France declared war, whether he should follow the old Schlieffen Plan or try a different route of attack against France – all these areas showed how difficult he found it to come to a final decision. Often it would take days before he made up his mind on military options with often disastrous consequences as a result of his indecision.

A final failure on his part was his inability to grasp the significance of scientific and technical developments that could have changed the outcome of the war. He never understood how crucial fighter aircraft were to winning an aerial war; he never grasped the potential of rocketry as a weapon and he blew hot and cold on the nuclear programme with the result that delays and even unnecessary meddling prevented the Nazis from developing the bomb earlier. All these failures were avoidable and must be laid at the door of his personality.

Unstable State

The Nazi regime boasted of its *gleichschaltung* – co-ordination – but was chaotic in every area of life. Ministry clashed with ministry, local authorities with federal ones, organization with organization. Nazi Party members tried to assert themselves as local powers but faced a constant battle with the SA and SS who in turn rampaged with little or no check upon their excesses. Hitler was not remotely interested in the administrative side of government and actively encouraged petty rivalries among his followers. He foolishly believed that "divide and rule" was a successful way of running a country.[1] It had the opposite effect where constant confusion and paralysis reigned and where decisions were reversed or ignored with no real sense of the consequences or importance of these failures.

In theory the Enabling Act brought every aspect of government and public life under the control of the Nazi government. The practical reality was very different. Political parties were banned and the Nazis were the only permitted political organization. Non-Nazi states were brought to heel by the appointment of Reich Commissars to force local authorities to adopt the same policies as central government.[2] This was quickly followed by compelling all existing organizations to appoint Nazi leaders and adopt Nazi policies.[3]

For all the apparent unification these measures were supposed to achieve, in practice they meant very little. Jews were discriminated against and often removed from positions and anti-Nazis suffered that fate to a lesser degree. It soon became apparent that there were frequent rivalries between local Nazis and local leaders and the central government. This led to long and costly delays in implementing policies. The judiciary became completely under Nazi control though individual judges and lawyers attempted to preserve a modicum of due process but were rarely successful in these attempts. As a result the whole system of law and justice became arbitrary.

The rule of law is an ancient one found in countries across the world. India had the laws of Manu, Babylon the Code of Hammurabi, the Chinese the precepts of Confucius, and the Greeks and Romans saw law as one of the fundamental building blocks of society. The laws of the Medes and Persians became proverbial for their fairness and justice. Britain had its Common Law, the French and Americans their written constitutions. Every society or empire that lasted for a significant period of time relied on the rule of law as a guiding principle.

At a stroke the Nazis overturned thousands of years of legal precedents and jurisprudence. Law became an instrument of coercion and control rather than a means of administering justice and punishing offenders found guilty after fair trials. Instead judges handed down death sentences or prison terms on an arbitrary basis and the concentration camps became places where suspects were routinely detained, tortured and murdered without even the fig leaf of an unfair trial.[4]

Changes to the law gave a legal framework for persecution of the Jews. Civil servants took advantage of them to advance their careers with no regard for the lives and liberties of the people they were replacing. Judges were required to join the National Socialist League for the Maintenance of Law and those who refused were dismissed. Jewish judges and lawyers and political dissidents were forbidden to operate. The 'principles' of law were stated in different forms – often inconsistent – by Frank and other representatives of the regime but the most fundamental 'principle' was laid down as being "Nazi common sense."

Not only criminal or political law changed under the Nazis. Even civil law was radically transformed, particularly to the disadvantage of the Jews. The Nazi marriage law laid down both that people with genetic diseases were forbidden to reproduce and also that people of "different blood" were prevented from marrying or having children.[5] This discriminatory measure was at least not made retrospective although later even that approach was adopted.

In addition to the ordinary civil and criminal courts which of course were compelled to follow Nazi 'principles' and on the whole did so, two entirely new institutions were set up. Following the Reichstag fire "special courts" were established to deal with "treason to the German nation." In these courts the burden of proof was almost non-existent and the defendant's guilt assumed. There was no right of appeal against the court's sentence and retrospective "justice" was allowed. Harsh punishments were inflicted on political offenders.[6]

In 1934 the People's Court was created and became notorious for the blatant unfairness of its proceedings. Its original remit was to deal with those accused of political crimes but by 1938 its jurisdiction was extended to cover felonies and in 1939 it began trying minor offences. Defendants were not allowed to communicate with lawyers and defence counsel was frequently interrupted by the judges, particularly once Roland Freisler became the head judge in 1942. Freisler, a former Communist, became notorious for "berating and belittling" both the defendants and their legal representatives. There were three judges in the court and its verdicts could not be appealed against. Generally the defendant was executed as soon as he or she had been found guilty.[7]

The irrelevance of law to the Nazi regime led to the abrogation of impartiality and integrity. Quickly a society emerged where not only the police and judges could no longer be trusted but neighbours and family members were encouraged to inform on other people. Petty jealousies and imagined slights generated numerous false accusations and led to a complete breakdown of trust and an atmosphere of pervasive suspicion and paranoia.[8]

To confuse the situation even further, regional leaders were allowed considerable autonomy in their decision making. The one guiding principle was to "work towards the Führer" but leave the fine detail to others.[9] Hitler hated taking decisions and preferred delegating matters to his subordinates. He rarely gave written orders and his verbal instructions were often open to considerable interpretation. As Bormann grew in power he began to dictate policy as well as determine how it should be implemented. Hitler became more isolated and remote and though he remained the ultimate arbiter it was increasingly hard to contact him and achieve the necessary authorization for courses of action.[10]

There was nothing resembling Cabinet government in Nazi Germany and after 1938 the German Cabinet never met again. Hitler was the supreme arbiter of policy and Ministers had to lobby him to persuade him to adopt their plans which often proved difficult. The combination (after 1941 in particular) of Bormann as the guardian of access to Hitler and the Chancellor's own growing preoccupation with the war added to the chaos and disorder in the administration of Germany. It became increasingly common for people and groups to work out solutions to problems on their own, often with disastrous consequences. Ministers saw themselves not as colleagues but rivals for Hitler's favour and deliberately obstructed policies by other leaders and attempted to undermine them at every opportunity.[11]

Further unnecessary complications arose because the Nazis were not content to take over the existing government structure but also created entirely new departments. Frequently this led to pointless duplication of effort and resources, particularly with the Office of the Four Year Plan created in 1936 and the existing Economics Ministry. The result was that each office and department competed with others and attempted to make their own sphere of operation the one that enjoyed most influence with Hitler. There was never any clear chain of command or any process of accountability other than to Hitler himself and, increasingly, Martin Bormann, the "power behind the throne", waste, duplication of effort and failures of communications resulted with increasingly catastrophic results, particularly during the war.[12]

Bormann began his career as an anonymous Nazi member but when Hess made him his deputy he saw the chance to achieve power. He was a born administrator while Hess was shambolic so Bormann increasingly became an indispensable part of the Nazi machine. Relatively speaking, he was a competent bureaucrat though lacked any sense of vision and (as the war showed) placed his personal closeness to Hitler above the needs of the nation.

Regional leaders were particularly keen to assert their own sphere of influence and frequently defied or obstructed instructions from central government departments. In addition to this conflict of responsibilities the Nazi state was riddled with corruption and favouritism. This was particularly true at local level but applied even higher up the food chain.

The appointment of friends and family to positions regardless of merit made the machinery of government work even less smoothly. This became notorious in local authorities where each Gauleiter and party official behaved more like Mafiosi than administrators. During peacetime this merely resulted in inefficiency and stagnation but when war broke out the incompetence of the officials in charge became a major problem.[13]

The civil service was hampered both by the enforced degradation required through being compelled to carry out Nazi policies and the proliferation of competing agencies and departments. There were always at least two and frequently more areas of disputed authority with resulting paralysis and duplication of effort. Every aspect of German life saw a reduction in the effectiveness of administration. Incompetent Ministers, competing jurisdictions and nepotism combined to create a perfect storm where ultimate failure was almost inevitable.[14]

This dysfunctional process became worse as the Nazi empire expanded during the course of the war. The Wehrmacht, Nazi party officials, the SS and others competed for the new positions and for authority over the occupied territories. This meant that in addition to the senseless brutality and murder within those areas they were also chaotic and incompetent. No amount of appeals to Hitler had the slightest effect. He continued to believe that allowing this type of unnecessary competition was a price worth paying to retain power. The effect on the quality of administration throughout the Reich and its colonies was to hamper production, prevent effective distribution of resources and eventually assist in the loss of the war.

On their accession to power the Nazis worked hard to try and impose their values on the civil service. Superficially they were highly successful as Jews, socialists and other politically suspect individuals were purged from the national and local administration. In Prussia this led to a cull of 20% of the existing bureaucracy and in Germany as a whole of 10%. There was a sudden influx of civil servants joining the Nazi Party, earning themselves the derisive nickname from long-standing Nazis of "March violets."

On the other hand this sudden rush to join the party reflected political opportunism pure and simple and did not demonstrate any genuine adherence to Nazi ideology. German civil servants were overwhelmingly conservative and came from a culture where routine was the norm. They accepted the new dispensation but had no intention of altering their ways of working to suit their new masters. In addition the service had long required promotion to be on the basis of seniority and experience and fiercely resisted the attempts of eager Nazis to take over the many vacant positions.

This conflict was not because of any reluctance to carry out the instructions of the new government but was simply based on the principle of "Buggins' turn." In their eyes the Nazi attempt to introduce newcomers to the service without the years of experience that had been the norm was a threat to them personally and risked losing the professionalism on which they prided themselves.

In the existing established departments they were relatively successful in maintaining the principle of seniority but in the newly created government agencies it was a different story. Goebbels in particular staffed his Propaganda Ministry with young and highly ideological Nazis who worked under him and sought to enforce his vision on their department.

Civil servants were continually pressured by the party and their "loyalty" to the new regime was under constant scrutiny. Their telephones were tapped and friends and acquaintances monitored by the secret police. They were investigated to discover their previous political leanings and their private lives were subject to intrusive examination. Their racial heritage and eugenic characteristics were also studied.

Huge pressure was put on them to marry and have children. They were required not only to subscribe to Party newspapers but to attempt to obtain new readers. A civil servant in Prussia was dismissed from his post for not reading any newspapers.[15]

Civil servants were required to contribute to the Nazi "People's Welfare" scheme or face dismissal. They could even be dismissed if their wife behaved in a way considered to be unsuitable for a woman married to a state employee.[16] Educating a child at a private school was grounds for dismissal as was failure to enrol children in the Hitler Youth.[17]

They were discouraged from attending church, forbidden to belong to church associations, forbidden to belong to Niemöller's Confessional Church, and forbidden to be Freemasons. Even previous membership of the Masons was grounds for dismissal. They were also forbidden to shop at department stores.[18] In 1937 they were ordered to report any "subversive" activity which sometimes led to envious colleagues "reporting" others but on the whole this instruction was ineffective.

Wilhelm Frick, the Minister of the Interior, attempted to centralize the entire civil service system in Germany. He tried persistently to achieve this aim but was unsuccessful and when he clashed with Himmler over the increasing use of concentration camps he lost favour and became sidelined. It is arguable whether if he had succeeded in his attempt to Nazify the civil service the result would have been greater efficiency. Certainly he failed to streamline the structure and the administrative bureaucracy continued to follow its established methods of working.

As the regime tightened its grip on power there was a greater degree of Nazification within the service but except in the new departments little change in working practices took place. The Nazi assault on the civil service was only partially successful.

An overriding problem for the Nazi state was its pervasive control of ideology, belief and news. From the point of view of the regime this was a good thing in terms of maintaining control but it soon proved to be a double-edged sword. It was not only the German people who were kept in ignorance of the truth through the relentless barrage of propaganda by Goebbels and others. Even Nazi leaders frequently had no idea about events beyond their own narrow world view. Hitler in particular was so entrenched in his prejudices that he simply refused to listen to counter-arguments or ideas or proposals that ran counter to his narrow ideological fortress.

In addition to the nefarious effect of prejudice on the reception of unwelcome news or dissenting ideas there was a generally inadequate provision of genuine information. This made it harder to form a more complete and rounded picture of things and take decisions that might have been more appropriate in the light of those factors. Instead there was a general reliance upon "approved" sources of news and information. The result was woeful ignorance of everything from the attitudes of foreign governments to the nature of scientific advances that could have helped the Nazis during the war.

It was not only the all-pervasive censorship preventing access to wider sources of news and information including control of newspapers, books, magazines, drama, films, music and radio. It became a criminal offence to criticize the Nazi regime in 1934 and even humour and satire had to be extremely circumspect. All anti-Nazi sources of news or information were closed down and the permitted sources were tightly controlled in terms of what they could report or say. In 1933 there was a wholesale public burning of books that the Nazis considered "un-German" and even during the war soldiers writing home had their correspondence rigorously censored.

The regime engaged in extensive propaganda and removed, rewrote or wrote new textbooks for the use of students in which Nazi ideology, anti-Semitism and the glorification of Hitler were staple ingredients.

All this machinery of repression and indoctrination helped promote the regime among its citizens but soon created a situation where the Nazis themselves found it increasingly hard to distinguish between propaganda and reality. The growing unwillingness to believe any news or opinions that conflicted with the accepted ideology led inexorably to a greater degree of ignorance and dogmatism.

This unfortunate attitude was merely inconvenient and wasteful in peacetime. Once the war had begun and particularly once the campaign against Soviet Russia had been launched it was vital for information and hard facts to be readily available to the political and military leaders.

Instead, information was withheld and in particular bad news was kept from Hitler. Even Himmler, Goering and Goebbels were unable to persuade Hitler of military realities and not until the last week or so did it dawn on him that the war was irretrievably lost.

It was not simply an absence of information and a reluctance to bring bad news to the table. More damaging was the way in which it was deliberately withheld from him, particularly by Bormann. When Goebbels sent a detailed account, complete with maps and diagrams of destroyed buildings, showing the catastrophic effect of Allied bombing, Bormann returned them to Goebbels with a curt note stating that "the Führer does not wish to be troubled by such trivialities."[19] This shortage of genuine information combined with Hitler's reluctance to face unpleasant facts and the increasing power of Bormann made it difficult for bad news to reach Hitler. This was a potent cocktail almost certain to lead to defeat.

Hitler's judgement became progressively poorer as it was increasingly based on prejudice and inadequate information. He was notorious for his ability to mesmerize even seasoned generals into silence or agreement with his plans. Time and again they saw him and prepared to give him bad news and suggest alternative ideas to salvage the situation but all too frequently found themselves overwhelmed and tongue-tied in his presence. As a result they either did not present their case at all or allowed Hitler's personality to persuade them to agree with him against their better judgement.

A considerable problem for the regime was its visceral anti-intellectualism. Hitler and most of the Nazi leaders despised intellectual activity. Goebbels attempted to use it for propaganda purposes and

Rosenberg imagined himself the creator of a new intellectual universe but the general trend throughout the Third Reich was hostility and suspicion. The official mantra was "thinking with the blood" and the regime was shot through with all kinds of irrational beliefs and behaviour. The quasi-religious veneration of Hitler, the bizarre mythological fantasies of Rosenberg, Himmler's cocktail of occult beliefs and Hess' utter gullibility about every conceivable "alternative" belief were simply the tip of the iceberg.

Nazi Germany was swamped by a flood of irrationalism which went far beyond its racial mythology and encompassed huge areas of life that should never have been subjected to that kind of approach.

What the historian James Webb called "the flight from reason" began with the growing development of science and the consequent reduction in religious belief. This was accelerated by the effect of Darwin's theory of evolution and the nineteenth century saw a considerable turning away from rationalism and an increasing search for alternatives to traditional religious belief.[20]

It is ironic that Germany not only gave the world some of its greatest composers, artists and writers but was also to the forefront in terms of philosophers and scientists. In spite of its eminence in these fields, rationalism became increasingly unpopular. In many ways it was blamed for the carnage of the First World War and the collapse of traditional social structures in Europe. This climate of disillusionment was partly fuelled by some rationalist thinkers such as Westermarck's whose concept of "ethical relativity" led many people to regard all values as subjective. A misapplication of Darwinian theory into the societal field created additional problems, particularly in terms of his concept of "the survival of the fittest". It became easier in this environment for irrational ideas and belief systems to not simply gain a foothold but achieve widespread support.[21]

There was a considerable vogue from the 1890s onwards for what was described as an "organic" society. These ideas were particularly popular in Germany and were often associated with *völkisch* movements.

Although there was a huge growth in "personal fulfilment" cults during that period there was also a big increase in the opposite tendency. Mystical thought became widespread and was frequently turned from the spiritual to the political context. Instead of the mystic seeking the dissolution of self through unification with God, the new goal became the abandonment of individuality in the service of society or State. The influence of Hegel and his disciple Marx grew and reinforced this growing tendency.

These ideas were particularly influential on Himmler and Hess but were widespread among *völkisch* movements. Their prevalence greatly assisted the Nazis both in terms of their quest for power and their ability to keep the public broadly supportive of them almost to the very end.[22]

Many societies have had irrational elements in their politics but only under the Nazis were they so powerful and even mainstream. It was not simply in terms of the racist mythology that dominated much of the regime, but wild fringe theories which had been abandoned by the majority of people elsewhere in the world. Hörbiger's World Ice theory; Bender's hollow earth fantasies – which captured not only Goering but the German Navy; Himmler's obsessions with the Teutonic knights, reincarnation, herbalism and ritual, physiognomy, phrenology and Hess' gullible belief in every occult notion going were simply the most obvious and pervasive aspects of this flight from reason.[23]

The Nazi accession to power saw a rapid exodus of some of the finest minds in Germany. Hitler was openly contemptuous of that area of life – perhaps surprisingly for an artist – and spoke derisively about intellectuals, saying: "Unfortunately we need them. Otherwise one might – I don't know – wipe them out. But, unfortunately, one needs them."[24]

Under the Nazis 2500 writers went into exile or were deported.[25] Numerous artists, composers and musicians abandoned Germany and made new lives elsewhere. It represented a huge brain drain and although it led to a huge cultural impoverishment it could be argued that this was an acceptable price to pay for Nazification. That wanton sacrifice of talent did not apply to the flood of scientists and engineers who emigrated. Many of them were Jewish and among them were some of the greatest names in science. Their departure was an irreparable loss to Germany.[26]

Of course, many first-rate people remained in Germany throughout the Nazi era. Some fell silent and went into what became known as "internal exile." Others tried to make small acts of resistance and some tried to adapt. A tiny minority even embraced the regime, at least for a time. The most notable examples of the last tendency were the writers Gottfried Benn, Agnes Miegel and Gerhardt Hauptmann, the sculptor Georg Kolbe, the painter Emil Nolde and the composer Richard Strauss. All of them ended up having their hopes dashed and their worst fears realized beyond even the darkest imaginings of their spirit. This completely unnecessary exodus had a huge impact on both the cultural and scientific life of Germany. It was a blunder that ultimately played a significant part in losing the war for Hitler.[27]

Another completely mistaken policy by the Nazis was the war against the churches. It was one of the few areas in which public opposition forced Hitler to compromise to some degree but it remained true throughout the Third Reich that Christianity was frowned upon, actively discouraged and to a considerable extent persecuted. Himmler actively promoted his neo-pagan religion and Rosenberg disseminated his anti-Christian views through various media channels. Hitler remained technically a Catholic and in general retained that pretence in public but other ministers were openly hostile to Christianity. Hess, Goebbels, Ley and Streicher were as opposed to Christian values as Himmler or Rosenberg and so, in private, was Hitler. Even Martin Bormann remarked: "Christianity and National Socialism are irreconcilable."[28] Goebbels also wrote, concerning "the Church question," that "after the war it has to be generally solved ... There is, namely, an insoluble opposition between the Christian and a heroic-German world view."[29]

The situation was not helped by the concordat reached between the Nazis and the Vatican. This restricted the ability of the Pope and

Catholic clerics generally to speak out against the regime's policies. It was even more difficult for Catholic clergy to voice opposition once Pius XII became Pope in 1939, the very man who as Cardinal Pacelli had concluded the concordat with Hitler. His predecessor Pius XI had at least been critical of the regime and in 1937 issued an encyclical in German, *Mit brennender sorge* (With burning concern) in which he condemned the Nazi attacks on Christianity and in particular the policies of Rosenberg.[30]

The encyclical was printed and distributed in secret and read from the pulpits of Catholic churches in Germany. It aroused Hitler and the regime to fury and every copy that could be discovered was seized and destroyed.

The bulk of the document was written by Cardinal Michael von Faulhaber of Bavaria who was one of the few Catholic clerics in Germany who consistently criticized Nazi policies. Even he was silent on the persecution of the Jews, who had almost no defenders among the non-Jewish population, at least in public.

In spite of his criticisms of the Nazis there is little doubt that the Cardinal was anti-Semitic. In 1933 he made a statement affirming the importance for Christians of the Old Testament and praising Jews before the time of Jesus. The following year he was asked if he extended his praise to Jews born after Christ's time and immediately made it clear that he did not look on them as people of God in the same way as the Jews of the Old Testament.[31]

Faulhaber described the Weimar Republic as having its origins in "perjury and treason."[32]

The Vicar-General of Mainz condemned "Jewish influence" in the media and the press.[33]

Other Catholic clerics were braver than Faulhaber and a few of them paid for their courage and faith with their lives. On the whole the Concordat between the Vatican and the Nazis muted any serious criticism of the regime, particularly once Pius XII became Pope in 1939. It has been definitively proved that the Pope knew about the

Holocaust yet not only failed to condemn it but was completely silent on the matter.[34]

The Concordat committed the Catholic Church to staying out of politics. Probably the Vatican imagined that it would be honoured in much the same way that the Concordat between Mussolini and the Church had been and they would be left alone by the regime. They soon discovered that the Nazi regime was full of anti-clerical Ministers and it was not long before problems began to arise.

In 1933 all church associations were forcibly dissolved and education in church schools was actively discouraged. The following year the head of Catholic Action was murdered by the Nazis. In spite of these direct attacks on the Church the Vatican and its representatives in Germany remained silent.

Occasionally some Catholic bishops and priests raised their voice in protest but only at the treatment of the church by the authorities. Never a word of condemnation was heard about the persecution of the Jews. Even though it was to be another eight years before the full horror of the Final Solution began they knew that Jews were being beaten up, having their property stolen or damaged and being discriminated against in every area of life and yet remained silent. Only when the regime directly attacked the Catholic Church or its clergy or congregation did they voice their opposition.

Protestant clerics were equally guilty of anti-Semitism. The Lutheran Bishop Dibelius declared that "one cannot fail to appreciate that Jewry plays a leading role among all the disruptive phenomena of modern civilization."[35] Dibelius also endorsed Hitler in the 1932 Presidential election.[36] When the Nazis organized a boycott of Jewish shops in April 1933 Dibelius praised it as being a way of removing "Jewish over-representation in business life, medicine, law and culture."[37]

In spite of these attitudes Protestants were slightly more courageous in their condemnation of acts by the Nazis. Even so they remained silent on the whole. The regime began by attempting to force them into the

German Christian movement. This was founded during the Weimar Republic and combined a formal Christianity with huge elements of German nationalism, anti-Semitism and *völkisch* racism. For a time it enjoyed strong support and grew rapidly. Then a combination of the tactlessness of its leader and a growing realisation by Protestants that the Nazi regime was pursuing policies in stark contradiction to the Christian message led to a falling away in support. As opposition began to mount, so did the persecution by the Nazis of Protestant clergy. This cowed many into silence but a few were brave enough to continue their struggle against the regime.

Hitler worked hard to infiltrate the German Christian movement into positions of power in the Protestant Churches. They won three-quarters of the votes in the church elections and seemed on the verge of Nazifying the churches. In November 1933 they introduced an "Aryan" paragraph into the church but then overreached themselves by demanding that the Bible should be "cleansed" of all "non-Aryan" elements such as "the scapegoat and inferiority theology of Rabbi Paul."[38]

This heavy-handed attempt to strip Protestantism of all its Jewish elements backfired spectacularly. The "German Christian" leaders lost all credibility and a new breakaway movement was formed. This soon became the Confessional Church and its leading light was Pastor Martin Niemöller.

Niemöller was an unlikely opponent of the Nazis. He had been a U-boat captain in the First World War and strongly supported Hitler's appointment as Chancellor. He described himself as "anything but a philo-Semite"[39] and was mainly focused on defending Protestantism against the neo-pagans and "German Christians." He certainly spoke out periodically against the regime but did not raise the issue of Nazi persecution of the Jews. Niemöller declared publicly that even baptism could not turn a Jew into a Christian.[40]

The Confessional Church was deeply divided and in 1935 rejected a motion by Dietrich Bonhoeffer – one of the few clergymen to show courage under the regime – to condemn the Nuremberg Laws. These robbed Jews in Germany of most of their civic rights.[41] Not until 1943 did the Confessional Church publicly condemn the treatment of the Jews in a message read from the pulpits of its churches.[42]

Niemöller's anti-Semitism was open and pronounced. He publicly wrote about the Jews as follows:

> "We see a highly gifted people which produces idea after idea for the benefit of the world, but whatever it takes up becomes poisoned, and all it reaps is contempt and hatred because over and anon the world notices the deception and revenges itself in its own way."[43]

On 17 December 1941 seven Evangelical leaders issued a joint statement describing Jews as "born enemies of the world and Germany" and demanded "the severest measures against the Jews be adopted and that they be banned from German lands."[44]

The only occasion when the Churches publicly protested against Nazi policies except to protect their own position was over the Nazi euthanasia programme to kill people with mental and physical defects.[45] This policy had been advocated by Hitler for years and was sporadically carried out before 1939. For two years it was undertaken on a large scale with 70.000 victims murdered, initially through lethal injection but then by the use of gas.

Before long the facts came to the notice of Church leaders as many of the victims were patients in their hospitals or homes for the incurable. The full scale was not initially realized but once it became clear that its intention was the extermination of all mentally and physically defective people protests began.

The first church leader to raise opposition to the Nazi euthanasia programme was the Protestant pastor Friedrich von Bodelschwingh. He was followed by another Protestant pastor, Theophil Wurm. Reinhold Sautter complained to the Nazi State Councillor in Württemberg and received the response that "The fifth commandment, Thou shalt not kill, is no commandment of God but a Jewish invention."[46]

Only after several Protestant leaders had protested did Galen finally deliver sermons on behalf of the Catholic Church rejecting the programme. He had known about it for over a year before he finally spoke out.[47]

The effect of these protests was remarkable and clearly shocked the German people. Even though it was two years after the inception of the programme its open condemnation led to such public outrage that the regime was compelled to discontinue it. Instead of direct murder the inmates were left to die of starvation or neglect but the fact that mass murder had been aborted as a result of public pressure shows how effective the churches could be in opposing Nazi policies. If they had shown the same resolution in condemning the regime's vicious anti-Semitism and genocide it might have made a difference, but not one clerical voice was ever raised in public to defend the Jews. Even in private the Protestant Bishop Wurm was the *only* prelate ever to condemn the genocide against the Jews and he only did so in a private letter to Hitler. It is doubtful whether Hitler ever received the letter but even if he had he would have taken no notice.[48]

Given the prevalence of anti-Semitism, extreme nationalism and hostility to democracy and liberal values among the clergy of both Catholic and Protestant churches it is astonishing that they fell foul of the regime. The persecution of Christians under the Reich was unnecessary and counter-productive. Most German Christians were patriotic and were puzzled by the open hostility of the Nazis to their religion.

In spite of the general support for the regime by the churches Hitler, Himmler and Rosenberg continued their attack on both Catholics and Protestants. Some priests, monks, nuns and pastors were imprisoned, sent to concentration camps or even executed. Prayers in school were no longer compulsory and religious instruction was reduced to one lesson a week. The State also progressively appropriated church revenues to finance the war.

Niemöller ended up in a concentration camp though he survived the war. Bonhoeffer was less fortunate and was executed for his part in the 1944 bomb plot.

In addition to the attempts to "Aryanize" Christianity there was also outright anti-Christian propaganda and neo-pagan movements. The two main sources for these tendencies were Rosenberg and the German Faith Movement. Rosenberg's *Myth of the Twentieth Century* attacked Christianity in such violent terms that Cardinal Galen wrote a rebuttal of it entitled *Studies on the Myth of the Twentieth Century*.[49] This led Hitler to reassure Catholic leaders that the *Myth* was only "a private publication."[50]

The other focus of anti-Christian sentiment and activity was the German Faith Movement. Its members were a loose conglomeration of neo-pagans rather than an organized group with a coherent ideology or theology. It held pagan rituals for birth, marriage and death and was particularly popular among members of the SS and Hitler Youth.[51]

There is no doubt that if the Nazis had won the war – a far less impossible idea than is often assumed – they would have swept away the power of the churches and broken their hold over the people for good. In an occupied part of Poland they attempted to do just that. Though the Catholic church in the area managed to survive, it was hanging by a thread and would certainly have died out after a few more years of the open attempt to destroy it.[52]

The persecution of Christianity was both a moral and a practical mistake. It served no useful purpose and simply aroused opposition without sufficient reason. Church leaders were overwhelmingly conservative and nationalist and most strongly supported Hitler even in the final stages of the war. Whether Hitler felt more threatened by the Protestant insistence on the primacy of the individual conscience or the prestige and authority of the Pope and the Catholic Church is uncertain. Perhaps he had become drunk on the virtually religious veneration in which he was held by millions of Germans and saw any opposition as being treason or even heresy.

Whatever the reason for his strange crusade against Christianity it was an unnecessary distraction from more important issues. It is hard to find any rational explanation for this campaign which in spite of its often brutal repression ended in failure.

Another disastrous political mistake was his constant meddling in affairs that were either unimportant or outside his competence. His military misjudgements were the most lethal in terms of their consequences but some of his pre-war mistakes were as bad. He fantasized about massive architectural projects that had little chance of being realized without greater resources than his nation possessed. He showed no understanding of other points of view or of the constraints, attitudes and policies of the leaders of other nations. His racism played a huge part both in depriving him of gifted Jewish scientists at home and in terms of his choice of allies abroad and his failure to recognize what was most likely to be effective. Hitler combined a lackadaisical and dilettante reluctance to focus on detailed planning when it mattered with a fatal wish to intervene and micro-manage in areas where it would have been preferable to leave matters to those with greater knowledge and experience than he possessed.

His personal defects combined with a series of poor political decisions led inexorably to his ultimate defeat.

The Twists and Turns of Foreign Policy

Hitler's approach to foreign policy once he became Chancellor was a series of gambles of which some were successful while others ended in failure. He gambled that there would be no negative consequences for Germany if the country left the League of Nations, in spite of the horror and fear the move produced in the officials of the Foreign Ministry. He gambled that his public announcement that Germany now had a Luftwaffe in flagrant defiance of the Treaty of Versailles would lead to nothing more than protests. He gambled that his invasion of the demilitarized Rhineland would not lead to war. He gambled that his takeover of Austria would not lead to military action. He gambled that Britain and France would back down over Czechoslovakia. He gambled that Britain and France would not go to war over Poland, especially after the Nazi-Soviet Pact was signed.

In addition to his impetuous habit of gambling for high stakes he made mistaken choices in terms of his allies. He vastly overrated Mussolini as a leader and Italian military and naval capacity and considerably underrated the power of Japan. His abrupt renunciation of the established German foreign policy of co-operating with the Soviet Union was also a mistake.

To examine the often strange aspects of Hitler's foreign policy it is necessary to go back in time to the early years of the Weimar Republic. Foreign policy under both the Republic and the Nazis was dominated by resentment and rejection of the terms of the Treaty of Versailles. The return of Alsace-Lorraine to France and the cession of Moresnet and Eupen-Malmedy to Belgium were not particularly controversial and even the cession of North Schleswig to Denmark raised few protests.

What angered the majority of Germans was the new settlement in Eastern Europe. The Allies, particularly the French, were determined to create a series of buffer states to hold Germany in check. To this end the Hultschin district was given to the new Czechoslovakia and Memel to the newly independent Lithuania. These raised far less indignation than the forcible cession of the provinces of Posen, West Prussia and a third of Upper Silesia to Poland. Danzig was declared a "Free City" under the overall supervision of the League of Nations, although Poland enjoyed a customs union with the city and control over its foreign policy. East Prussia was isolated and the Polish frontier was now a mere 100 miles (160.94 kilometres) from Berlin.[1]

Britain and France continued to believe until late 1919 that the Bolsheviks could be defeated in the Russian civil war. German politicians and military leaders were more realistic about the chances of the "White" Russians. In 1920 the German High Command secretly negotiated with the Bolsheviks about the possibility of both countries launching a joint invasion of Poland and dividing the newly independent country between them. After the defeat of the Russians at Warsaw and Pilsudski's success in preserving Polish independence this plan was dropped but the German Chief of High Command, General Hans von Seekt continued to be committed to an "Eastern" foreign policy. He believed that France and Britain were both determined to keep Germany weak and that only an alliance with Russia offered any realistic prospect of the nation recovering its military strength. He wanted to revive Bismarck's old foreign policy of a formal German-Russian alliance but this was too much for the Weimar government.[2]

The provisions of Versailles led to huge economic disadvantages for Germany with the loss of all its colonies and much of its arable land and industry. In addition, the reparations bill imposed upon it by the Allies inevitably led to hardship. Successive German governments tried with varying degrees of success to moderate its terms. In 1920 and 1921 Britain and France were still in vengeful mood and unwilling to entertain any attempts to modify the Treaty. As the German government tried to dally and evade its provisions the British issued the "London Ultimatum" on 15 May 1921. This demanded immediate steps to begin disarmament, put "war criminals" on trial and pay 132 billion Marks and a quarter of the value of German exports. Faced with an inflexible position by the Allies, the German government had no choice but to comply. There were some half-hearted protests but it was the economic aspects of the Ultimatum that hurt most. Germany began conducting economic negotiations with Russia which went extremely well once Lenin was securely in power. Perhaps by chance or possibly as a gesture of defiance the news of these new trade and economic deals was announced the day after the London Ultimatum was received.[3]

In 1922 the world was stunned by the Treaty of Rapallo signed between Germany and Bolshevik Russia. Both nations were still pariahs on the international scene and the treaty gave them a combined strength neither enjoyed on their own. It was welcomed by the German army and its (banned) air force though the navy consistently refused to co-operate with the Russians. Opposition to the treaty came from the left and right with the German Nationalists and Social Democrats both unhappy about the idea of signing a treaty with Communist Russia, let alone any kind of military collaboration.[4]

Seeckt had wanted to go much further than the treaty and for several years remained a force behind the scenes in German politics. He continually urged a closer relationship with the Russians. He was unconcerned about the fact that Russia was a Communist country and in his eyes it was simple *Realpolitik* for his nation to ally with them. France continued to be "*revanchist*" for some time and Rapallo actually had a salutary effect on the French government and led them slowly to adopt a more conciliatory approach to Germany.[5]

The benefits of Rapallo were not only economic. It enabled the German military to test illegal aircraft and other weapons in Russia and so evade many of the provisions of Versailles that aimed at preventing Germany from developing powerful armed forces in the future. It gave the politicians of Weimar a bargaining chip by suggesting they might be willing to go further in terms of their collaboration with Russia. This threat alarmed Western governments and made them willing to be more conciliatory towards Germany. It also led to sporadic discussions between Russian and German military leaders about "revising" the boundaries of Poland. German leaders, particularly the military, were obsessed with the idea of a possible joint attack on their country by France and Poland which in their weakened military position they knew would be impossible to withstand.[6]

The main objective of German foreign policy throughout the Weimar Republic was to overturn the Treaty of Versailles and re-establish German influence in Europe. In pursuit of these goals successive Weimar governments sought to detach other Eastern European countries from Poland. The result was a series of trade deals and economic agreements.

Although Rapallo came as a shock to France and Britain and Poland it represented the culmination of three years of painstaking diplomacy by the German government to evade its isolation and poor economic position. It took advantage of the fact that most Eastern European nations were struggling economically and trade was used as a bargaining chip to improve the economic and political position of Germany.

The French relied on a system of alliances in Eastern Europe which they believed would hold the Germans in check. In March 1921 France signed a treaty with Poland and in 1924 another with Czechoslovakia. The Polish treaty included a secret military protocol guaranteeing military assistance if either country was attacked by a third party.[7]

Eastern European countries established other alliances. On 17th March 1922 the Warsaw Accord between Poland, Estonia, Latvia and Finland was signed and all parties agreed to defend each other in the event of an attack by a third party. In south-eastern Europe the Czechs and Yugoslavs signed a treaty of mutual defence on 14th August 1920. On 23rd April 1921 the Czechs and Romanians signed a similar defence agreement and on 5th June 1921 the Yugoslavs and Romanians signed a similar treaty.[8]

In an attempt to protect themselves from the consequences of their encirclement successive German governments signed trade deals. The first was with Czechoslovakia in 1920 and an agreement with Latvia followed. 1921 saw trade negotiations with all three Baltic states. The newly independent Eastern European countries were anxious to expand their economies and industrialize and German capital and trade was a means for them to achieve their objectives.[9]

These treaties were part of a German policy to mend fences with their Eastern European neighbours – with the notable exception of Poland – and extend German economic and political influence throughout the region. In many ways these trade deals foreshadowed the Treaty of Rapallo and by developing closer links with Russia they isolated Poland from other Eastern European nations. The implied threat of joint German-Soviet military action against Poland acted as a brake on Polish militarism. During the French invasion of the Ruhr in 1923 Russia actually warned Poland not to join the French in attacking Germany.[10]

Weimar policy continued to regard Poland as an enemy and attempted to isolate it by a series of alliances with neighbouring states. Hitler viewed the matter differently and saw in Poland a possible ally against the Soviet Union. He knew that Germany was militarily weak and that he needed time to build up its armed forces. Unlike the Weimar governments that were obsessed with regaining the German territory lost after the First World War, Hitler had quite different priorities. His ultimate goal was the conquest of Russia and turning it into a colony for German settlers. He was always motivated more by his racial mythology than *realpolitik* and was prepared to – at least temporarily – abandon the issue of Danzig and enlist Poland as an ally against the Soviet Union.

The Polish-German non-aggression treaty 1934 came as a total surprise to everyone. It was one of the most daring of all Hitler's foreign policy surprises. For years successive German governments had viewed Poland as a mortal enemy and were particularly incensed about Polish possession of Danzig and Upper Silesia. Seeckt was not the only German to consider allying with Russia to dismantle Poland and Hitler's abrupt change of policy was deeply unpopular in Germany.

Of all the territories the nation had lost after the First World War the loss of Danzig was resented most deeply. The population of the city was overwhelmingly German and the idea that it was cut off from the rest of Germany by the new buffer state of Poland rankled. As an Austrian, Hitler felt less deeply about the issue than the Germans but was well aware of the resentment in the country. He planned to use it at some future date as a means to pursue his ultimate goal of acquiring vast territories in the Soviet Union.

There were several reasons why Hitler and the Poles signed the treaty. For some years the Franco-Polish alliance had been weakening and the Poles felt that the French were now allied to them in name only and would not come to their assistance if they were attacked. The Poles were more nervous of the growing power of the Soviet Union than of the still weak Germany and saw an alliance with Hitler as an insurance policy against Russian attack.

On Hitler's part there were a variety of reasons that led him to adopt this abrupt departure from the established *Ostpolitik* of the Weimar Republic. He admired the Polish leader Josef Pilsudski who ruled his country as a dictator. The Polish government was nearly as anti-Semitic as the Nazis and as fiercely anti-Communist as them. Hitler also wished to create a series of satellite states in Eastern Europe to act as a deterrent to possible Russian aggression. He believed this would prevent Britain and France from using the eastern states as brakes on his long-term aims. With these factors presenting both sides with motives for signing a non-aggression pact it is perhaps easier now than it was at the time to understand this utterly unexpected *volte face*.[11]

The new relationship between Germany and Poland stunned and alarmed France. They attempted to organize a new regional alliance to counterbalance the situation which would include Poland, Germany, Russia, Finland, Estonia, Latvia and Lithuania. Britain opposed the plan and both Germany and Poland refused to become involved in the project. Neither the Baltic states nor Finland were willing to see Russian involvement in their affairs so the plan failed.[12]

For the next few years the Poles proved surprisingly helpful allies to Hitler. They moved progressively away from their formerly close relations with France and became more aligned with Germany. They failed to condemn the remilitarization of the Rhineland in 1936 or the Austrian *Anschluss* (the annexation of Austria in 1938). During the Czechoslovakian crisis they joined with Hungary in making territorial demands on the Czech government which were conceded as a result of Munich.

What Hitler failed to appreciate was that the Poles saw the alliance with Germany as a purely defensive measure against possible Soviet aggression. They had no desire to go to war with Russia any more than they wished war with Germany. The effect of the Polish alliance was to fatally tie Hitler's hands over Danzig and prevent him from raising the issue until 1939 when events had turned against him as a result of his own hubris and lack of awareness of foreign opinion.

Britain and France were well aware that of all Germany's territorial grievances the loss of Danzig was the most justifiable. The population of the city was overwhelmingly German and the demand of its citizens for reunification with Germany grew progressively louder. If Hitler had made Danzig his first territorial demand – at least up to 1938 when Britain and France began to turn against him – it is virtually certain that the Poles would have been pressured into conceding the territory to Germany. A Munich style agreement would have been achieved and it is highly possible that the Second World War would never have occurred.

By his sudden friendship with Poland and abrupt break with Russia Hitler threw away the economic and military benefits that eleven years of co-operation between Germany and Russia had produced. It was a major factor in the rapid development of the Luftwaffe. Under the terms of Versailles Germany had been forbidden to possess an air force and as a result of the agreements with Russia they were able to develop and fly aircraft. This not only allowed them to evade the prohibition but gave a huge boost to German military aviation. Hitler's shift of policy caused alarm in the German High Command who feared that the country's aeronautical development would suffer. They were also alarmed by the sudden prospect of war with the Soviet Union in the light of the current military weakness of Germany.

Too many of Hitler's foreign policy decisions were made on an *ad hoc* basis rather than as the result of long-range planning. He certainly had overriding goals but few of his decisions were arrived at after careful consideration. His decision to move troops into the Rhineland was a gamble but at that stage of his career he was still anxious to stay on good terms with Britain. He favoured the union of Austria with Germany but until 1938 was prepared to wait and adopt an indirect strategy to draw the country into his orbit. His policy in Eastern Europe, and to a lesser extent Austria, was to create a series of satellite states. He viewed their conquest as unnecessary as long as they remained essentially allied to Germany. Events, first in Austria, then Spain and then Czechoslovakia, forced him to react and in all three cases his decision was mistaken.

The first example of Hitler's failure either to plan or take full advantage of the situation occurred in 1934 when Austrian Nazis attempted a coup. The Austrian crisis was not of Hitler's making and began when the Austrian Chancellor Engelbert Dollfuss carried out a coup d'état and destroyed Austria's fledgling democracy. This led to a brief civil war during the course of which Austrian Nazis attempted to seize power themselves. Their actions were neither instigated nor directed from Germany and the rising was a purely indigenous affair.

Throughout the crisis Hitler remained in a state of indecision and failed to formulate a coherent policy towards the situation. He neither assisted nor condemned the rebels and simply allowed Munich radio to broadcast messages of support for them. Privately he admitted that he might have to wait years before Germany and Austria were united and certainly gave no public support to the Austrian Nazis.

At this point the German Foreign Office arranged a meeting between Hitler and Mussolini in Venice. This was the first time the two dictators had met and was inconclusive. Mussolini refused to use an interpreter and his bravura German was often hard for Hitler to follow and Hitler's German dialect often escaped Mussolini. Hitler also persisted in quoting from *Mein Kampf* which bored and irritated Mussolini intensely. He was so unimpressed by the German leader that after the meeting he described Hitler as "a silly little monkey." At the meeting Hitler assured Mussolini that he had no intention of annexing Austria and suggested that a new Austrian government should be formed including Nazi Ministers. Mussolini insisted that the Nazis should abandon their campaign of violence and that if they did so it might be possible for them to enter the government.

All these promises were rendered irrelevant when the Austrian Nazis murdered Dollfuss and attempted their own coup. The already strained relationship between the two men worsened immediately and Mussolini hastily moved troops to the Austrian border. The new Chancellor, Kurt von Schuschnigg, suppressed the Nazi revolt. Mussolini was furious with Hitler and he was forced to disown any connection with events in Austria. This was largely true – the uprising had been carried out without his knowledge or involvement – but it represented a humiliation and by failing either to support or oppose the uprising he offended everyone.[13]

The background to this and subsequent crises in Eastern Europe is complex. From 1924 onwards successive British governments had come to view the Versailles settlement as unfair to Germany and began taking steps to unpick aspects of it. By 1925 Mussolini felt secure enough to attempt to make Italy a great power. He regarded Austria and south-eastern Europe as his "sphere of influence" and in spite of his hostility to France and Russia had no desire to see Germany take over in the area. He intended to turn Austria, Albania and Hungary into satellite states of Italy. The Nazi uprising in Austria not only shocked him but forced him to draw closer to Britain and France. France attempted to form an alliance of Eastern European states against Germany but Poland's refusal to join doomed the project. Instead, France signed a pact with the Soviet Union but the terms were so vague that it was unlikely ever to be implemented.[14]

Hitler swallowed his humiliation over the Austrian debacle and countered it by reintroducing conscription. This flagrant violation of Versailles brought a last gasp of resistance from the Western Powers. Britain, France and Italy met at Stresa and announced their determination to maintain existing borders in Europe and resist any attempt to forcibly change them.

Hitler rightly imagined that the "Stresa Front" was no more than an expression of intention and would not lead to any meaningful action. He promptly renounced all the disarmament clauses of Versailles though still promised to respect its territorial decisions.

Events soon played into Hitler's hands as Mussolini, for reasons that remain obscure, decided to attack Abyssinia in October 1935.[15] Britain and France held different views on the outcome of the invasion with the French expecting a rapid Italian victory and the British predicting a long and draining war. Both were mistaken as the war dragged on until May 1936 when Haile Selassie went into exile and Abyssinia became an Italian province.[16]

Public opinion in Western countries was outraged and at the time, at least in Britain, support for the League of Nations and its supposed ability to deliver "collective security" was at its height. At first Britain tried negotiations with Mussolini which would have allowed him to possess half of Abyssinia but leave the rest to the Emperor. Initially Mussolini rejected the proposals outright but as the war began to stall he was willing to accept it. At that point the details of the proposals were leaked to the public and there was fierce opposition to the plan. Britain actually approached France with a view to military action against the Italians. This failed to produce results but was the last time either nation showed any willingness to resist aggression until 1939.

Instead the League imposed sanctions on Italy which merely infuriated Mussolini, were widely evaded and had no effect in preventing an Italian victory. The League lingered on with an increasingly unreal existence – it did not even register the outbreak of the Second World War in September 1939 – until 1946 but 1936 dealt it a mortal blow.

Hitler had initially been anxious that sanctions might bring Italy to heel and that if that happened it would force him to moderate his own plans. Temporarily he reduced trade between the two countries but when he recognized that sanctions were empty gestures without teeth his response was to occupy the Rhineland.[17]

This action on Hitler's part was a huge gamble. In spite of the strains between Britain, France and Italy the Stresa Front showed that resistance to German militarism was not entirely dead. It was of course a direct violation of the 1925 Treaty of Locarno so it may be useful to give a brief note on what the Treaty entailed on the participants, the intention behind it and the consequences of Hitler's violation of Locarno. The treaty was divided into several parts of which the most important were the ones regarding France and Belgium. One part guaranteed the existing frontiers of France, Belgium and Germany and was guaranteed by Britain and Italy. The second and third parts declared that in any future disputes between Germany and Belgium or Germany and France there would be arbitration. France wanted to apply the same treatment to Eastern Europe but Germany refused to agree to an "Eastern Locarno." This alarmed Poland and Czechoslovakia so further parts included arbitration treaties in case of disputes between Germany and Poland and Germany and Czechoslovakia.[18]

The effect of Locarno was entirely different on Western governments from its reception by Eastern European leaders. Poland in particular was contemptuous of the treaty and regarded it as a betrayal of the alliance with France. As Józef Beck remarked bitterly, "Germany was officially asked to attack the east, in return for peace in the west."[19] Beck's response was unfair given the type of government in power in Germany at the time but once Hitler became Chancellor the Poles had every reason to be nervous. They were as grateful and surprised as everyone when Hitler approached them with his plans for a non-aggression pact and were happy to be, as they wrongly imagined, free from the threat of German attack.

In addition to the territorial clauses in Locarno it reinforced the provision in the Treaty of Versailles that the Rhineland must be a permanently demilitarized zone. The French were still anxious to contain Germany and prevent it from launching an aggressive war and hoped that the agreements signed at Locarno would achieve that.[20]

Hitler knew he was taking a huge risk by sending 3000 German troops into the Rhineland but gambled that Britain and France would stop short of military action. He knew that the French army could have responded instantly and forced the German troops to pull back. That would have been a huge blow to Hitler's prestige and might have compelled him to be less reckless in his foreign policy. Instead they consulted their allies and found that only the Czechs were willing to join France in an invasion of the Rhineland. The other Eastern European leaders stated that they would only come to France's assistance if Germany attacked France directly. The French overestimated the number of German troops in the Rhineland and were too sanguine about the condition of their own military. As a result, after a brief consultation with the British, they did nothing.[21] The British government did not seem concerned about the German move but the consequences were far-reaching. Instead of the Rhineland acting as a buffer zone between France, Belgium and Germany, the French and Belgians now faced German troops directly on their borders.

France had been increasingly adopting a defensive policy since the late 1920s and the changed situation in the Rhineland made this mindset even more pronounced. The belief that the Maginot Line was impregnable created a fatal complacency in French political and military quarters.[22]

Ironically Hitler had not planned to remilitarize the Rhineland until 1937 but the failure of the Allies to restrain Mussolini and the breach between France and Eastern European nations emboldened him to take this radical step. Hitler was still cautious enough to ask Mussolini if he objected to German renunciation of the Locarno Treaty but on receiving assurances that he would take no action against Germany Hitler felt confident enough to send in the troops.[23]

Military occupation of the Rhineland was a gamble but because of a weak response by Britain and France cannot be considered a blunder. That is certainly *not* true of German involvement in the Spanish Civil War which was unquestionably a major mistake.

The war began soon after the election of a Popular Front government that included Communists as part of the coalition. It was anti-clerical and the Catholic Church began to protest against the new government's policies. In 1936 Spanish troops based in Morocco launched an uprising. The original leader of the rebels, General José Sanjurjo y Sacanell, died in an aircraft crash and it remains a matter of dispute whether or not his death was an accident. In any event General Francisco Franco took over the leadership and began to organize his troops into a fighting force.

Initially both Britain and France expected the Republican government to collapse and for Franco to win quickly and easily. In fact Spanish government forces held their own and began to push the rebels back. At that point Mussolini and Hitler decided to become involved in the war and give direct military assistance to the rebels.[24]

The Republican government had overwhelming superiority in terms of air power and of course had regular troops under their command. Franco needed to ferry troops and equipment to Spain from Morocco and in that task Hitler and Mussolini assisted him. Twenty Junkers Ju52s were flown by German pilots and carried Franco's army into Spain in an operation codenamed Operation Magic Fire. This involved airlifting 13,500 soldiers, 36 pieces of artillery and 126 machine guns from Morocco to Spain. In October of that year Franco's forces gained control of the sea between North Africa and Spain which allowed them to transport men and equipment by ships.[25]

Neither Hitler nor Mussolini embarked on the venture from a desire to spread fascism or to expand the area of their influence. The Italian dictator had a hope that a victorious Franco would allow him to use Spanish naval bases in pursuit of his aim of controlling the Mediterranean but beyond that had no real reason for becoming involved. That was even truer of Hitler where *no* vital German interests were involved and both men ran the risk of becoming involved in a world war. They realized the danger and would happily have abandoned Franco if Britain and France had shown resolution and threatened war.[26]

The French government of the day was a Popular Front coalition and initially wanted to assist the Republicans to defeat Franco. The Premier Leon Blum went to London and spoke with the British Prime Minister Stanley Baldwin asking if Britain favoured a strong policy in support of the Republican government. Baldwin, knowing Britain's military weakness, gave an evasive answer and instead put forward the farce of "non-intervention" as a policy. Blum, already struggling to control his unstable coalition, leapt at the idea and promptly both France and Britain adopted it as their policy.

If it had been genuinely applied it might still have been possible for the Republicans to win the war but Britain and France's refusal to sell arms or give assistance was not matched by Germany and Italy. The Italians in particular gave major assistance to the rebels in spite of their public protestations of support for "non-intervention." As a result the military balance began to tip in favour of Franco's forces.[27]

Stalin was alarmed at the prospect of a fascist victory and decided to send Russian aid to the Republican government. This undoubtedly helped to slow down Franco's advance but Stalin, like Hitler and Mussolini, was not motivated by altruism. He was determined that the Spanish Communists would take over the leadership of the Republican government and his troops spent as much time attacking anarchists, Basque and Catalan separatists and the more moderate elements of the governing coalition as they did in fighting Franco's troops.[28] Quite apart from the damage this did politically and militarily to the Republicans it alienated and alarmed the British government which was terrified of the spread of Communism.

Eventually the Russians scaled back their help to the Republicans and the inevitable result was that Franco won. German forces had been involved in assisting him but only on a minor scale with the substantial aid to the Falangists coming from Italy. The German troops formed what was named the Condor Legion which had mixed fortunes on the battlefield though greater success in the air.[29] Germany essentially used Spain as a training ground for their aircraft.[30] The involvement of their ground troops was smaller in number and relatively unsuccessful with German soldiers being defeated in several battles. The naval involvement was even less impressive with ships sunk and submarines destroyed.[31]

Militarily and politically German involvement in the war produced *no* obvious benefits. Hitler was not even motivated by ideological considerations although for public consumption he pretended that the war was a crusade against Communism and to extend fascism. When the war began he expected Franco to lose and saw the adventure in Spain as an opportunity to try out his armed forces and particularly his air force in terms of their combat readiness.

He was so anxious for the war to continue as long as possible – not least because he felt it might lead to war between Italy and the Western powers – that when things began to go badly for the government he seriously considered switching sides and aiding the Republicans. His pose of intervening in the war to fight Communism and extend fascist influence to Spain was, even by his standards, utterly dishonest. By 1937 he had abandoned any kind of naval warfare following severe reverses and from that point on the Condor Legion played a smaller part in ground warfare. Only the Luftwaffe remained heavily involved and their greatest "achievement" was the mass bombing of Guernica. Even then he failed to learn the lesson that bombing alone was insufficient to win a war.[32]

Other than the continuing involvement in the Spanish Civil War 1937 was a quiet year in terms of foreign policy. Then on 5th November 1937 Hitler called a high-level meeting at which a document known as the Hossbach Memorandum was drawn up. The meeting arose as a result of Admiral Raeder's complaint to Hitler that the Navy was not receiving its fair share of resources.

The minutes of this meeting have become known as the Hossbach Memorandum and their status and importance has been fiercely disputed ever since. Hitler spoke of the need for *lebensraum* though without naming specific areas for this expansion. He described Britain and France as "hate filled enemies" and outlined three possible scenarios that might lead to war. He first suggested that war would not break out before 1943 by which time German military might would be at its height. His second scenario was a civil war in France which he believed would mean that "the time for action against the Czechs had come." The final scenario was a war between France and Italy. Hitler knew that Mussolini had ambitions to recover Savoy and Nice – ceded to France in 1859 – and had designs on Corsica. Mussolini also saw the Mediterranean as "an Italian lake."

None of the three scenarios materialized and there is no reason to suppose that Hitler viewed them as a plan of action. In fact he believed that Germany could fulfil her goals without the need for war and that Britain and France would be cowed into submission by the mere threat of force.

Count Friedrich Hossbach wrote up the minutes of the meeting from memory five days later. No one took notes at the time which in itself is unusual. The original document disappeared and the copy produced at the Nuremberg Trials was considerably shorter than the original. Most fundamental of all is that there is no reasonable doubt that the Hossbach Memorandum was simply a general announcement of a policy of increasing rearmament rather than a specific programme for action.[33]

1937 saw Hitler greatly assisted by a new emphasis in British foreign policy when Neville Chamberlain became Prime Minister. Chamberlain served as an officer on the Western Front during the First World War and had a horror of any repetition of conflict. His predecessors Ramsay McDonald and Stanley Baldwin shared this view and attempted to deal with the threats posed by Italian expansionism and German militarism by seeking to reach comprehensive agreements on possible causes of war.

Chamberlain followed this approach but took it to a new level by adopting a policy that became known as "appeasement." He believed that by acceding to Hitler's demands war could be avoided. To this end he sent Lord Halifax to meet Hitler at Berchtesgaden in November 1937. Halifax told Hitler that he regarded Germany as "the bulwark of Europe against Bolshevism" and declared – with particular reference to Czechoslovakia, Austria and Danzig – that "possible alterations might be destined to come about with the passage of time." This entirely unnecessary communication was naturally interpreted by Hitler as a green light to begin the process of subverting these territories. Halifax did insist that such changes must come about peacefully but as Hitler had no wish to risk a European war that made little difference to his plans.[34]

Hitler began to consider destroying Czechoslovakia which in addition to being the only democracy in Eastern Europe also possessed a powerful army and a strong series of defensive fortifications. He encouraged the German minority to begin agitating for greater rights and autonomy within the country.

Hitler saw Austria as a less pressing problem with Schuschnigg effectively within the German sphere of influence. In spite of his preference for dealing with Czechoslovakia first his hand was forced. Austrian Nazis became increasingly belligerent and not even reproofs from Hitler and counsels of caution and patience could hold them back. They persisted in stirring up trouble and Hitler's attempts to damp down their agitation were notably unsuccessful. Schuschnigg appealed to Mussolini for support but the Italian leader was not simply unhelpful but positively hostile. By now Mussolini realized that he needed Hitler as an ally to fulfil his own ambitions, at least by diverting attention away from Italian plans. If the price of alliance with Hitler was sacrificing Austrian independence then Mussolini was prepared to pay that price.

Having failed to secure Italian support Schuschnigg took action against the Austrian Nazis. In early January 1938 he raided their offices and discovered plans for an uprising. He also made a rousing speech in which he declared that:

> *"There is no question of ever accepting Nazi representatives in the Austrian cabinet. An absolute abyss separates Austria from Nazism ... We reject uniformity and centralization. ... Christendom is anchored in our very soil, and we know but one God: and that is not the State, or the Nation, or that elusive thing, Race.'*[35]

Following these events Schuschnigg decided that there was no point in appealing to Mussolini. Instead he contacted Franz von Papen who was then the German Ambassador to Austria. At this meeting Schuschnigg gave Papen details of the plot and expressed a wish to meet Hitler.

Ironically Papen was dismissed from his post as Ambassador shortly after the meeting but met with Hitler at Berchtesgaden the next day. Papen brought with him both news of the Nazi plot and Schuschnigg's desire to meet Hitler. Hitler agreed at once and two days later Papen returned to Vienna with an invitation to meet the German Chancellor. On 12th February Schuschnigg arrived at Berchtesgaden.[36]

What happened when the two men met has been the subject of considerable controversy. There is no doubt that Hitler blustered and attempted to intimidate Schuschnigg but in spite of these tactics Schuschnigg held his nerve and negotiated a settlement that gave him most of what he requested. Arthur Seyss-Inquart was appointed as minister of security with control of the police force and another Nazi, Hans Fischbock, became Minister of Finance. His task was to prepare for economic union between the two countries. All Nazis currently imprisoned in Austria were to be released. A hundred officers were also exchanged between the German and Austrian armies.

All these points have been described as an ultimatum and handing over control of the country to the Austrian Nazis. That is not remotely correct. As early as 1931 Austria and Germany had attempted to conclude a customs union but were forced to abandon the project owing to opposition from France, Italy, Poland and Czechoslovakia. The plans for economic union were favoured by both Hitler and Schuschnigg so this policy was anything but an ultimatum or a violation of Austrian sovereignty. Fischbock's appointment was simply a measure to smooth the path for the economic union that both countries desired. In the same way the appointment of Seyss-Inquart was not objectionable to Schuschnigg and the two men were close friends. The release of Nazi prisoners and the exchange of officers between the two armies was more of a gesture than a sign of any significant alteration in the nature of the relationship between Germany and Austria.

In return for these largely cosmetic changes Hitler was forced to condemn the Austrian Nazi attempts to subvert the country. He met with their leader Leopold and gave him a harsh reprimand and demanded that he and most of his followers relocate to Germany. Hitler publicly confirmed the frontiers and the territorial integrity of Austria and its status as an independent sovereign state. For all Hitler's ranting and raving Schuschnigg had got the better of him in this particular set of negotiations.[37]

Whether this success went to Schuschnigg's head or whether on his return to Austria he felt he had conceded too much the Austrian Chancellor certainly began to renege on aspects of the agreement. He cracked down hard on the Nazis within his country in spite of confirming the appointments he had agreed with Hitler. In a fatal misjudgement of his position Schuschnigg decided to hold a referendum on Austrian independence. Even the wording of the referendum was phrased in such a way that it not only infuriated Hitler but virtually guaranteed a conflict between the two nations.

Schuschnigg told Mussolini of his intentions but the Italian leader simply replied that "it is a mistake." In spite of this warning Schuschnigg pressed ahead with his plans. Contrary to the version of events he peddled to the West this would have been a totally rigged referendum and he would have engineered the result Schuschnigg's referendum would have been as carefully orchestrated as the plebiscites organized by Hitler were "managed." The idea that Schuschnigg's vote on independence would have been a free and fair one is nothing more than propaganda to justify his actions after the event.[38]

A furious Hitler spoke with his Generals and told them he would invade Austria to punish Schuschnigg. He would then install Seyss-Inquart as his replacement in a puppet regime that would be loyal to Germany.

When Schuschnigg realized the storm his proposed referendum had caused he tried to contact Mussolini for support but the Italian leader refused even to answer the telephone. At that point he withdrew the proposal hoping that jettisoning the vote would be enough to mollify Hitler.

Though he was furious with Schuschnigg Hitler remained cautious about the course of action to adopt. Chamberlain told Ribbentrop that he favoured greater understanding between Britain and Germany "once we had all got past this unpleasantness."[39] Hitler then sounded out the Czechoslovak government who informed him that they would not march to Austria's assistance if he decided to invade. Mussolini went even further, telling Hitler that he had no interest in the future of Austria and would support the Germans in whatever action they undertook.[40]

At this point Hitler still hesitated, wavering between direct invasion with an attendant risk of war and pressuring Schuschnigg into capitulation. Goering decided to take the lead in the matter and began by issuing a series of demands. The entire affair, bizarrely, was conducted via a series of telephone conversations.

Goering telephoned Seyss-Inquart and told him that Schuschnigg must resign and be replaced by him. Schuschnigg resigned but President Wilhelm Miklas refused to appoint Seyss-Inquart as his successor. Goering then telephoned Miklas and warned him that German troops were on the border and would enter Austria unless the President changed his mind. Miklas still refused so Seyss-Inquart proclaimed himself the new Chancellor and telephoned Goering asking him to postpone the invasion. Goering refused and German troops entered Austria.

It was hardly a triumphal procession as most of the armoured vehicles broke down on their journey to Vienna. Hitler made a public speech at Linz and announced the *Anschluss* from the town hall balcony. The incorporation of Austria within the German Reich – even the day before the invasion this had not been the plan and once again Hitler reacted to events rather than controlling them – followed and was quickly confirmed by a plebiscite.[41]

Was the Anschluss a mistake in itself? There is little doubt that most Austrians wished to be united with Germany. What alarmed Britain and France was not the joining together of the two countries. They would have been willing to accept their union if it had been carried out in a peaceful manner but the fact that the threat of force had led to the surrender of an independent country shocked them. The lesson was not lost on Hitler though sadly it produced no significant change of policy among the leaders of Britain and France.[42]

Hitler was flushed with hubris after his successful annexation of Austria and proceeded to make his next foreign policy mistake. He should have raised the issue of Danzig where everyone except the Poles agreed that German claims for its return were fair, legitimate and justified. In 1938 – even after the annexation of Austria – he would certainly have been able to persuade the Western Powers to lean on Poland and grant him Danzig. Instead he began encouraging a campaign of subversion by the German minority within Czechoslovakia.[43]

Why Hitler chose to make Czechoslovakia his next target has never been satisfactorily explained. There are four possible reasons for this poor choice. One is the fact that Hitler was an Austrian and grew up regarding the Czechs as subject people. Another is his awareness that Czechoslovakia had the best army in Eastern Europe and strong defences. The Czechs had a strong network of alliances with France, Russia, Romania and Yugoslavia. They were also the only democratic state in Eastern Europe. All these factors might explain his attitude and perhaps a combination of them played a part in his thinking.

He was greatly assisted by the fact that though Britain and France had momentarily woken from their slumber after the *Anschluss* they soon resumed their previous passivity. Hitler received the impression from Halifax and Chamberlain that they would support a peaceful solution to the Sudeten German minority in Czechoslovakia so expected no serious protests or opposition from Britain. France was if anything even more wedded to appeasement than the British so Hitler felt confident that he could exert maximum pressure on the Czechs without fear of intervention by the Western Powers. He was helped considerably by the attitude of the Czech government which seemed unwilling or unable to recognise the danger signs and to believe that somehow they would be able to survive through diplomacy. The fall of Austria should have made them more realistic about the prospects of obtaining support from Britain and France but they did not heed the warning.

Benes had strong alliances but failed to use them. He relied too heavily on France and either underestimated or did not wish to summon aid from his Eastern European partners and the Soviet Union. He placed little confidence in his alliances with Yugoslavia and Romania and made no attempt until the last moment to seek assistance from the Soviet Union. He believed that negotiations could be satisfactorily concluded even with the Nazis though to be fair to him the British government shared that illusion.

Further problems arose from the gross overestimation of Germany's military capability and the inverse underestimation by France and Britain of their own strength. An additional problem for Benes was that he knew how fragile Czechoslovakia's nationhood was. The Czechs dominated a nation of Slovaks, Poles, Hungarians, Ruthenians and Germans and the country had been artificially created at the end of the First World War out of the ruins of the Austro-Hungarian Empire.

The Soviet government took the initiative after Benes failed to approach them. In March 1938 it proposed raising the problems of Czechoslovakia with the League of Nations. Halifax rejected the suggestion out of hand.[44]

The French proposed issuing a joint warning to Germany by Britain and France but the British ignored the idea. Soon the French government fell and the new regime simply called for the British to take a lead in the issue. Pressed further on the matter by the Czechs the French Foreign Minister replied:

> *"The Czechoslovak government should not consider that if war breaks out we shall be on its side. France, like Britain, will not go to war."*[45]

At this stage Hitler was sitting back and allowing Benes and the Sudeten leader to negotiate. On 24 April Henlein demanded that Czechoslovakia should become "a state of nationalities" which effectively meant autonomy not only for the Sudeten Germans but the Polish minority in Tesin and the Slovak, Hungarian and Ruthenian minorities. He demanded that the Czechs abandon their pro-Western foreign policy and follow Germany's lead in foreign affairs. They were also required to renounce their alliances with France and Russia.

The intention of these demands was both to break Czechoslovakian power and to turn the country into a German satellite. Hitler preferred obedient vassal states to the risk of war and gambled that the Czechs would back down without the support of Britain and France.

Faced with this open demand for them to surrender the independence of his country Benes decided to make a show of Czech military strength. On 28 May troops manned the borders and reservists were called up. It was a clear message of defiance and intended to deter Hitler but sadly produced the opposite effect Not only did Czechoslovak defiance enrage Hitler but Britain and France were thrown into panic by the prospect of war.

Chamberlain discussed the matter with his Cabinet and with the French and decided to begin pressuring the Czechs to make concessions.

He even contacted the Germans and asked them what they would consider an acceptable settlement of the Czechoslovakian question. Hitler was delighted at this unexpected development and immediately instructed Henlein to make demands that were so extreme that it would be impossible for the Czechs to agree to them.

Benes still clung to the illusion that he could persuade the French at least to come to his aid if the Nazis refused to be reasonable. He continued to ignore suggestions by the Soviet Union that the Czechs should ask for its assistance. Meanwhile the French and British refused to ask the Russians for help. The Soviet government bluntly asked the French to persuade the Poles and Romanians to allow the passage of Russian troops through their territory if it was necessary to defend Czechoslovakia but the French refused even to make the enquiry. They knew that Eastern European countries were more frightened of the Soviet Union than they were of Germany.

Poland, seeing the growing pressure on the Czechs, decided to make demands of its own.

Not only did it present the Czechs with a formal demand for the return of Tesin to Poland but the Polish government began direct talks with the Germans on the basis of a joint military attack on Czechoslovakia. The Polish Foreign Minister Beck instructed the Polish Ambassador to Germany to encourage Goering to launch an attack on Czechoslovakia, adding:

> *"We have at our disposal forces under arms capable of action. Relative to the development of the situation we could take prompt action following the outbreak of a German-Czech conflict."*[46]

Benes continued to show defiance even though he was aware of the new threat from Poland. Again he refused to believe that the British and French would let him down. Hitler decided on a final diplomatic effort and sent Henlein to London to persuade the British to support the Sudeten position.

The British government remained split with Halifax increasingly unhappy with the Germans and Chamberlain becoming angry with the Czechs. Eventually Henlein left without any specific commitments but with a strong sense that Chamberlain would back the Sudetens over the Czechs. He reported back to Hitler on the lack of appetite for war in the British government.

Hitler decided to crank up the tension but once more Benes decided that he was bluffing and decided to put him to the test. He summoned Henlein and the Sudeten leaders and told them to write out their own terms. They sat there in stunned silence and refused to sign anything or even make a formal written list of their demands.

Both the Czechs and the British sounded out the possibility of American involvement in the dispute. They met with a resounding rebuff from the United States. Roosevelt simply urged them to appeal to the League of Nations. The US Ambassador to London, Joseph Kennedy, was even more blunt in his pro-German and anti-British attitudes. American politics were still deeply isolationist and as late as 1939 Roosevelt conducted a military exercise based on the possibility of America going to war with Britain. Nor is it clear that he even wanted Britain and France to go to war. Roosevelt was preoccupied with domestic politics and the growing threat from Japan and had no desire to become entangled in European conflicts.[47]

At this point, far too late in the day and in a half-hearted fashion, Benes finally decided that Britain and France were proving unreliable allies so approached the Soviet Union. He made a formal enquiry about their willingness to support Czechoslovakia militarily in the event of a German attack if France joined with her. The Russians agreed to his request and also stated their willingness to assist the Czechs under the League of Nations terms and conditions. This was vague but promising and Benes approached Gottwald, the leader of the Communist Party in Czechoslovakia. He asked him if Russia would support the Czechs militarily even if it meant acting alone. Gottwald refused to be drawn and told Benes to approach the Soviet Union directly. He was reluctant to do so and the last chance of avoiding the fall of Czechoslovakia was missed.

The next step was the Four Power conference at Munich where Mussolini, Hitler, Daladier and Chamberlain made their own agreement which ceded the Sudetenland to Germany without any regard for the Czech state. As well as the Sudetenland Czechoslovakia lost its strong fortifications, most of its coal, iron and steel and its electric power. The effect was to drastically impoverish and weaken the rump state. Roosevelt's comment on hearing the news was "good man."[48]

Benes resigned and went into exile. His successor Emil Hacha was a weak and ill man who was considered senile by many Czech politicians. He was soon confronted with demands from Poland and Hungary for large slices of the remaining Czechoslovak territory.

With Czechoslovakia out of the way Hitler began planning his long desired war against the Soviet Union. He had every reason to believe that Poland would continue to support him and be a willing partner in the war against Russia. The Polish demand for Tesin had been the final threat forcing Benes to concede the independence of his country.

Hitler, still regarding Poland as an ally, raised the issue of Danzig with the Poles in October 1938. They did not agree to cede it to Germany but did not rule it out absolutely. In fact the Poles and Germans promptly began discussions about a possible joint attack against Russia. These plans were mentioned several times between the two countries as late as March 1939.[49]

Then in March 1939 everything changed. As so often in the years leading up to war it was not the result of any premeditated plan on Hitler's part. The Slovaks demanded independence from the Czechs in a development that took Hitler by surprise. He had no control over this unexpected move but believed it could be used for his own benefit. Goering encouraged the Slovaks to become more militant in their demands and on 14th March 1939 Slovakia declared itself an independent state. He commented cynically that this made the Czechs "even more completely at our mercy."

The initial Czech instinct was to crush them by force but Hacha was bewildered and frightened. He asked to meet Hitler the day after the Slovakian declaration of independence and once again Hitler achieved his aim by bluff.

He told Hacha that he intended to occupy the rump of Czechoslovakia and that Slovakia would be independent while the rest of the country would become the Protectorate of Bohemia and Moravia. If Hacha refused, Hitler told him, German planes were ready to bomb Prague into submission.

The reality is that the weather was so bad and the fog so dense that not a single plane could have left the ground but Hacha, probably already tired after months of internal struggle, signed away his country on the basis of a threat that was incapable of being carried out. Once more Hitler had bluffed his way to success. It was to be the last time that he carried out this trick successfully.[50]

The effect was not at all what Hitler had expected. Britain and France reacted furiously to the news and two days later Chamberlain declared that although he was "not prepared to engage this country by new unspecified commitments operating under conditions which cannot now be foreseen" he added "any attempt to dominate the world by force was one which the democracies would resist." The effect of these words was lessened by the British recognition of the German protectorate over Bohemia and Moravia and handing over six million pounds of Czechoslovak gold to the Nazis.

British panic was partly caused by a sense that Hitler had broken his word and partly by an alarmist message on 16th March from the Romanian Minister in London. He declared that his country faced an immediate threat of German invasion. This was a false alarm but it threw Chamberlain into panic. On 19th March he prepared a declaration of "collective security" and invited France, Russia and Poland to sign the agreement. This document was *not* designed to protect Poland but to act as a deterrent to the imagined threat to Romania. The French agreed to sign and the Russians expressed their willingness if France and Poland signed first. The Poles refused and remained determined to avoid any involvement with the Soviet Union.

Then Beck made a fatal blunder. He pretended to the British that the Danzig question had almost been settled and suggested instead a British-Polish agreement. Given the pro-German policy of Poland the British feared that they might be forced into acting together against Russia.

On 22nd March Memel in Lithuania was surrendered to Germany. Like Danzig it had an overwhelmingly German population and had been taken over by the Lithuanians at the end of the First World War.

Meanwhile the Poles and Germans continued to discuss Danzig and future co-operation once the issue had been settled. Hitler was quite clear that he did *not* want to resolve it by force and wanted the Poles as allies. At this point some anti-Nazi German generals told a British journalist, quite falsely, that Hitler was preparing to attack Poland. He reported this news to London and in the atmosphere of increasing panic Chamberlain made a fatal mistake that ultimately led to World War Two. In a misguided attempt to counter a non-existent threat to Romania he drafted a declaration of support to the Polish government. It read:

> *"If any action were taken which clearly threatened their independence, and which the Polish government accordingly felt obliged to resist with their national forces, His Majesty's Government and the French Government would at once lend them all the support in their power."*

This declaration was another example of Chamberlain's poor judgement. Not only was it a guarantee to Poland when the alleged threat was against Romania but he made this commitment on behalf of France without consulting the French beforehand. They were furious at being treated in this cavalier fashion but reluctantly agreed. They told the British that they believed Poland was not in any immediate danger and they doubted the fighting abilities of the Polish armed forces.

In addition to these difficulties the declaration was fundamentally flawed by making it impossible for Britain and France to urge the Poles to make concessions. Only the Poles could decide whether or not British and French assistance was necessary. It encouraged Poland in the foolish belief that the Franco-British declaration strengthened their hand over Danzig. The reality is that without the "guarantee" a compromise settlement would almost certainly have been achieved.

When Hitler heard the news he flew into a rage. He not only broke off the discussions with Poland but on 3rd April told his armed forces to be prepared to launch an attack on the country. He reassured his generals by telling them that this operation would only be instigated if the Poles fought alone. On 28th April he addressed the Reichstag and declared that he wanted a negotiated settlement over Danzig. He called on the Poles to renounce their alliance with Britain and France and remain German allies.

At this stage Hitler still hoped for a peaceful solution and the British were already regretting the blank cheque that their guarantee to Poland had been. They told Beck that the alliance would only operate if Polish independence was "clearly threatened." This belated attempt to pressure the Poles into making concessions over Danzig had no effect.[51]

Curiously Hitler fell silent on the question for some months. Instead various factions within the Nazi leadership attempted to resolve the situation. Goering tried to reassure the British about the threat of war while also seeking to pursue discussions with the Soviet Union. Hitler allowed the various differing viewpoints to follow their own policies while remaining out of the fray and waiting for events to resolve the situation.

There followed a tragi-comic interlude of musical chairs between Russia, the Western Allies and Germany. France became increasingly desperate to secure a military alliance with the Soviet Union and put pressure on Britain to engage in negotiations with the Russians. There was little enthusiasm for the idea in the British Government though

Churchill, Lloyd George and the Labour Opposition began to demand that the British and Soviets should join forces to resist Nazi aggression.

This was difficult for a variety of reasons ranging from the visceral anti-Communism of Chamberlain's government to a fear of Russian intentions if she became militarily involved against Germany and a general though mistaken underestimation of Soviet military capability. The negotiations were conducted in a desultory manner with the Russians on the whole offering their proposals and responses to British ideas very quickly while the British dragged their feet and were slow to reply.

Various theories as to what happened over the next few months have been put forward. Soviet historians were (and many Russian ones still are) convinced that the West was never sincere in seeking to reach an agreement and hoped that the Germans would launch an attack on the Soviet Union and destroy it. The Nazis believed that the British and French were trying to encircle Germany but that they failed because of Soviet doubts about their intentions. Some Western historians believe that the Russians were never truly interested in the discussions and intended all along to sign a peace deal with Germany to protect themselves.

In hindsight it can be seen that there is some truth in all these theories. France was always more interested than Britain in an alliance with Russia and the British certainly distrusted Stalin and were not at all anxious to see the spread of Communism into Eastern Europe. To that extent the Soviets were right but the archives clearly show that however mismanaged and full of doubt and hesitation the British approaches to Russia were they do appear to have been sincere.

The Nazis were also correct in seeing the British and French aim in negotiating with Russia as being to encircle Germany but that was primarily designed as a deterrent rather than as a means of making war against the country.

Equally there is some truth in the claim that the Russians were not exactly wholehearted in their pursuit of a Western alliance. They were almost as wary of the British who distrusted the Soviets and their subsequent conduct after 1945 showed clearly why Britain had good reason to fear their expansionist ambitions in Eastern Europe.

The ultimate reason for the failure of the British-Soviet talks was because Russian political and military demands could not be met. The Soviets insisted on being able to move their troops into Poland and/or Romania which from a purely military point of view was totally reasonable. The problem was that both the Poles and Romanians doubted that Russian troops would leave once they had defeated a German invasion.

That military difficulty might have been capable of compromise but what made agreement between the Soviets and the West was their political demands. They insisted that the Baltic states of Estonia, Latvia and Lithuania should be "taken under their protection" which everyone knew was code for annexation to Russia. Having already betrayed Czechoslovakia it was impossible for Britain and France to do the same to the Baltic States.

It was not helped by the refusal of both the Polish and Romanian governments to allow the passage of Russian troops through their territory. Faced with this insuperable obstacle the talks between Russia and the West ended in failure.

Elements in the German government continued their negotiations with the Russians and finally Hitler became directly involved. He suggested that his Foreign Minister Ribbentrop should fly to Moscow and conduct high level discussions between the two countries.

Even at this stage Hitler was not planning an attack on Poland but hoped to frighten Britain and France by his negotiations. He saw a putative Nazi-Soviet agreement not as a blueprint for war but a means to keep the Western Powers quiet and force the Poles to reach an agreement over Danzig.[52]

At this stage the Hungarian Prime Minister wrote to Hitler and told him that "in the event of a general conflict Hungary will make her policy conform to the policy of the Axis" but also said "Hungary could not, on moral grounds, be in a position to take armed action against Poland."[53]

On 12th August Ciano, the Italian Foreign Minister, arrived to meet with Hitler. He had been instructed by Mussolini to keep Italy out of the war at all costs. Ciano explained that he felt it would be impossible to confine the war to Poland and Germany and his country was not ready to take part in a war against Britain and France and possibly the Soviet Union as well. Hitler retorted that "he was absolutely certain that the Western democracies would shrink from a general war" and that the whole conflict would be over by mid-October.[54]

Then events came to Hitler's assistance once more. The Anglo-Soviet talks broke down on 17th August and on 21st August the French tried to go it alone, agreeing to sign the terms required by the Russians. The British and Poles refused to accept them and in the meantime the Germans took action. On 14th August Ribbentrop sent a telegram to the German Ambassador in Moscow declaring that:

> *"There exist no real conflicts of interest between Germany and Russia. There is no question between the Baltic Sea and the Black Sea which cannot be settled to the complete satisfaction of both parties."*[55]

The Russians responded with a query about the willingness of the Germans to sign a pact of non-aggression between the two countries. Ribbentrop immediately replied that not only were they prepared to sign such an agreement but would make a joint guarantee with the Soviet Union of the Baltic States and were prepared to mediate between Russia and Japan (at the time both countries were engaged in border clashes.) In spite of this message the Russians continued to proceed with the negotiations at a leisurely pace and it took a telegram from Hitler to Stalin on 20th August to break the deadlock. The result was that Ribbentrop was invited to Moscow and on 23rd August the two countries signed a public non-aggression pact. They also signed a secret agreement to divide up Poland between Russia and Germany and allow the Soviet Union to take control of the Baltic States.

Both the Russians and Germans imagined that the treaty would bring an end to the Danzig question and that without Soviet help the Poles and Western Powers would be forced to yield and conclude an agreement with Hitler. Neither side imagined that the treaty would pave the way to a second world war yet that is exactly what happened.

On 25th August it finally dawned on Hitler that war was imminent. Two events that day made him hesitate and try to withdraw from his military preparations. The first was that the British government told Hitler they would stand by Poland in the event of war. The second was that the Italians informed him they would not be able to participate in any military operations.

Hitler's response was immediate. He summoned Keitel, his chief of staff, and told him he needed time for negotiations. The military plans to invade Poland were put on hold.

Negotiations between Germany and Britain were hastily resumed but without any satisfactory agreement. Then on 29th August Hitler asked the Poles to send a plenipotentiary to Germany to negotiate a settlement. The Poles refused and after two days of fruitless attempts to persuade them to try to reach an agreement Hitler reluctantly gave the signal to attack Poland. With even greater reluctance the British government declared war on Germany two days later. The whole affair had been a disastrous blunder on Hitler's part and showed his failure to grasp foreign public opinion.

He was right to believe that Chamberlain was desperate to avoid war but the anger against Germany after the fall of Czechoslovakia and his foolish blank cheque to Poland made it impossible for Chamberlain to withdraw from his commitments. Hitler failed to recognize that the British guarantee to Poland was of a different type and order from its previous assurances to Czechoslovakia. He should have realized that his own stubbornness was dragging his country into war and it was impossible for him to avoid fighting Britain and France as well as Poland.

Other foreign policy issues again show the way in which Hitler's ignorance of the outside world and his failure to perceive public opinion abroad led to mistaken decisions. It is difficult to see the value of the alliance with Japan. It brought no visible benefit to Germany – politically, economically or militarily. Only in the event of a joint German-Japanese attack on the Soviet Union might it have made military sense but as that not only failed to happen but was never a realistic prospect the purpose of the alliance seems dubious. It led at least partly to the disastrous and incomprehensible decision to declare war on the United States after the Japanese had destroyed the fleet at Pearl Harbor.

Of all Hitler's poor Cabinet appointments, the choice of Ribbentrop as Foreign Minister was one of the worst. He lacked tact and had little understanding of foreign affairs and almost every foreign policy decision he took was wrong. There were people in the Foreign Ministry who tried to give sensible advice but they were ignored. He was despised by the other Nazi leaders with Goebbels saying scornfully that "he bought his name, he married his money and he swindled his way into office."[56] Ribbentrop's only reasonable foreign policy idea was to oppose the war against the Soviet Union and to beg Hitler to make a separate peace with Stalin. Other than that his tenure as Foreign Minister was an unmitigated disaster.

Economy in Crisis

German agriculture had been in decline for years with the growing industrialization of the country. This process was dramatically accelerated by the Depression and smallholders were hit particularly hard. Punitive taxation on agriculture under the Weimar Republic created additional difficulties for farmers. Young people preferred to abandon a life on the land and seek employment in the cities where wages were higher and the work less strenuous. The combination of a shortage of agricultural workers, high costs and falling profits and the glowing promises made to the farming community by the Nazis resulted in growing support for the party.

The rising burden of debt and increasing poverty led to an explosion of popular discontent in 1932. Violent protests occurred across most of North Germany.[1]

German agriculture was largely unmechanized and most farms lacked running water. The majority of ploughing was carried out through the use of oxen and grain was bundled by hand. The labour-intensive nature of farming contrasted dramatically with the picture in Britain or America.

It is unsurprising that farmers were attracted to the Nazi Party. Once Hitler came to power the Nazis genuinely tried to improve the conditions of both farmers and agricultural labourers. Mortgage interest rates were limited to a maximum of 4½ % and the government gave credits to improve farm labourers' homes, silos and drainage. The Reich Food Estate was created which controlled 3 million farms, 300,000 food processing businesses and half a million stores selling food and drink.

The Food Estate fixed wages and prices, distributed resources and set quotas for production. It also dictated which crops were sown. The wages of farm labourers rose dramatically though remained below the level of industrial workers.

It was forbidden to sell or mortgage a farm above 7.5 hectares. In 1938 a law was passed dissolving family estates.

Nazi farming policy was intended to benefit the farmers and on the whole did so but was continually frustrated by the opposition of the Junkers with their vast landed estates and the military with its growing hunger for land. In spite of these factors the budget for agriculture rose by 62% between 1934 and 1939. Land reclamation programmes secured an additional 596,000 hectares.[2]

For all the attempts to grow more food within Germany it was impossible for the regime to achieve the self-sufficiency goal desired by the Nazis. Food imports declined in some areas such as grain but the need for foreign imports continued. The shortage of animal feed led to reduced livestock production and a growing reliance on chemicals rather than natural fertilizers.

Farmers and farm labourers endured long hours and poor living conditions. The fact that most farms did not even possess a radio added to the isolation of their lives. Young women preferred not to marry a farmer because of the hard life they knew agriculture entailed. The Labour Service for girls attempted to fill the shortage of farm workers but with mixed results.

Ultimately the government's aim of agricultural self-sufficiency could not be achieved without modernizing farms and making a life in farming a more attractive option. The Nazis preferred to spend money on the military, infrastructure and other prestige projects so agriculture remained the poor relation.[3]

The chaotic nature of business organization created severe problems through the pursuit of incompatible goals. Rigid restrictions were imposed and there was excessive central planning, but this was coupled with insufficient regulation of quality and design. Human resources were used in a highly inefficient manner, partly to reduce unemployment and partly as a result of corruption.

The Nazis came to power on a programme of goals that were fundamentally contradictory. Full employment was achieved though often at the cost of waste and increased use of part-time work. Industry recovered its former strength and rigid price and wage controls had both positive and negative effects in terms of achieving economic stability. The Nazi economy performed a curious balancing act that created problems of its own. An essentially anti-capitalist and anti-industrial spirit pervaded the Nazi movement which ran directly counter to their strident pursuit of rearmament. The regime's commitment to what would now be called "Green" policies also hindered the development of industry and even the military. Price control, while benefiting workers and consumers, made it harder for industry to develop rapidly and effectively.

In the early years of the Third Reich shorter working hours and a reduction of mechanization were methods employed to lower the unemployment figures. This created a labour-intensive working environment and hampered attempts to modernise industry. The regime also declared that "profit is to be kept within moderate limits."[4]

When business demanded tax cuts, preferential treatment in public service contracts and a laissez-faire approach by the government they were met with a flat refusal.[5]

In 1934 a group of businessmen was informed that "any organization that represents the interests of employers will be regarded as illegal."[6]

In 1934 an article condemned not only laissez-faire economics but even the profit motive itself, declaring that "the economy left to itself has neither the inner authority nor the discipline necessary to prevent serious damage," adding that "the profit drive is generally stronger than the moral edification to the general welfare."[7]

This inconsistency of objectives pervaded the Nazi regime and not until 1943 was the economy fundamentally restructured to put it on a war footing with other goals set aside unless they served the aim of victory. The inconsistency came from the very top with Hitler oscillating between a romantic mediaeval vision of a peasant society and an aggressive modernity of spirit.

For the first four years of the regime all kinds of wild idea were proposed, discussed, considered and generally dismissed. The nearest approach to economic equilibrium was provided by the Economics Minister Hjalmar Schacht. Even his contributions were not always successful since he attempted to combine two incompatible economic philosophies – Keynesian economics and deflationary policies. Schacht might have been nicknamed "The Old Wizard" but he remained too wedded to antiquated fiscal concepts which made his expansionary policies less effective.

It is ironic that when Goering took charge of the economy following Schacht's dismissal the situation improved. Although the government kept tight control on wages and prices the rearmament programme would inevitably have led to inflation. Foreign currency restrictions made exporting more difficult and reduced the opportunities for German businessmen to gain experience by working abroad.

Various ideas for economic organization were considered and generally rejected during the six years preceding the outbreak of war. These ranged from the Italian Fascist *Carta del Lavoro* model to the revival of the mediaeval guild system. Feder and others on the left of the party championed a corporate model while Schacht and Walther Funk favoured a fundamentally capitalist social order. Neither side achieved their objectives and the economic chaos resulting from the lack of a clear and consistent policy was entirely avoidable.

The threat of inflation posed by the pursuit of a policy of deficit financing alarmed Schacht and the shortage of foreign currency reserves also hampered the government's room for manoeuvre. His solution was an export drive but Germany's shortage of raw materials and a concern among the Nazi leaders that a reliance on exports might affect the push for self-sufficiency led to its rejection. Instead the government preferred to adopt Goering's Four Year Plan. This produced mixed results with its demands for increased production of iron and steel, increased development of synthetic fuel and rubber and domestic production of raw materials rather than reliance on imports being only partially successful.

The chemical industry embraced the plans enthusiastically with the result that I G Farben became one of the wealthiest companies in Germany. Steel producers were reluctant to follow the plans which led to Goering setting up a government-funded rival organization that soon became one of the biggest semi-public corporations in the country. The existing steel businesses had surplus stocks and saw no reason to expand when there appeared to be no purpose in adopting that course of action. Goering, always conscious of the needs of the military, thought ahead to the prospect of a possible war and used his new quango to impose a production drive on the steel industry.

Foreign debt remained high and the balance of payments continued to show a deficit. Trade agreements and tight import controls were insufficient to overcome the inherent economic instability. In spite of the successful drive for autarky in many areas and the development of *ersatz* – substitute – products it remained essential to import food and other raw materials from abroad. This dependence on imports continued to handicap the economy and eventually made the prosecution of the war far more difficult than it might have been.

The outlook for small businesses was difficult. In theory they benefited from Nazi rule with public contracts being reserved for them and authorities or public bodies being forbidden to deal with department stores or chain stores. In May 1933 the creation of new chain stores was forbidden and they were also prohibited from expanding. They were not allowed to sell new product ranges or to open restaurants. Department stores were subject to punitive tax rates on their revenue.[8]

Big business was also handicapped by limiting dividends to 6% and any profits above that amount were compelled to be converted into Reich bonds. The wealthy contributed nearly half of government revenue from taxation.

The manner in which the Nazi economy operated was a great hindrance to the war effort. Until 1941 for example Krupp sold better quality weapons to Greece, Turkey and even the Soviet Union than they provided to the Wehrmacht. This was because better raw materials were reserved for export sales rather than the domestic market.[9]

The military was also affected by wider-ranging economic problems. Germany was deficient in almost all raw materials except coal which meant that oil, rubber, metal and many other essential items had to be imported. This increased the balance of payments deficit and led to a growing shortage of foreign exchange.

Fuel was crucial both for domestic energy requirements and to accelerate the process of German rearmament. In spite of considerable investment in synthetic fuel plants to convert coal into petrol by 1938 only 25% of fuel reserves were available for military use.

The Luftwaffe and Navy were particularly badly affected by Nazi economic policies. By 1938 the Germans were forced to *reduce* the amount of steel that had been allocated for armament production. By January 1939 the shortage of raw materials and foreign exchange had become so acute that it was necessary to make further reductions on the amount made available for military purposes.

The Luftwaffe was short of both fighters and bombers and the lack of sufficient industrial capacity made it impossible for Hitler and Goering to realise their dream of using aircraft as a weapon of terror to cow their enemies into submission. A lack of suitable engines and the relative backwardness of German aviation development compounded the problem.[10]

Further unnecessary difficulties were created by the nature of Nazi administration. Central planning was extensive in many areas and control of prices and wages were maintained successfully. On the other hand unnecessary competition between government, Party and quasi-governmental bodies that all operated independently and all made demands for preferential treatment. The result was waste, duplication of resources, a lack of co-ordination and an absence of effective research and development or forward planning.

Limitations on dividends and capitalization discouraged business expansion and the organizational side of companies was often almost anarchic. Lack of adequate quality control affected production with the result that defective goods were often released on to the market. There were also logistical problems in distributing essential components.[11]

As Burton Klein demonstrated in his still classic analysis of the Nazi economy, Germany was completely unprepared for war in 1939.[12] Hitler continued to believe that the threat of war would be sufficient to bluff his enemies into conceding his demands and neither the military nor the economy was in any shape to prosecute an effective military campaign. If, as has often been wrongly maintained, he had been preparing for war ever since his accession as Chancellor in 1933, he would have organized the nation on a far more effective basis. In spite of Rudolf Hess' remark that 'guns will make us powerful; butter will only make us fat,' as late as 1943 the Nazis consistently put butter *before* guns. Hitler was desperate to keep the civilian population fed with vivid memories of the revolution in 1918 always before his eyes. As a result he continued to prioritize the material welfare of the Home Front above that of the demands of the military.

By 1934 the shortage of foreign currency was so acute that drastic restrictions on imports were introduced. This handicapped the development of both agriculture and industry since domestic foodstuffs were in short supply and the raw materials needed by industry were lacking. In spite of the attempts to produce alternatives domestically there was neither the time nor the capacity to do so except over a much longer timescale than was possible.[13]

Further attempts to reduce the balance of payments deficit were made by preventing the export of capital from Germany. Foreign companies were compelled either to retain their money within the country or use it for building projects. It was forbidden to export more than ten marks a month.

The planned export drive failed in its objectives. There were relatively few areas where manufacturing could produce goods that other countries were willing to purchase from them. A further difficulty for the policy was that as Germany increased its exports other countries began imposing higher tariffs upon their goods.[14] Schacht's "New Plan" was introduced in September 1934 and attempted to use permits for foreign exchange to restrict imports to the same level as exports. Schacht's plan failed partly because foreign companies were reluctant to buy most German goods but primarily since the hunger for raw materials – particularly metal – made it almost impossible to achieve the desired reduction in imports.

By March 1935 Schacht realized that his policies had failed. The result was that imported goods were drastically limited. This Draconian measure produced a temporary surplus in the balance of payments but was unsustainable in the long term.

A more effective method of controlling imports and exports was through the use of barter. Under the guise of bilateral trade agreements Germany imported food and raw materials and paid for them, not in cash but by supplying weapons or materials for public works projects. This led to increasing German influence in many countries though eventually it was resented by some of its recipients, particularly Greece and Bulgaria.

As with so many of Schacht's economic experiments, he failed through being insufficiently bold. He was willing to operate on the basis of deficit finance but insisted on a grossly overvalued mark and refused even to countenance devaluation. The memory of the 1923-4 hyperinflation led him to pursue a deflationary approach to the economy in harness with a programme of large public spending.

Of course the government's hands were tied by the economic difficulties they inherited from the Weimar Republic. Germany had very little in the way of gold reserves or foreign currency and it was difficult to fund capital projects through borrowing. This was partly because of the continuing distrust of the country and partly because the worldwide recession made banks and governments less willing to take risks with foreign lending. On the other hand, Schacht's policy of what would nowadays be called "quantitative easing" made more sense if it had been combined with a policy of increasing consumer spending to refloat the economy rather than being pursued in tandem with strict wage and price control and cuts to many existing government programmes. Schacht's economic policies attempted to reconcile two policies that were fundamentally incompatible and not until they were effectively abandoned in 1943 did the German economy function more smoothly. By that time, of course, the war was in full flow and Germany's defeat was inevitable, a process that relentless Allied bombing only accelerated.

The drive for economic self-sufficiency remained the Nazi hope but it could never be more than a Utopian dream. In spite of the continuing development of *ersatz* materials and Darré's successful drive to improve agriculture it was never realistic to assume that Germany could produce enough food or raw materials to sustain itself. Bauxite, tungsten, nickel, antimony and even vegetable oils could not be manufactured at home and the shortage of these and other items could only be overcome through imports. The process of rearmament demanded greater quantities of these materials and so it was inevitable that the volume of imported goods would increase rather than decrease.

The world prices of raw materials were rising in the 1930s while the prices of manufactured goods were falling. This made it impossible to correct the imbalance of trade and the bilateral trade agreements which essentially substituted payment in goods for payment in cash were a desperate expedient. How long this process would have continued had the Second World War not occurred is difficult to say but there is little doubt that the gains in political influence were counterbalanced by the increasing dependence on the client countries for these essential materials. In some ways the policy was more suited to a war economy than a peacetime one and perhaps without the outbreak of war the German economy might have buckled under the strain.[15]

Another device used to refloat the economy was privatization. The companies and institutions involved ranged from banks, iron and steel companies, shipping businesses and public transport.[16] The privatization of these enterprises reduced state expenditure (although the massive increase in armaments and public works easily outweighed this reduction), created a network of companies that owed varying degrees of gratitude to the regime. It also released more funds for the government to spend on weapons and public building projects.

As a policy, privatization ran counter to the official Party policy but was not entirely a cynical expedient to reduce the public debt or to reward possible supporters. There was a genuine dichotomy in Nazi economic philosophy between its attachment to a loosely socialist form of economic organization that remained championed by Goebbels, Himmler and other leading Party leaders and its desire to use the state to control rather than directly own enterprises. This inner tension was compounded both by the desperate need to increase revenue and the fact that the conservative wing of the Party consistently opposed anything beyond the minimum level of State intervention in the economy. The privatization programme was an attempt to reconcile incompatible objectives and philosophies and in that respect was typical of the Janus-faced nature of the Nazi regime. It gave support to business with one hand and took it away with another. It gave the majority of workers a better standard of living (on the whole) but denied them the right to strike or to organize except within the narrow parameters of the Nazi-controlled Labour Front.

A consistently socialist or capitalist approach might have been more successful just as a consistently followed policy of deficit financing might have avoided some of the problems that increasingly hampered the development of the economy. The idea that the Nazis were the tool of big business and their rise to power was largely founded by financial support from industrial magnates such as Thyssen has long since been exploded. Only after Hitler became Chancellor did business begin to switch its support to the Nazis and even then it was not until he had been in power for two years that it became the norm for them to do so.

One measure that the Nazis took ran directly counter to their pre-election pledges to support small business. They began to favour the growth of cartels which resulted in the merger of companies into large conglomerates and increasingly led to the failure of smaller firms. This gave huge advantages to the larger corporations but the downside was that it became easier for the government to control them. Even the most powerful combines found that it was inadvisable to reject Nazi policies. A few did so without incurring serious consequences but in the majority of cases flouting the will of the regime led to economic penalties. These ranged from denial of government contracts, restrictions on access to raw materials or in a handful of cases attracting the unwelcome attentions of the Gestapo.[17]

The position of cartels was established under a law passed in July 1933. This gave the Minister of Economics the power to stabilize the economy by compelling businesses to form cartels. Within three years of this decree 1600 smaller businesses were merged into larger cartels. The downside from the point of view of the consumer was a restriction in choice and competitiveness; from the perspective of business the negative aspect was increased control by government of every aspect of their activities and the compulsory fixing of prices.[18]

The Ministry of Economics assumed sweeping powers over the cartels, dictating the quantities and even type of products they manufactured or sold; they were forbidden to expand their productive capacity without the express consent of the government.[19]

In spite of the drive towards cartelization small business initially benefited from Nazi rule. Government and local authority contracts were reserved for them and no public contract could ever be given to chain stores or department stores.[20]

Businesses had to endure high taxation, limitations on the dividends payable to shareholders, currency control, a ban on the issue of new shares, import restrictions and (effectively) a tax on profits. Any profits over 6% had to be converted into Reich bonds which of course contributed enormously to government revenue. In 1935 the interest rate on mortgages was reduced from 6% to 4½%. Corporation tax was increased to 25% in 1936 and to 40% in 1939.[21]

Goering's Four Year Plan – whatever its other merits may have been – involved a revival of the mediaeval system of "benevolences" – forced loans. The Herman Goering Works became a large quasi-public company with 70% of shares owned by the government and businesses compelled to purchase the remaining 30% at 4½% interest. Goering essentially compelled business to subsidize his industrial empire.[22]

Another example of Nazi inconsistency was their treatment of the co-operatives. These had arisen in the late nineteenth century primarily as a means of allowing workers to save and obtain credit. Some also became involved in the housing market.

By the early twentieth century most co-operatives were affiliated to the Central Union of German Consumers' Societies. In 1932 949 societies belonged to the Central Union and their members controlled nearly 11,000 shops, 48,000 workers and had 2.8 million members.

Even in opposition the Nazis had denounced the co-ops in a typically inconsistent manner as being both tools of Marxism to destroy private business and as being capitalist ventures to exploit the workers. The Nazis set out to pit small business owners against the co-ops and to paint them as being enemies of the people.

Once in power the campaign against the co-operatives intensified. Shop windows were broken; many of the enterprises had their assets seized and SA members even engaged in brutal violence against the businesses and their staff and owners. The situation became so difficult that leading members of the co-operatives approached the government directly asking for protection and help.

Characteristically the response was a mixed one. Hess issued a public declaration that no one should be either physically attacked or discriminated against because of their membership of a co-operative society. On the other hand, in May 1935 the government passed a law forbidding the co-ops to expand, requiring them to liquidate their existing funds and to work towards ending their co-operative nature and transforming themselves into small businesses. Further problems for the co-ops occurred in 1938 when anti-Semitic policies intensified and the co-operatives were required by law to exclude all Jewish members and Jewish firms from membership. By 1941 the Nazis decided that all existing co-operatives would be shut down but of course the war made this more an aspiration than a reality.

The campaign against the co-operatives was economically unnecessary, reduced consumer choice and access to credit and savings outside the government-approved firms and had no impact on either inflation or unemployment. It was ideologically motivated and ended up being positively harmful to the nation. In spite of the success in drastically reducing the numbers of co-operatives it failed to eliminate them completely.[23]

Skilled workers and artisans benefited considerably from Nazi economic policies. In November 1933 the government passed a law requiring artisans to belong to a guild and possess "a major certificate of qualifications." Each trade had its approved guild and belonged to the local *Handelskammer* (Chamber of Trade.)[24]

These groups had struggled under Weimar particularly following the Depression. With the vast expansion of public and private projects their skills were in demand and they prospered as a result.

Of course the nature of the guilds was not that envisaged by either the left of the Nazi Party – who saw them as a replacement for the former trade unions – or by the romantic right who wished to revive them on the old mediaeval basis where they dominated trades and were able to control their own destiny. The Nazis saw them as a counterpart to their control of the business sector and ensured that admission to them was restricted to those considered to be politically reliable. In spite of these restrictions on their freedom of action the results of Nazi economic policies were to enrich them considerably.[25]

The Nazi treatment of the guilds was a half-way house between feudalism and the corporate state ideal promoted by Mussolini and championed by many Nazis including Feder, Himmler, Goebbels and Ley. In many respects it granted a demand that artisans had been making since the late 19th century. On the whole from 1933-1939 the economic policies of the regime made the artisans extremely happy with their situation.[26]

Of course these conditions were beneficial to the artisans during peacetime but the advent of war made things more difficult for them. Mass production was needed for the war effort and although they were vastly more mechanized than in previous centuries they remained essentially handicraft workers and so were less able to contribute to the needs of the military machine.[27]

Business and employers represented only one side of the economy. Mistakes in that sector were matched by errors in terms of labour. The Nazi Party contained a considerable proportion of workers in its membership and a far larger number who voted for them in elections. The socialist wing of the party remained strong even after the "Night of the Long Knives" with Feder, Ley, Rust, Goebbels and Himmler all sympathetic to its vision.

Unemployment stood at six million when Hitler came to power and many of the methods he adopted to reduce it were effective and could even (particularly in hindsight) be considered to be sensible measures. Others were neither effective nor sensible.

One measure that in the short term reduced unemployment but in the long run had negative consequences was the attempt to remove most women from the work force and replace them with men. In peacetime this strategy worked reasonably well but once the nation was at war it severely hampered the ability of Germany to operate as effectively as the Allies. Britain, the United States and the Soviet Union used female labour from the earliest stages of the war and not until 1943, on the desperate insistence of Goebbels, did the Germans even begin to make use of the productive capacity of women.[28]

When the Nazis came to power they bided their time for a few months and then brutally suppressed the existing trade unions and seized their assets. This removed a source of opposition and placed their funds under the control of the Nazis. What followed was a year of characteristically inconsistent approaches. The socialist wing of the Party advocated the idea that the NSBO (Factory Cell Organization) which was dominated by Nazi leftists should take over the role of the former unions. Goering and Hess bitterly opposed this idea and cast around for an alternative.[29]

The solution they came up with was the formation of a new body, the Labour Front. For a variety of reasons this was a disastrous mistake. One reason was the character of its leader, Robert Ley. He was an alcoholic whose drunkenness grew worse the longer he stayed in post and who was incapable of effective organization. Another problem with the Front was that it rapidly turned into a sprawling bureaucratic nightmare with departments fighting other departments and a consequent paralysis on decision-taking. Ley had no previous experience in labour relations and his "leadership" was a disaster.

The proliferation of departments and functions of the Front made it not simply unwieldy but wasteful. In spite of its success in providing subsidized holidays, better working conditions and even improved wages for the majority of workers it remained a body that floundered in a welter of contradictory objectives.

The Front soon expanded its activities to control economic activity, legal aid, social services and career advice. It employed around 40,000 people and its membership ran into millions. Schacht soon clashed with the Front on economic issues but increasingly fought a losing battle. In spite of Ley's alcoholism and general incapacity for high office his organization grew increasingly powerful.

The Front might have purged the socialists of the NSBO from any positions of power but it remained on the left of the Nazi Party. It was common to hear Ley and his subordinates declare that "the industrialists are a gang of conspirators."[30] The Front may not have wished to become a revised form of the trade unions but it certainly loathed capitalism and in its own bizarre fashion genuinely attempted to represent and advance the interests of the workers.

Industrial disputes were now settled through a "court of honour" which consisted of a judge, an employer and a member of the "shop council." In spite of claims to the contrary, the majority of decisions by the court went in favour of the workers rather than the employer. Far from being a device to enable employers to act with impunity the "courts of honour" held businesses to account and could fine or otherwise take punitive action against them.

Above the courts stood the Reich Trustees who were responsible directly to the Ministry of Labour. They had the power to fix wages and working conditions and approve or reject cases of dismissal of employees.[31]

The Front took over the Labour Service that had been created in the dying years of Weimar and in that area turned it into an effective body. It conscripted civilian labour in the same way that military service had added to the numbers and calibre of the armed forces.

The main tasks of the Labour Service were forestry and land reclamation. The youths cleared swamps and moorland, drained marshes, built irrigation channels and reclaimed land from the sea. Sometimes they would work on road building projects but on the whole that was untypical. The regime preferred to use the unemployed for that type of work.

Generally youths working in the Labour Service found themselves on the land with 80% of young men and 90% of young women working on farms. This undoubtedly helped to assuage the dire problems faced by agriculture with an acute shortage of workers and the low level of mechanization requiring physical labour to make farmland productive. In that respect the Labour Service was a beneficial idea and one that assisted the farming community to overcome their deep-seated difficulties in achieving a satisfactory lifestyle.[32]

The acute shortage of agricultural labour could not be filled by Labour Service youngsters alone. This led to restrictions on freedom of movement with older workers retained in towns and cities and youngsters directed to work on the land.

Soon skilled workers were forbidden to move or change their employment without permission from the local Labour Exchange. Aircraft workers were forbidden to move without a "certificate of release" signed by their former employer. Labour passes were also issued which meant that labour shortages could be identified and the movement of labour strictly controlled and directed.[33]

Nazi policy remained a mixture of stick and carrot. The stick was the fear of the Gestapo and concentration camps and the carrot was both the way in which the Front genuinely gave the workers a sense of "belonging" and of having their interests looked after and the expedients it used to try to win the loyalty of the working population.

The most obvious and effective way in which the "carrot" approach was used was through the *Kraft durch Freude* (Strength Through Joy) programme. Cheap holidays, often on cruises to Madeira or Norway, were the most popular part of the KdF activities.

Other KdF projects included education classes, sporting activities, subsidized theatre shows, exhibitions, dances and films. Around half the workers in Germany benefited from at least one of the KdF offerings. It was an expensive programme and of course the war forced its curtailment but it achieved its objective of using the tried and tested "bread and circus" model of pacifying the population.

The regime's drive for full employment and increased productivity was overwhelmingly focused on men. In the beginning of Nazi rule women were forced out of work to make room for the male unemployed but by 1936 the number of women in employment rose again.

It was no longer possible to fill the new labour shortages by the use of youngsters alone but the attempt was made. In 1939 it became compulsory for young women to join the Labour Service (previously it had been a voluntary choice for them) and they too found themselves compelled to work, almost entirely in the field of agriculture where the labour shortages were most acute.

There was a fierce disagreement among Nazis over the status of women. The more modern-minded ones like Goebbels had no objection to using female labour as freely as that of men but the conservative wing of the Nazi Party objected strongly. One of the great ironies is that the 1920s and early 1930s saw the apparent paradox of German feminists overwhelmingly supporting the Nazis.

In the 1920s Elizabeth Zander put her feminist organization entirely at the service of the Nazis and became a strong supporter. By 1930 three fiercely feminist women – Guida Diehl, Lydia Gottschewski and Sophie Rogge-Börner – were prominent, even militant, Nazis while not renouncing a single one of their feminist principles. All the Nazi feminists were eventually sidelined though for a while Gottschewski was in charge of the largest women's organization ever seen. Even Gertrud Scholz-Klink, who succeeded Gottschewski as the head of that body, insisted that confining women to the role of motherhood was a mistake. She declared firmly that there were no good reasons for excluding women from the work force.

By 1938 employers recognized that women were capable of performing a wider range of work than was previously believed and the severe labour shortages acted as an additional incentive to fill the gap with female labour. They began recruiting women to produce food and clothing and even to work as electricians, chemists and in factories. It was discovered that many women were particularly good at working in chemistry. The increasing degree of mechanization in industry also made it easier to recruit and employ women.

In spite of the increasing labour shortages and the growing demands by employers to recruit more women for traditionally male roles there remained opposition to the idea. This came directly from Hitler as well as conservative Nazis. In peacetime this hampered economic activity but was not a serious problem. Once the country was at war the reluctance to employ women became a major negative economic factor. Even during the last two years of the conflict when the military situation was desperate the use of women for war work remained far below the level of Britain and America.[35]

Another way in which the regime sought to overcome the labour deficit was through the use of forced labour. Between 1933 and 1939 this was carried out by Germans and (after 1938) Austrians who were either political opponents of the regime or were Jews or gypsies who were condemned on racial grounds. After 1939 Poles and Czechs also suffered from the forced labour programme with the French, Dutch and Belgians being subjected to it after 1940 and the Soviets from 1941.

Forced labour has often been confused with foreign labour. A surprisingly high number of foreign workers volunteered to work in Germany. 16% of Poles worked there voluntarily, for example, and Spanish and Italian workers were also employed as free labourers rather than slave labour. They were paid and their working conditions were on the whole tolerable.

There was a long tradition of hiring Polish migrant workers for German farms so the number of volunteers from Poland is less surprising than it might otherwise appear. Most Poles who chose to work in Germany were directed to agricultural labour; they were fed and housed and their working conditions were on a par with German farm labourers. Their employment on farms not only helped fill the shortage of agricultural labour but was also partly due to a reluctance to send them to work in urban areas.

It was a different matter for the forced labourers. No consideration was given to their welfare and they received subsistence rations at best and worked in appalling conditions.

As the war continued and the military situation worsened the use of forced labour increased dramatically. This was not only cruel and immoral but wasteful and inefficient. It is hardly surprising that many who were compelled to serve in this way attempted to sabotage the projects on which they were employed.[36]

Horrific as the forced labour system was it was exceeded in its barbarity and futility by the extermination programme. Instead of giving priority to military and economic needs that would have benefited the war Hitler preferred to respond to the prospect of defeat by accelerating the genocide campaign. The extermination programme was indefensible morally and even in practical terms. Resources were wasted on killing innocent people with no resulting benefit to Germany either militarily or economically.

The Holocaust was not simply a "mistake;" it was an act of needless cruelty. There is perhaps a kind of poetic justice in the fact that instead of helping to win the war it accelerated Germany's defeat.

From the Blitzkrieg to the Battle of the Bulge

Keitel might have nicknamed Hitler *Grofatz* – the greatest Field Marshal of all time – but almost every military decision he took was mistaken. Initially he tended to leave decisions to his generals and when he followed that approach the results were more successful.

The conquest of Poland was easy, especially with the Soviet Union also attacking from the east. What followed was not simply a failure to grasp the new political reality but a fundamental military miscalculation.

For eight months not a blow was struck in anger either on the ground or in the air. It was different at sea where U-boats fought a brutal war against the Royal and Merchant Navy to devastating effect.

Why did Hitler pause other military operations? Why did he not follow up the conquest of Poland by a direct attack on France?

The first and most fundamental reason is that Hitler feared a repeat of the stalemate of the First World War with German armies bogged down on French soil and ultimately being worn down. He knew – and his generals knew – that Germany was not equipped to fight a war of attrition. The Germans were short of tanks, aircraft, ships, submarines, fuel and raw materials. A long-drawn out conflict would inevitably drain their resources.

Neither Hitler nor his generals imagined that the French army would collapse suddenly. The fear of a long war led him to take the advice of his generals and postpone an attack. In hindsight that was almost certainly a mistake.

The second reason was a fundamental misjudgement of the mood of the British government. Hitler despised Chamberlain and was far too ready to accept Ribbentrop's assurances that the "Peace Party" in Britain would persuade the government to abandon the war. There is no doubt that advocates of appeasement existed within the British government but they were no longer dominant. Chamberlain refused to consider any peace deal that did not involve Hitler standing down as Chancellor and full withdrawal of all German forces from Poland. Hitler's dream of British acceptance of his conquests was never more than a fantasy.

The third reason for his failure to act was poor advice from his generals. They were overly cautious and believed that an invasion of France would be costly in terms of lives and equipment and be halted early in the campaign. They even overestimated the problems of the weather.

The failure of Britain and France to attack during the "Phoney War" has often been criticized but German inaction was equally indefensible from a military perspective. A lightning attack might not have succeeded as easily as the 1940 campaign but was certainly worth the risk.

When the decision to invade France was finally taken the original idea was to follow the Schlieffen Plan of attacking through Belgium. This had failed in World War One and it is probable that it would have been equally unsuccessful in 1940.

What changed events was an intelligence fiasco known as the Mechelen Incident. A plane carrying the plans for the invasion crashed in Belgium and although an attempt was made to burn the documents it was unsuccessful. Belgian intelligence studied the plans and passed them on to the Dutch and French authorities.

The discovery of the German invasion plans made Hitler abort the original strategy and follow an alternative course of action suggested by Manstein. This envisaged an invasion of France via the Ardennes. Pure chance avoided a military fiasco in 1940.

On the other hand the Mechelen Incident made Hitler distrust his generals and begin to meddle more in strategy. This led to significant errors of judgement that eventually cost him the war.

However questionable the failure to attack the Allies in 1939 might be there is no doubt that when the Germans finally overran Holland

and Belgium in 1940 and launched their surprise invasion of France via the Ardennes they were on the brink of victory. The French army was in full retreat and utterly demoralized and the British were unable to press forward in spite of desperate appeals by Churchill for them to continue the attack.

A bold assault by tanks and ground forces would undoubtedly have led to a crushing defeat for the Allies and the capture of almost all British troops and many French ones. In that event it is difficult to see how Britain could have continued the war. The country might have been able to fight a rearguard action for a time but with almost no trained troops available it is hard to see how they could have effectively defended themselves against a German invasion. The RAF and Navy would have fought hard to protect the nation but they would almost certainly have been overwhelmed and the war lost.

Instead the German advance halted for three crucial days and neither tanks nor infantry played any part in the German attempt to destroy the Allied forces. The Luftwaffe engaged in heavy bombing raids but otherwise the Germans were militarily inactive. The result was that almost all British armed forces were evacuated and many French troops as well.

The reason for the German failure to attack with ground troops has been debated for many years. A variety of different explanations have been put forward and one of the most obvious approaches is to blame Hitler. It has been claimed that Hitler ordered the troops to halt the attack either out of fear of losses or because he was reluctant to crush Britain. The truth is that Hitler played no part in the decision and the pause in fighting was entirely the result of an over cautious attitude by the German commander Rundstedt. He was concerned about damage to his tanks and expected to encounter much fiercer resistance from the French. Rundstedt wanted to pause to repair his Panzer divisions and prepare them for the forthcoming invasion.

This error of judgement by Rundstedt was compounded by the hubris shown by Goering who assured Hitler that the Luftwaffe could destroy the ground troops on its own. Not only was the Luftwaffe incapable of doing so but a combination of bad weather, heroism by RAF pilots and the Navy as well as a flotilla of small boats ensured that the bulk of the Allied forces were able to escape and regroup.

Even though this was a massive defeat for the Allies and led directly to the subsequent collapse of the French armed forces it represented a golden opportunity for victory that was thrown away by Rundstedt's over cautious approach. Hitler was not directly to blame for the failure but if he had issued instructions to attack it would have been the correct military and political decision.

Even after Dunkirk the British army was shattered. It had been forced to abandon nearly all its heavy weapons and tanks. Morale was at its lowest ebb and only Montgomery's 3rd Infantry Division remained a viable fighting force. The remainder of the army had obsolete equipment, few modern tanks and their spirit was all but broken. In spite of Churchill's attempt to present Dunkirk as a miracle of deliverance the truth is that it was a disastrous defeat. If Rundstedt had shown more courage and daring the British army would virtually have ceased to exist. The remnants left behind would have stood little chance against German troops if they had invaded the country.

Guderian later admitted that the failure to capture the Allied troops at Dunkirk was the biggest military mistake of the war. It not only saved Britain from almost certain defeat but had profound consequences for the future history of the world. Without Britain and its Empire continuing the fight against Germany Hitler would have had a free hand to attack the Soviet Union with every prospect of winning that war.

The United States would have continued to sit on the sidelines and Roosevelt's loathing for the Nazis would not have been enough to propel them into war with Germany. Hitler would have dominated Europe and large parts of Asia and even America would have had to regard him as too powerful for them to attack. With their Japanese allies dominating most of Asia and the Germans controlling Europe it is hard to see the Americans being able to do more than at most apply economic pressure against the Axis powers.

The results of what would have happened if the Germans and Japanese had obtained control over oil, gas and other natural resources are problematic. It is likely that the US would have enjoyed an uneasy stalemate with the Axis powers and that neither side would have wished to attack the other. The entire shape of the world would have been different, with the British Empire being dissolved much earlier than it was and the new German and Japanese empires replacing it in its former colonies. Perhaps the West Indies and Canada might have become American protectorates but the British dominions in Africa, Asia and probably Australasia would have been lost.

Following the Allied defeat at Dunkirk and the rapid capitulation of the French Hitler had his best chance to win the war. Even allowing for the presence of dispirited British troops on home soil there was never a better opportunity for Germany to invade Britain.

At that point a curious combination of factors conspired to save the British. Two were directly attributable to Hitler and a third to Goering. The first mistake was to imagine that Churchill would decide to sue for peace rather than continue to fight. Hitler was so confident that Britain would abandon the war that he began demobilizing. This was hardly a sensible way to prepare for an invasion and yet again Hitler's refusal to recognize the determination of the British government led him to make poor judgements.

The second problem – which recurred throughout the war – was Hitler's failure to grasp the importance of naval warfare. However shattered the British army was in 1940, at that time Britannia still ruled the waves. The German Navy was incapable of facing it in battle so a "second Jutland" was inconceivable.

Hitler failed to understand that a full-scale invasion might not be necessary. All that was needed were sufficient vessels to carry enough troops to capture part of the coast. This could have formed a bridgehead for other troops following up through this central foothold. An additional reason why a small invasion force would have been almost unstoppable was because at that time the Luftwaffe enjoyed complete air superiority and could have protected the invasion force.

The third factor was Goering's arrogance. Though his aircraft had failed to destroy the British troops at Dunkirk he insisted that he could force Britain to surrender through air power alone. This idea appealed to Hitler though it proved to be yet another failed strategy.

Even though these factors predisposed Hitler against the idea of invading Britain with ground troops he ordered a plan to be drawn up for the purpose. It was codenamed Operation Sea Lion and demanded 90,000 troops to be ferried across the Channel. The plan was grandiose but completely unrealistic.

The German Navy did not have the capacity to carry such a large body of troops across the Channel. There were few surface ships available and most of the best naval vessels had been lost during the needless Norwegian campaign.[1]

There was little enthusiasm for Operation Sea Lion in the German high command. Both Raeder (in charge of the Navy) and leading generals raised all kinds of technical objections. They magnified the difficulties of the operation and made extravagant and impossible demands for weapons and raw material. It was clear that they had no faith in a successful invasion and worked hard to persuade Hitler to abandon the project.

With all these factors working against the idea of a risky but almost certainly successful assault on Britain the plan was essentially shelved until the Luftwaffe had achieved its goal of supposedly reducing Britain to surrender through air power. That too was a costly failure and the blame for that fiasco rests squarely with Goering.[2]

Sea Lion was a bad plan and it is clear that even its advocates – whether by design or through incompetence – saw it as being unrealistic. A scaled-down version of it involving a small body of German troops seizing a part of the coast and using it to spread outwards with other troops following up would certainly have succeeded. The demoralized British army would have fought but been overcome, especially with the Luftwaffe adding to their woes. As often happened during the war, Hitler's indecisiveness cost him victory. A bold thrust by a small number of troops would have been a risk worth taking and would almost certainly have brought a rapid end to war, at least in the West.

Eventually Hitler "postponed" – in reality abandoned – the idea of Sea Lion and instead began making preparations for war against the Soviet Union. The result was to ensure his defeat although it might have turned out completely differently if alternative military and political strategies had been followed.

The next military problem was not of Hitler's making though it does reflect upon his poor judgement in terms of assessing the quality of his allies. Hitler had been working hard and with considerable success to draw the Eastern European countries into the German orbit. With one rash move Mussolini undid all the diplomatic and economic gains that Hitler's policy had achieved. On October 28th he informed Hitler that Italian troops had invaded Greece and confidently expected to conquer the country soon. Hitler was appalled and had previously attempted to deter Mussolini from any foreign adventures but *Il Duce* refused to listen to the advice of his fellow dictator. His jealousy of Hitler's annexations of territory from France, Belgium, Czechoslovakia and Poland led him to imagine foolishly that it would be easy for him to overcome the Greeks and add their country to his empire.

There were political as well as military reasons for Hitler's reluctance to see Mussolini invade Greece. One was that Eastern Europe was full of nations with territorial disputes with their neighbours including Greece. Another was the fear that Russia might decide to aid the Greeks and as the Germans were still virtually allied to the Soviet Union conflict with the Greeks would be at the very least an embarrassment for Germany. He also felt, with justification, that it was the wrong time of year for the Italians to invade and he doubted their military capability. All these fears except that of possible Soviet involvement turned out to be correct.

The overconfident Italians soon ran into trouble. The Greek army fought well and the result was that the advance stalled and the Italians were pushed back. After this initial repulse the Italian troops regrouped and attacked once more but again the Greeks pushed them back. By March, not only had they driven the Italians out of Greece but had pressed forward into Italian-occupied Albania.[3]

The Greeks were greatly assisted by British troops and particularly by the RAF. The result was that the Italians were on the verge of collapse and the British were contemplating using Greece as a base to bomb the Romanian oil fields that provided the bulk of German oil.[4]

With the Italians also being attacked in North Africa by a small British force and faring poorly against them Hitler felt that he had no choice. Against his will he felt compelled to intervene to rescue his hapless ally. The result was militarily a success but politically a disaster for Germany. It drove wavering Balkan nations firmly into the Allied camp and alarmed both the Russians and other nations who feared that it was the beginning of a new series of conquests. To the Soviet Union the Balkans was important both symbolically and strategically and the idea of the region falling under German domination filled them with anxiety.

It also had longer term military consequences, as Hitler himself recognized some years later. As he told the filmmaker Leni Riefenstahl later: "if the Italians hadn't attacked Greece and needed our help, the war would have taken a different course. We could have anticipated the Russian cold by weeks and conquered Leningrad and Moscow. There would have been no Stalingrad."[5]

Not only was it a campaign that could have been avoided if Mussolini had been prepared to hold back but it was a costly conflict in terms of lives and equipment. Crete in particular was nearly held by the British against strong German forces and General Kurt Student later described the island as "the graveyard of the German paratroops" and as the conquest of Greece as being a "disastrous victory."[6]

The waste of time, resources, money and lives on the Greek campaign was bad enough but the further military campaign against Yugoslavia was completely unnecessary. Having forced the Yugoslav king to agree to his country becoming a German satellite the result was a popular revolt. This led to his overthrow and a pronouncement by the new government that they had no intention of becoming involved in hostilities against Britain. Hitler became furious and refused to heed advice to do nothing. He had already drawn up the plans for the attack on the Soviet Union and this act of open defiance by Yugoslavia led to him losing all sense of proportion. Hitler raged against "the mad Yugoslavs" and swore to destroy them as a nation. The result was that he invaded Yugoslavia and faced fierce opposition from its brave if outgunned armed forces.

As well as German troops who formed the bulk of the attackers the Romanians, Hungarians and Italians also took part. Just as had been the case in Albania the Italian troops performed poorly and the Yugoslavs drove them back into Albania.

The Yugoslav military collapsed rapidly and within twelve days the official war was over. It had been less costly for the Germans than expected and of all the Axis powers it was the Italians who suffered the greatest losses. Following the capitulation of the Yugoslav government the country was divided. The fascist movement in Croatia proceeded to run its own area on brutal and racist lines just as if the Nazis themselves were in charge.

Of course, the end of formal military conflict did not end the war as partisans immediately began conducting guerrilla operations against the occupying powers. It is often forgotten that of all the resistance movements in occupied Europe the Yugoslav partisans – both the royalists under Mihailovic and the Communists under Tito – were by far the most effective and posed the greatest threat to German rule.

The Greek and Balkan campaigns not only involved loss of lives, equipment and aircraft but delayed the projected invasion of the Soviet Union by a few months. Since then it has been a point of contention among historians to what extent this delay affected the outcome of the war against Russia. Hitler, admittedly with hindsight, certainly blamed it for leading to the campaign opening later than originally planned and exposing his troops to the Russian winter as a result. Others believe that it had no impact and that it was unlikely that Germany could have invaded earlier because of the heavy rains that made the ground sodden and so more difficult for tanks to traverse easily.

Probably both perspectives have merit. There is no doubt that the Balkan adventure alarmed the Soviets and turned many wavering nations against the Axis. The campaign showed the weakness of Italian troops and makes Hitler's choice of allies questionable. It also gave British troops an opportunity to fight the Germans directly and they acquitted themselves well in the conflict. On the other hand it is difficult not to imagine that an earlier date for the invasion of Russia without the premature entanglement in the Balkans might have made a difference.

The initial plan for Operation Barbarossa – the code name for the invasion of the Soviet Union – was flawed from the outset. Perhaps the most surprising aspect was the complete absence of any planning for the hardships of a Russian winter. This failure might have been more understandable had it been the result of Hitler's overly optimistic approach. In this case it also represented a serious lack of professionalism on the part of the German generals.

It is certainly true that many of them regarded the invasion of Russia as unnecessary and were nervous about the chances of success but even given those misgivings – which were certainly not uniform among the high command – the failure to plan for a possible winter campaign in the Soviet Union is extraordinary.

Barbarossa began life as Operation Fritz. The earliest formulation of the plan is found in Franz Halder's diary. On 22nd June 1940 he wrote:

> "To defeat the Russian army, or at least to occupy as much Russian soil as is necessary to protect Berlin from air attack, it is desired to establish our own position so far to the east

> that our own air force can destroy the most important areas of Russia."[8]

This initiated a series of discussion among senior military leaders. General Erich Marcke drew up the first detailed plans for an invasion of the Soviet Union and its conclusion was that the capture or destruction of Moscow was the primary military objective and that its fall would lead to the state falling apart. On 5th December 1940 the plan was presented to Hitler.

Unknown to the planners of Fritz, Hitler asked Jodl to consider other options. He turned the task over to Baron von Lossberg who drew up a radically different scheme for the invasion. The Lossberg plan did not regard Moscow as a primary target and instead believed that victory could be achieved by operating on a broad front.

Hitler, for reasons that defy logic, preferred the Lossberg strategy and rejected Operation Fritz out of hand. He changed the name of the plan to Operation Barbarossa and ordered the generals to prepare for war on the basis of the new proposals.

As a historian wrote of the new project:

> "The directive thus contained a large number of disconnected objectives with priority given to none. Hitler was about to send the German army into the Soviet Union on a four-year will-o'-the-wisp chase after seaports, cities, oil, corn, coal, nickel, manganese and iron ore."[9]

Thanks to Hitler's preference for an inferior line of approach and complete disregard for the careful planning of the German staff Barbarossa was flawed from the outset. Its lack of focus and failure to prioritize military objectives meant that from its very creation the plan carried within it the seeds of its own failure.

It is quite possible that Operation Fritz would have failed to win the war against the Soviet Union, especially as it failed to plan for a winter campaign. Nevertheless it represented the best and most realistic chance of success. Hitler's cavalier dismissal of it and enforced adoption of the inferior Lossberg strategy made defeat in the war far more probable.

There were also intelligence failures which will be dealt with in the relevant chapter. The transfer of Richthofen to the Soviet borders was a mistake which virtually telegraphed to the Russians that an invasion was imminent. Only the complacency of Stalin and his refusal to believe that the Germans were preparing for an attack prevented the Russians from taking precautions and being ready to meet the forthcoming assault. If they had been alert and prepared the initial stages of Barbarossa would have been as disastrous as the later ones.

The Germans launched the invasion with a poor plan, no provision for a Russian winter and inadequate transport. Much of the equipment was transferred to the Russian front using horses. Many of the tanks were obsolete models that were not suited to such an ambitious military operation.

In spite of these handicaps the attack took Stalin by surprise and the incompetence and complacency shown by the Russians nearly resulted in defeat. The Luftwaffe destroyed large numbers of Soviet aircraft and tanks and the rapid German advance swept everything before it. Many Russian soldiers simply fled. The British were dismayed at the prospect of a Russian collapse and Churchill immediately allied Britain with the Soviet Union. He also began organizing the Arctic convoys to provide supplies and equipment to Russia. This aspect of the conflict will be examined in the chapter on the naval war.

On June 30 Goebbels made one of the most hypocritical speeches ever delivered by a Nazi leader. He sent "war crimes investigators" into occupied Soviet territory and they quickly found evidence of Russian atrocities. Ironically this was not a case of manufactured human rights violations but genuine victims of Stalin's terror. Even so the brutality of the Nazi regime even before the Holocaust hardly entitled them to take the moral high ground. The revelations of Soviet atrocities shocked the German public and led to an upsurge of popular enthusiasm for the war.

The initial stages of the war went so badly for the Russians that Stalin retreated into isolation and passivity. Even when he finally emerged from this state of inaction he remained sunk in gloom and discussed with Beria – head of the secret police – and his Foreign Minister Molotov what peace terms Hitler would consider. Stalin proposed ceding the Ukraine, Belarus and the recently conquered Baltic states in the hope that it would satisfy German ambitions. Whether these proposals – that were never put before Hitler for consideration – would have brought an end to the war is doubtful. The Nazi leader's obsession with the fantasy of "Jewish Bolshevism" would probably have led him to reject them. In the event nothing came of these plans. The Russian troops rallied and held the line and Stalin recovered his nerve.

Soon the Germans received an unpleasant surprise in the form of Russian tanks. These advanced and sophisticated vehicles shocked the Wehrmacht and their very existence was unknown to the Germans before their appearance in battle. This represented yet another intelligence failure on the part of the Germans who were completely unprepared for these powerful and effective tanks.

Then, as so many previous invaders of Russia had discovered, the weather began to come to the assistance of the defenders. By mid-July heavy rain turned the roads into mud and that dramatically slowed the progress of the German tanks. A further hindrance for them was the scorched earth policy that the Russians adopted which included destroying bridges, burning crops and evacuating factories. The Soviets managed to move entire plants, transferring steel and munitions by rail to Siberia where they were out of reach of German attack. They destroyed most of the rolling stock on their railways which led to serious difficulties for the Germans whose railways ran on a different gauge from the Soviet system.

In spite of these difficulties, by August the Germans had made significant progress and at this point in time – with the Luftwaffe still enjoying air superiority – an immediate advance on Moscow would almost certainly have led to the fall of the city. Instead, as so often became the case, Hitler intervened with his own flawed strategy.

He ordered the Germans to continue their advance on too broad a front and in particular became obsessed with capturing the oil fields in the Caucasus. He directed them to make that their main priority but also dissipated his forces by instructing them to make an assault on Leningrad. This unnecessary splitting of his troops made their task more difficult and if a single objective had been chosen the results would probably have been quite different.

The attacks continued in the face of stubborn Soviet resistance but then by October an early winter began. Snow and ice now appeared on top of the mud, causing tanks, armoured vehicles, artillery and aircraft to ice up and German soldiers to suffer from frostbite. They began to run low on fuel and Rundstedt wanted to pause the offensive and wait in winter quarters before resuming the attack when the weather improved. He was overruled by Hitler who in his arrogance imagined that willpower alone could overcome the problems of a severe winter and lack of fuel.

On 6 December the Soviets finally counterattacked, Stalin having ordered Moscow to be held at all costs. Zhukov, the most competent Russian general, drove the invading forces back in a slow but relentless drive. By the end of the month it was clear that further German progress was impossible and the only sensible strategy was to dig in or even make tactical retreats. Hitler refused to countenance either approach and insisted that his troops must find a way to continue the assault. Bock defied these instructions and managed to manoeuvre his soldiers into safety so that later they were able to launch fresh attacks. Other generals failed to follow his example and the result was increasingly heavy losses of men and equipment and the gradual establishment of air and ground superiority by the Soviet forces.

From the moment of Zhukov's counterattack all serious prospect of a German victory had gone. The best course of action would have been to adopt a defensive strategy and hope that the still effective German armed forces could prevent the Russians from advancing any further. That would have enabled the Germans to maintain control of the territory they held and allowed them to hold out and perhaps hope for reinforcements in men and equipment. Hitler's inability to grasp the truth of Clausewitz's maxim "defence is the stronger form of war" doomed his invasion to defeat. German troops and aircraft threw away their lives needlessly in a series of failed assaults.

Surprisingly, Spring brought a renewed chance of German victory. This was largely due to some ill-considered and reckless Russian attacks. The Soviet offensives failed and gave the Germans fresh hope. By May 1942 the Russians had been defeated once more.

This gave Hitler a fresh burst of overconfidence and in June he ordered the Germans to begin a new assault on Soviet positions. Once more he insisted on spreading his forces too thinly and so negated the chance of a successful concentrated attack.

He soon became mesmerized with the vision of capturing Stalingrad. Hitler saw this as a symbolic gesture that would affect morale so badly that it would force the Russians to surrender. Instead it was the most brutal and bloody battle in world history and the city became the graveyard of German troops and snuffed out the last lingering flame of hope for a German victory.

Although conflict on the Eastern Front continued for another three years and in 1943 the Germans made another ill-advised attack on Kursk, that was the last time they were able to take the offensive. Instead the story was one of slow retreat and ever increasing casualties.

Militarily the war against the Soviet Union was badly handled from start to finish. But for the incompetence of the Russian side the invasion could probably have been stifled at the very beginning. A few transitory victories were far from enough to make up for the death toll, the needless sacrifice of lives and the utter futility of the whole campaign.

The conduct of the war was far from sensible but an equally important factor was the bigoted racism of Hitler. In spite of pleas from Rosenberg and others to treat the Soviet people as future allies and equal citizens of an expanding Third Reich he utterly refused to consider the idea. He declared that those people who were not killed would become slaves to their German masters. Hitler offered the subject peoples nothing. His behaviour contrasts sharply with every successful empire in history.

When the Germans entered the Soviet Union they were welcomed as liberators almost everywhere. The hatred of Stalin was so intense that it would have been easy to recruit the people to join in revolt against Communism and so help the Nazi invasion to succeed. Instead the Wehrmacht was swiftly followed by the *Einsatzgruppen* and the SS and the result was an orgy of terror and the beginning of the programme of genocide. The result of these atrocities and the German plunder and looting of the people's supplies and possessions was naturally to turn them against the invaders. What could have been a powerful support base for the Germans crumbled and only the most vicious anti-Semites continued to back the Nazis. The ordinary people decided that even Stalin was a lesser evil than Hitler.

To call the genocide programme or even the widespread atrocities committed by the Nazis "mistakes" is to undervalue their horror. These aspects of the regime will be considered in the chapter on racial mythology.

The next theatre of war to be considered is North Africa. Again Hitler was forced to intervene as a result of Italian incompetence. Mussolini's troops had attempted to sweep towards Egypt but instead were repulsed and a British counter-attack was in danger of driving the Italians out of their African empire altogether.

Hitler sent Rommel to North Africa to rescue the Italians but failed to send him more than brigade strength in troops. This was totally inadequate for a serious campaign and only Rommel's brilliance as a general and the ineptitude shown by the British commanders till the arrival of Montgomery avoided its early failure.

Further difficulties for the North African campaign were transporting weapons and supplies to the Germans. The British Navy and RAF operated expertly and it became increasingly difficult for any supplies to reach Rommel.

German difficulties were increased by the reluctance of Hitler to allot more than a small number of troops to the campaign. Instead he relied on the Italians to do the bulk of the fighting and they proved both unwilling and incapable of being an effective military force.

It is often forgotten that the campaign in North Africa was fought on a very small scale. Until 1942 British and Commonwealth troops fought alone against the Germans and Italians. Their position was precarious and they experienced difficulties in transport and supplies. The Germans and Italians almost reached Cairo and Hitler's failure to adequately supply them with men, tanks and supplies on an adequate scale doomed them to an unnecessary defeat. Rommel pleaded for more troops and equipment but was granted a fraction of what he asked for. So fine was the balance between victory and defeat that a relatively small amount of additional resources would have turned the tide and given victory to the Axis forces.

North Africa represented a golden opportunity for Hitler to achieve a relatively easy victory with long-term consequences for the course of the war. Particularly in 1941 when America was still neutral a small commitment of additional troops and equipment would have seen Rommel overcome the almost equally disadvantaged British and Commonwealth forces and given Germany control of the Suez Canal and the whole of North Africa. This would have opened the door for possible campaigns in Asia that would have threatened the British Empire on some of its most vulnerable fronts. It would also have made the Mediterranean theatre of war far more difficult for the Allies.[10]

Why did Hitler fail to seize the opportunity? Obviously he was considering the invasion of Russia and that dominated his thinking. On the other hand he could have spared a small quantity of resources for Rommel's campaign and that limited expenditure would have reaped huge dividends. Primarily it comes back to Hitler's inability to see the wider picture. He regarded North Africa as a diversion and hardly worth significant expenditure in time, money, troops and equipment. He also failed to grasp the strategic necessity – or at least advantages – of controlling the Mediterranean. Hitler was incapable of grasping even the basics of naval warfare and this lack of vision cost him and his country dearly.

From 1942 onwards the war on land was leading to a series of German defeats. El Alamein saw Rommel's troops routed by Montgomery and from that point onwards it was a case of mopping up operations for the Allied forces in North Africa. In the Soviet Union the Russians were slowly winning the war and the only sensible strategy would have been to accept that Germany now needed to fight a defensive war and to prioritize the areas that needed to be defended.

That strategy was urged on Hitler by most of his generals but he steadfastly refused to entertain the idea. To him retreat was a sign of cowardice and ceding territory or time to prepare to repulse an attack was inconceivable. He insisted on an offensive posture at all costs and if that was not possible then the only alternative he accepted was standing firm and fighting to the death. As a result of this blinkered attitude the lives of thousands of service personnel were lost as well as countless civilian casualties.

In 1943 the military picture unravelled swiftly. From North Africa and with control of the Mediterranean now in Allied hands the invasion of Sicily was launched. The island fell rapidly and the result was that mainland Italy was assaulted. Mussolini fell from power and Hitler reacted in a characteristically mistaken manner.

He would have done better to abandon the Italian front and concentrate on defending his borders in Austria, Central Europe, France and Eastern Europe. Instead he sent crack troops in to rescue Mussolini and fight the Allies with the result being a needless waste of lives and the death or capture of some of his best soldiers.

In 1944 D-Day again showed Hitler's poor judgement in military matters. The landings were precarious and the Allied strategy deeply flawed. Rommel advised Hitler to attempt to prevent the landings on the beaches but he refused. Once the Allies had established a bridgehead Rommel asked for permission to retreat to a more defensible position. Again Hitler refused with his obsession that any retreat was an admission of failure and a sign of cowardice. As a result more lives were lost in a futile attempt to hold fast in positions that were indefensible rather than moving the line to one that was strategically viable.

Hitler's mistaken strategy once the Allies had landed in France resulted in more German casualties than the previous four years of war – even including the horrific losses at Stalingrad.

One of his few sensible decisions at this time was to give Goebbels the power to wage "total war." As Goebbels remarked acidly to an aide, "it takes a bomb under his arse to make Hitler see reason." Goebbels had been pleading for the power to wage total war since early 1943 but Hitler steadfastly refused. Whether Goebbels was correct in assuming that if he had been granted those powers earlier he could have changed the course of the war is a moot point but it would certainly have assisted the war effort if the nation had been fully organized on that basis.

D-Day marked the beginning of the end but Hitler the gambler attempted one final reckless throw of the dice. The Ardennes campaign – the Battle of the Bulge – was in itself a good plan. As the military historian Liddell Hart wrote:

> "It was a brilliant concept and might have proved a brilliant success *if* he had still possessed sufficient resources, as well as forces, to ensure a reasonable chance of success in its big aims."[11]

After the failure of the Ardennes campaign nothing remained beyond increasingly hopeless resistance on every front. Throughout the war Hitler's military misjudgements hampered the armed forces at best and at worst led directly to total defeat.

The Fall of Eagles

Germany began the Second World War being outclassed and outnumbered in the air. The RAF had over 10,000 aircraft in service and 3.500 were in operational units. Half the planes at their disposal were antiquated but the other half included the ultra modern Spitfires and Hurricanes, planes that were soon to prove their value.

By contrast the Luftwaffe had only 4,200 aircraft although they had 373,000 personnel in the air force, 208,000 of them being aircrew. It was not equipped to fight a long war and suffered from a series of handicaps that reduced its fighting ability.

The most fundamental problem for the Luftwaffe was the head of the service. Goering might have been a fighter pilot during World War I but had no sense of strategy and was a poor organizer. His choice of subordinates was generally mistaken with Ernst Udet being a particularly poor choice. He performed so badly in his role that he committed suicide after a series of abject failures. The effective administrative and supply side of the air force was handled by the vastly more competent Erhard Milch but time and again Milch's calm and reasoned strategy was thwarted by Goering or his cronies.

A more widespread problem was the prevailing notion – not confined to Germany but believed throughout the Western World – that bombers were unstoppable. There was a saying "the bomber will always get through" and the former head of the RAF, Lord Trenchard, was furious when Baldwin decided to favour the cheaper option of fighter planes over his own advocacy of heavy bombers. Trenchard claimed that "this decision might well cost us the next war" but events proved that he was wrong. The civilian Baldwin was right to focus on fighters even though his motivation was their relative cheapness rather than a strategic decision taken on military grounds. As a result of Baldwin's policy the RAF was equipped with the Spitfires and Hurricanes that won the Battle of Britain. By contrast the Luftwaffe had numerous bombers, particularly the Ju87 Stuka dive-bomber, but no fighter that could match the best RAF aircraft.

Throughout the war Hitler and Goering remained obsessed with the notion that bombers could win the war and fighters were no more than auxiliaries. In spite of the fact that indiscriminate bombing had failed to break the spirit of either Britain or the Soviet Union the Germans persisted in this mistaken strategy. The British recognized that fighters played a crucial part both in terms of escorting bombers and of destroying enemy bombers with their superior manoeuvrability. Again and again the Germans prioritized bombers over fighters and even compelled excellent fighters – most notoriously the Me109 – to be converted into bombers with an obvious and dramatic reduction in their offensive and defensive capability.

In spite of Milch stressing the importance of fighters for the German war effort his words fell on deaf ears. Goering and Hitler were mesmerized by the idea of bombing their enemies into submission.[1]

The historian David Irving commented on the poor fighting state of the German air force as follows:

> *"Milch knew, perhaps better than anyone else, how unprepared the Luftwaffe was. They still lacked trained commanders at every level. They had fuel stores sufficient for six months of operations at most. The bomb dumps held enough bombs for about three weeks' hostilities against a small enemy and most of these were 10-kilogramme bombs secretly purchased by the Reichswehr a decade ago. Only 182,000 tonnes of steel had been allocated to air force equipment in the year ending 1 April, 1939."*[2]

In the campaign against Poland at the commencement of the war the Luftwaffe lost over750 crew and 300 aircraft with a further 279 damaged so badly they needed substantial repair work. The loss of nearly 500 aircraft in terms of operational combat capability against a relatively weak opponent in Poland was not a glowing testament to Luftwaffe strength. They were soon to face more formidable enemies in Britain and France with a considerably depleted air force against stronger odds.[3]

Following the declaration of war in September 1939 the RAF took the offensive. On 3 and 4 September they attacked harbours at Wilhelmshaven and killed eight German seamen. They followed up by attacking ships at Cuxhaven and Heligoland. On 10 December the Battle of Heligoland Bight took place in which three squadrons of RAF bombers attempted to sink German ships. This daylight raid caught the Germans by surprise but they scrambled fighters to protect the ships and inflicted more casualties on the RAF than they suffered themselves. Both sides drew conclusions from the conflict but while the RAF drew the correct one – that daylight bombing, especially without adequate fighter protection, was too risky a strategy – the Germans drew a mistaken one, that they had adequate resources to protect their homeland from enemy attack by air. This led to a complacent attitude among the Luftwaffe leadership and meant that not until the Americans began bombing Germany did they finally understand the need for strategic defence against air attack.

On 16 and 17 October 1939 the Germans attacked Rosyth and Scapa Flow. Other than that the Luftwaffe made no attempt to attack Britain from the air. The RAF also did little after the Heligoland Bight battle and the air war became as "phoney" as the ground war.[4]

The next conflict in which the Luftwaffe became engaged was the invasion of Denmark and Norway. Operations began on 9 April 1940 and continued until 10 June when Norway surrendered. In Denmark there was little aerial combat though two Danish fighters did attack the German invaders but both were shot down and their pilots killed by Me110 fighters.

On 9 April the weather was poor and German parachute drops and infantry landings from the air went awry. The crew of six Me110s captured the Oslo-Fornebu airfield on their own as the expected reinforcements did not arrive until too late.

An earlier squadron had arrived at Fornebu but the Norwegian air force sent nine Gladiators to attack them. Two Me110s and their crews were lost but two Gladiators were destroyed. Later in the day a damaged Me110 crashed and had to be written off. A Sunderland flying boat was shot down by the Germans and two further Me110s and their crew were lost to the weather.

On 8 June the RAF lost ten Hurricanes and ten Gloster Gladiators with 18 pilots also meeting an untimely end. The conflict continued to go badly for the Allies and eventually all aerial activity by the RAF – and any further attempts to assist the Norwegians by the British – were abandoned.

In the course of the aerial war 57 Wellingtons, 12 Hampdens, eight Blenheims, 14 Hudsons, five Skuas, two Rocs, two Sunderlands, one Danish Fokker and five Gladiators – two of them Norwegian – were destroyed by the Luftwaffe in addition to the Hurricanes and Gladiators lost when their aircraft carrier was sunk.

The Germans were handicapped in the initial stages by the fact that for some months their commander was both drunken and unhinged. He threatened to shoot some of his crew and after appeals to higher authority was replaced. One of the most unusual German pilots operating during the Norwegian campaign was Himmler's deputy Reinhard Heydrich. He wrote off an aircraft by crashing it but did achieve some victories as an aviator.

British losses were heavy but the Germans also lost a considerable number of planes. According to official figures the total number of aircraft lost was 90 but the historian

François Kersaudy estimates the true number of losses at 240 in all.[5] Even on the lower figure the campaign resulted in significant damage to the fighting capability of the Luftwaffe.

Top of Form

The campaign against Holland, Belgium and France involved considerable activity by the Allied air forces. They were poorly equipped and although production of the Spitfire, Wellington and Blenheim aircraft was accelerated the RAF could only pit four squadrons of Hurricanes among their advanced planes. The rest were obsolete biplanes and unable to fight effectively against the Luftwaffe. The Germans also had many outdated aircraft but possessed more of the modern type of planes than the RAF was able to put into the field.[6]

The Luftwaffe – and the Wehrmacht – underestimated both the quality and resistance of the Norwegians. They made the same mistake when they attacked Holland and Belgium. The Dutch war ended quickly but in that brief period of combat they inflicted significant damage on the Germans and the Luftwaffe failed to learn lessons from the experience. They destroyed the Dutch and Belgian air forces within two days but lost 122 of their own aircraft. Considering how antiquated Belgian planes were that should have been a major worry to the Luftwaffe as should the excellent anti-aircraft defences of the Dutch.[7] In spite of that they were complacent which was foolhardy with a campaign against the superior French and British air forces still to come.

The Luftwaffe overrated the effect of their bombing of Rotterdam. This was the first example of "terror bombing" and while it accelerated the Dutch surrender it strengthened the Germans in the mistaken belief that aerial bombardment could win wars unaided. It could also have been a disastrous military error as at the time German troops were being hard pressed by fierce Dutch resistance and the planes would have been better employed in giving air support to the 22nd Infantry Division rather than unnecessarily bombing the city.

57 Heinkel He 111s dropped a combined total of 97 tons of bombs. 30,000 people lost their lives, most of them civilians. Churches, schools and hospitals were destroyed or severely damaged.

The key factor in the German success during the Dutch and Belgian campaigns was not the terror bombing of Rotterdam but the way in which the Luftwaffe and ground forces generally worked together. The Germans used aircraft to shield Rundstedt's troops as they advanced through the Ardennes. By 12 May they achieved complete air superiority and began attacking transport and supply networks rather than Allied troops. Paratroopers and glider troops captured bridges and even the fort of Eban Emael which was considered impregnable. As German troops continued to advance the Luftwaffe used its fighter planes and dive bombers to support them. The Junkers Ju52s provided an essential transport system for the Germans when fuel, spare parts and ammunition were running low. Once a forward position had been established at Charleville 2000 technicians were flown in to create a tank repair depot.[8]

The Germans were astonished at the fierce resistance they encountered and again failed to draw the appropriate conclusions. Both the Dutch and Belgians had inflicted casualties on the Luftwaffe and the British examined the campaign carefully, particularly after the humiliation of Dunkirk, and made appropriate changes in strategy and tactics.[9]

The British responded to the devastation in Rotterdam by asking the RAF to bomb targets in Germany. The brief was to bomb oil depots and industrial plants contributing to the war effort. The reality was rather different with most of the bombs missing their intended destination and instead hitting villages and towns. On the night of 7 May a single French aircraft managed to bomb Berlin. These Allied air raids caused widespread anger in Germany but at first the Luftwaffe did not retaliate. It was not until six weeks after the French surrender that they began to bomb targets in Britain.

Two days after the French pilot had bombed Berlin the Luftwaffe began to attack targets in France. By 11 May fourteen different areas of the country had been bombed with forty civilian deaths resulting.

The Dutch and Belgian campaigns highlighted a number of problems for the Luftwaffe but Dunkirk provided a glaring example of their limitations. The planes available to them lacked the range and manoeuvrability of the Spitfires and Hurricanes. German air bases were too far away to react quickly. When German bombers attempted to attack Allied troops the RAF was frequently able to prevent them from doing significant damage. Between 26 May and 2 June the RAF lost 177 aircraft but the Luftwaffe lost 240 planes. The Western offensive cost the Germans around a third of their aerial armada. This rate of attrition could not be sustained for long. Goering's empty boast that he could subdue the Allied troops by aerial bombing alone was shattered by the bravery and skill of the RAF.[10]

Following Dunkirk the battle for France began in earnest. Now that British troops had been evacuated along with a sizeable number of French soldiers the demoralized French armed services had to fight the Germans on their own. The air force was in a state of flux with many of their planes being antiquated but for all their deficiencies in quality the bravery and skill of the French pilots meant that the Germans were far from having an easy victory in the air war.

The French were certainly short of fighters with most of their complement being obsolescent twin-engine planes. The Germans outnumbered the French but not dramatically. The Me109 was certainly faster than any aircraft the French had and particularly their main fighter, the Morane-Saulnier MS 406. In spite of its relative slowness it performed well against the Germans.

It was a different matter when it came to bombers where the Luftwaffe had overwhelming superiority. Around 1500 German bombers faced around 400 Allied bombers, not all of them French. Most of the British bombers operating in France were single-engine Fairey Battles and carried a bombload of only1000 pounds.

In spite of these problems the bombing of aerodromes was not a great success. Only 31 French airfields were attacked and little damage was done. So inaccurate was the German bombing that they bombed

Freiburg in Germany by mistake resulting in the death of 57 civilians and a further 101 injured.

On 3 June a heavy bombing campaign was launched in the Paris region. 300 bombers were involved and they destroyed 16 French planes on the ground, killed 32 servicemen and 195 civilians. The escorting Me 109s shot down a further 17 French aircraft.

Accuracy on both sides was poor and the Germans and Allies seemed equally to blame for shooting down their own aircraft with anti-aircraft guns. On the first day of the German attack the French shot down five British planes. The ratio of accuracy did not improve for the duration of the conflict.

When the French tried to attack German tanks on 5 and 8 June they suffered heavy losses from flak. On other occasions French fighters engaging German pilots ran out of ammunition. Even the RAF – which was at least better organized than its French counterpart – was almost out of ammunition for its Hurricanes based in France.

The French frantically rushed a series of replacement aircraft into service but most of them were defective and could not fly. Aircrews were also in short supply. The procurement side of the conflict was chaotic with orders for new parts being delayed for around a month with obvious consequences for the crews trying to hold off the Germans.

A more fundamental problem for the French was that the commander-in-chief of the army, General Maurice Gamelin, was contemptuous of the air force. He declared that "there is no such thing as air battle, only battle on land.' Unlike the RAF, which had considerable autonomy, the French air force had to liaise with the army and try to persuade them of the need for air support. Almost invariably, the army response was that there was no work for the air force.

A lack of leaders of quality in the French air force did not help. Air Commodore Douglas remarked "There are few officers in the French Air Force of really first class mental calibre.' The former French aviation minister Pierre Cot was even more scathing, declaring that "*Armée de l'air* command bears the shame of having lost the battle without having fought it."

The ease with which the Germans won the air battle over France again led them into the dangerous habit of over-confidence. They imagined that they had now achieved total air superiority over the Allies when the reality was that French ineptitude and poorer quality equipment and planes was the main factor in their defeat. An even bigger factor was the army's complete lack of understanding of the need for air support to assist ground troops. The British knew they had been outfought in this particular battle but were equally quick to draw conclusions from German failures. The lessons they learned from the campaign were put to good use in the next aerial battle.[11]

Following the conquest of France the Germans prepared in a half-hearted way for the invasion of Britain. In spite of his failure at Dunkirk Goering insisted that the Luftwaffe was capable of defeating the RAF. He believed that he could establish air superiority over the British Isles and establish the conditions for a successful subsequent invasion.

German pilots were less sanguine about the prospects of an aerial war. They had been shocked by the performance of the Spitfires at Dunkirk that were in most respects superior to any plane the Germans could put into the field. Of course the bulk of the RAF aircraft were less deadly than the Spitfires but the planes created a fear factor out of proportion to their numbers.

The RAF had suffered heavy losses during the war in the West and it now faced the prospect of an imminent Luftwaffe attack with reduced capability. Of course the Germans also incurred heavy casualties but numerically they had more planes to throw into the field.[12]

The German mood as it prepared for the Battle of Britain was complacent and grossly overconfident. Even Jodl remarked that "the final victory of Germany over England is only a question of time." The Luftwaffe had seen the French crumble and imagined that defeating the RAF would be relatively simple and that once air superiority was established the British would be compelled to sue for peace.

Jodl drew up a plan for defeating the British with two possible approaches to victory. One was to attack the UK directly and the second was to control the Mediterranean. In terms of air strategy he proposed attacks on British supplies and industry and terror bombings on residential areas. He insisted on the need to achieve complete supremacy in the air. Aircraft factories also needed to be targeted to prevent rapid resupply to the RAF.

German intelligence grossly underestimated the performance capabilities of the Spitfires and Hurricanes. They were either unaware of or dismissed as unimportant Britain's radar system. Their conclusion was that "the Luftwaffe, unlike the RAF, will be in a position in every respect to achieve a decisive effect this year."[12]

Apart from its undue complacency the Luftwaffe failed to take into account the fact that their fighters had a limited range. They were only able at this stage of the war to attack southern England which enabled factories and RAF stations further away from the conflict such as Liverpool or Birmingham to operate with impunity. During the Spanish Civil War the Germans had experimented with oil drums that extended the range of their aircraft by 100 miles but failed to learn from this experience. None of the Luftwaffe planes were fitted with these devices that might have made the conflict more difficult for the RAF.

It has been suggested that the Germans could never have won the Battle of Britain because of the limitations of the distance their aircraft could travel. To some extent this is true but it remains the case that the margin of victory for Britain was extremely slim. The average age of RAF pilots was 19 and the appalling physical and mental toll the fighting took on the young pilots brought many close to breakdown. Some even went AWOL for a time suffering from the aerial equivalent of shell shock. The RAF was outnumbered, at least in the early stages of the battle, and German aircraft inflicted heavy casualties on it. Both sides lost planes and pilots in a spiral of attrition that could not be sustained for long and if the Luftwaffe had continued its assault on British aircraft in spite of the death toll they could still have won the

Battle of Britain. The contrast between the reckless disregard for human life shown by German ground troops and the astonishing reluctance to risk the continuing fatalities of pilots is extreme.[13]

The air battle was principally fought between the Messerschmitt Bf 109 and 110 on the German side and the Hurricanes and much less numerous Spitfires. At Dunkirk the Germans were surprised by the performance of the Spitfires though – at least until the Battle of Britain had been raging for some time – they preferred their own Bf 109s. The German aircraft was faster and had a higher climb rate than the Spitfire. The RAF plane was more manoeuvrable than its Luftwaffe counterpart but was less well armed. The Browning 303 machine guns hit and damaged German aircraft but rarely downed them. The Bf 109s had two 20mm cannons and two machine guns so their firepower was greater. The Bf 109 could also be used as a fighter-bomber as it could carry a bomb weighing 250 kilograms. While the Stukas were used as fighter-bombers they were unable to fight effectively against British planes after they had released their bombs while the Bf 109 could continue to fight. On the other hand it had a larger turning circle than the Spitfires and Hurricanes which made it more vulnerable.

Another German plane that was expected to play a large part in the battle but in the end played only a marginal one was the Bf 110C. It was faster than the Hurricane and nearly as fast as the Spitfire but had poor acceleration and lacked manoeuvrability. It was soon discovered to be unsuitable as an escort fighter for bombers and was rapidly converted to a dive bomber role. With this new use it was able to attack and destroy "pinpoint" targets.

The RAF also discovered that some of its own aircraft were not effective. The Boulton Paul Defiant had been reasonably successful at Dunkirk but during the Battle of Britain it suffered heavy losses and was withdrawn from daylight operations.

German bombers enjoyed varying degrees of success. The Ju 87 Stuka had been an effective dive bomber at Dunkirk and against France but its slow speed made it vulnerable and it was frequently caught by

British fighters. After heavy losses the Stukas were withdrawn from service over England and asked to bomb shipping instead.

The other German bombers were more effective but also had severe problems. The Dornier Do 17 had a small bomb load and was slow; the Heinkel He 111 had the largest bomb load; and the Junkers Ju 88 was the fastest. All three were vulnerable to fighter attack and the shortage of Luftwaffe fighters to protect them meant that they suffered heavy casualties.

British bombers came in three types. The Fairey Battle and Bristol Blenheim were light bombers and the Battle was an obsolete type that but for the war would probably have been retired from service. The Handley-Page Hampden was a medium bomber and relatively effective. The best British heavy bombers were the Armstrong-Whitworth Whitley and the Vickers Wellington. Blenheims were used more than the other aircraft and proved effective at attacking airfields, ports, factories and ships.[14]

Another problem the Germans faced was a further intelligence failure. They failed to realize that the British had cracked the early version of their Enigma code and were able to read their signals. This gave the British a huge advantage in anticipating German movements. The role of intelligence during the war will be dealt with in the chapter on intelligence failures.

On the military front there were both tactical and strategic mistakes made by the Luftwaffe. It was quickly discovered that the Bf 110 was incapable of eluding the RAF fighters and the Bf 109 became the main escort for bombers. Bomber crews with their slower aircraft demanded close protection from fighters which it was not always possible to provide. The Stukas proved particularly vulnerable to RAF fighters and were largely withdrawn from the campaign as a result.

Goering became concerned at the lack of progress and met with his unit leaders. The result was a policy known as "Free Hunts" where fighters would sweep an area before a raid by bombers in the hope of removing RAF fighters from the bombers' target areas. In spite of these measures attrition continued at a horrific rate and not until September did Goering provide the bombers with additional close fighter escorts. This meant the Bf 109s could offer greater protection to the bombers but exposed the fighter pilots to higher casualty rates because they were forced to reduce their speed to match that of the bombers.

The failure to equip the Bf 109s with long-range drop tanks until the closing stages of the battle meant that they were only able to fly for just over an hour. The pilots had to watch their fuel gauge and once it signalled "red" for low fuel they had to return to France. They were forced to make two flights over water under the hostile gaze of the RAF and this reduced their effectiveness during the combat.[15]

In spite of all these problems the RAF was losing planes and pilots at a horrific rate. The mainly young aviators were brave but utterly exhausted. They were traumatized by the ordeal of flying continual sorties under extreme pressure and the constant presence of danger. Pilots were dying and aircraft being destroyed at a faster rate than they could be replaced. The loss of pilots was critical as it took time to train new aviators. On a human level it resulted in a mood of continual weariness and nervous anticipation among the crews. By 30 August the mood in the RAF was sombre. It was the lowest point in the Battle of Britain and the time when the nation came perilously close to defeat in the aerial war.[16]

Further problems for the Luftwaffe were provided by the weather. On the first day of the air assault it was so bad that only the Third Air Force was able to fly. The Germans launched 500 bombing raids but did little damage with radar assisting the British defences. The RAF lost 13 fighters but 45 German aircraft were destroyed. Not until 15 August was Goering able to launch all three of his aerial armada. That day saw the RAF shoot down 75 German planes for the loss of 34 aircraft.

Four days of bad weather gave both sides a welcome respite. During the lull in hostilities Goering began by unfairly accusing his fighter pilots of cowardice and of breaking away from their duty to escort bombers when the weather was bad. He also decided to abandon daylight bombing raids in favour of attacks at night.[17]

23 August saw the first German attack on London. It was the result of a navigational error by a group of bombers and their intended target had been an aircraft factory. Nine people were killed in the raids.

Hitler was furious and warned the Luftwaffe to be more careful. He was desperate to avoid retaliatory raids on Germany and at the beginning of the campaign gave strict instructions that civilian targets were not to be bombed. It was one thing in his eyes bombing Rotterdam but he knew that Britain had far greater air capability than the Dutch and had no wish to provoke them into bombing Germany.

The RAF reacted by bombing Berlin the following night. The raid achieved little but profoundly affected German morale. Goering had promised that Germany would never be bombed yet Berlin had been successfully attacked.

At first this made no difference to German tactics with Hitler and Goering continuing to avoid attacking civilian targets but three days later the RAF launched a second raid on Berlin. Two people were killed and 29 injured. Two more evening raids by the RAF followed.

These assaults did relatively little damage but outraged German public opinion and forced Hitler and Goering to abandon their policy of not hitting civilian targets. Instead they decided that retaliatory raids were now essential to restore confidence among the German people and also hopefully break the morale of the civilian population in London.

Goering decided to launch a massive attack on the London docks. On 7 September over 1500 aircraft swooped on London. The intention was to cripple the dockyards and draw the RAF out into the open in the hope of smashing it in one last aerial battle.

However understandable from a political and psychological viewpoint the change in tactics from fighting the RAF and bombing military and industrial targets to attacks on civilians might have been it was a huge mistake. The RAF had been on the verge of collapse with low morale, huge losses of pilots and aircraft and a growing fear of defeat. In spite of the horrific German casualties if the fight against the RAF had continued to be prioritized it is possible that the course of the battle might have gone differently. By changing the focus of the attack to London it gave them a breathing space and enabled them to rebuild, re-equip and train new pilots. Tactically it was a major blunder by the Luftwaffe and cost them any remaining chance of victory in the aerial war.

Strategically the campaign was flawed from the outset. It was never clear what the focus was and the primary – if not sole – job of the Luftwaffe ought to have been to eliminate the RAF and aircraft production. Too much emphasis was placed on bombing installations and attempting to destroy aircraft on the ground rather than maximizing the use of German fighters to destroy the RAF's fighting capability. The crucial importance of fighters was not realized until far too late in the campaign and the general strategic assumption had been that bombing alone would be enough to force the British to surrender.

Another fundamental mistake was in assuming that the air war would be over quickly. The Luftwaffe underestimated the quality, quantity and resilience of the RAF and aircraft factories and had made no plans for a long war. The belief that the campaign would be a short one led them to fail to make provision for supplies, reinforcements, repairs and training new pilots. As a result of the RAF's bravery and skill the war was prolonged to a point where issues of supply in particular became crucial. On that front Britain was better prepared and better able to adapt to and recover from its losses. In a war of attrition it was clear that the British were better equipped to survive.

They were also able to draw on the vast resources of their empire while the Germans could only rely on those of the occupied countries to supplement their own needs. None of these factors had been seriously considered at the planning stage of the campaign and the Germans paid the price for this strategic failure.

A huge strategic mistake was not recognizing the importance of radar. On 15 August Goering ordered the Luftwaffe to end its attacks on radar installations which the Germans had been bombing with great success. The bombing had a significant impact on radar capability and the cessation of these raids was a monumental blunder. Britain had time to rebuild its radar network which played a key role in detecting German attacks and protecting installations against their assaults.[18]

By 17 September Hitler was forced to admit failure in the air attack. He began dismantling air loading equipment at airfields in the Netherlands. Churchill exulted at the news and realized it meant the end of the Battle of Britain. The RAF had defeated the hitherto invincible Luftwaffe. Churchill compared it to the victory over the Spanish Armada.[19]

The failure of the Battle of Britain led to the beginning of the Blitz. This campaign did not simply target military and industrial objectives but also aimed to strike terror into the British population. Raid after raid saw huge quantities of bombs dropped on the country but though death and destruction was extensive German losses were considerable. The RAF and anti-aircraft defences worked tirelessly to reduce the success of the German bombers and the spirit of the British people was not broken by the onslaught.

The Blitz too suffered from a diffusion of objectives. It was not simply a concentrated and focused attack on military capacity. It was not simply a directed attack against British industry. It was not simply an attempt to cow the population through terror bombing. The Luftwaffe tried to achieve all three of these aims and ended up fulfilling none of them.

The Blitz began on 7 September 1940 and lasted until 11 May 1941. This sustained attack lasted for over eight months. 43,000 civilians were killed, 139,000 injured and two million homes were destroyed or damaged. This represented 60% of the housing stock in London.

The first day of the Blitz came as a surprise to Londoners but was less deadly than later attacks.[20] The RAF and civil defence forces struggled to contain the damage and save lives but as the air assault continued and grew in intensity their task became increasingly difficult.

15 September saw the largest bombing raid to date. It was a daylight assault and in spite of the scale of the operation achieved little in the

way of damage. The slow speed of German bombers continued to be a problem and as there remained a shortage of escort fighters they were vulnerable to attack by the RAF and ground anti-aircraft fire. The principal German bombers – the Dornier Do 17, Junkers Ju 88 and Heinkel He 111 - were only capable of delivering relatively small bomb loads which again reduced the effectiveness of the bombing campaign.

As so often with German military planning the lack of a focused objective made their task more difficult. The Luftwaffe's leaders could not decide whether to concentrate on aircraft factories, industrial and supply targets or simply terror bombing of civilians. The result was that they vacillated between all three approaches with a consequent failure to accomplish any of those goals.

The attempt to attack ports and shipping and to restrict imports might have been productive but the Luftwaffe had neither the numbers nor the range to attack many targets outside the south of England. The British had anticipated a possible German assault by air on these facilities and so moved as many of them as possible out of reach of the enemy bombers.

The attack on 15 September was mainly directed against the docks and the rail network. It put the railways out of action for three days but otherwise failed to do significant damage. Air battles between the RAF and Luftwaffe raged throughout the day's conflict and resulted in the loss of 18% of the German bombers.[21]

By 7 October German losses became so great that daylight raids were abandoned in favour of night bombing. 14 October saw the heaviest night attack with 380 bombers hitting London. 200 people were killed and 2000 injured.[22]

Throughout October the bombing continued with around 10% of the assaults being daylight raids. The Luftwaffe continued to pound London but also attacked Birmingham, Coventry, Liverpool, Glasgow, Manchester and Hull. That month saw 8,200 tons of bombs dropped by the Luftwaffe. Curiously the Germans barely touched Fighter Command's airfields but instead attacked those of British bombers.

By November 13,000 civilians had been killed and 20,000 injured. Then the Luftwaffe began to adopt a different strategy. It shifted its focus away from London and attacked the industrial cities of the West Midlands. 13/14 November saw a devastating night attack on Birmingham and the following night saw one of the worst aerial bombardments of the war, the raid on Coventry. This involved 449 bombers and 470 tons of bombs being dropped as well as 127 parachute mines. Only one German aircraft was lost in spite of desperate RAF attempts to drive away the Luftwaffe bombers. It was difficult for both sides to operate fighters effectively at night time and not until later in the war was this problem overcome.

On 29 December a bombing raid on the City of London with a combination of high explosive and incendiary bombs created a devastating firestorm. 130 bombers dropped 10,000 firebombs and the ancient historical centre of the City of London was destroyed.[23]

The Blitz led to appalling human suffering in terms of loss of life, destruction of property, devastating fires and homelessness. It was perhaps the most intensive period of bombing civilians ever endured and although its military impact was limited it affected the morale of the population. The bravery of the RAF and civil defence forces and the difficulty on the German side of sustaining this attack, given the heavy losses the Luftwaffe suffered, held the foe at bay until they were compelled to reduce the level and intensity of the bombing.

Eventually Hitler recognized that the terror bombings had failed to accomplish the defeat of the British and began exploring alternative strategies. At that point he again failed to show a proper understanding of priorities and his mistaken decisions contributed directly to the defeat of Germany.

The next direct combat in which the Luftwaffe became involved was the result of the Italian collapse in North Africa and Greece together with the destruction by the RAF of much of the Italian fleet. January 1941 saw the arrival in Sicily of *Fliegerkorps X* (Flying Corps X). Soon after they were in position German bombers and fighters began attacking the Royal Navy and British communications in the Mediterranean. This activity had a huge and immediate effect on British resources.[24]

The Luftwaffe strategy alarmed the British and if it had been given a higher priority – just as Rommel should have been given more resources – it would have been almost impossible for Britain to hold on in North Africa and the Mediterranean theatre. The Suez Canal would have been in German hands and the Mediterranean totally under Axis control without any realistic prospect of being challenged by Britain. In these circumstances both Spain and Vichy France might have considered joining the Axis and certainly the closure of the Mediterranean would have struck a major blow against British supplies.

The Mediterranean was one of the few theatres of war where relatively insignificant numbers were involved. The situation in that region remained critical for Britain until 1942. Sustaining an intensive air assault in this area would have given the Germans a huge advantage over the British at a time when America and Russia remained outside the war. It is difficult to see how Britain could have continued any kind of offensive action beyond the most minimal level. Hitler's failure to see the crucial importance of controlling the Mediterranean and North Africa was a major strategic blunder. He could have acquired control of the entire region at relatively low cost yet never regarded the campaign in that area as anything more than a sideshow.[25]

Hitler regarded the Mediterranean campaign as unimportant but was obsessed with the Balkans. Mussolini's rash invasion of Greece compelled him to send assistance to the Italians. Hitler began preparing to fight the Greeks who were receiving assistance from Britain, RAF units being active in its defence. Hitler feared that Britain might send its aircraft to attack the Romanian oil fields on which Germany depended for the bulk of its fuel.

The attack on Greece had been planned for months but then Yugoslavian developments added to German problems. A reluctant Yugoslav government had been pressured into joining the Axis but a military coup overthrew the regime. It is unclear how much assistance Britain could have given to Yugoslavia but foolishly the new leader failed to request British aid.

Hitler was enraged by what he called "the mad Yugoslavs" and declared that "the city of Belgrade will be destroyed from the air by continual day and night bombings."[26] Around 600 aircraft were moved from other bases to take part in the campaign. When war began 1000 Luftwaffe planes were deployed in the assault.

The Germans were ordered to avoid bombing the transport network or industry in the hope that they could service the needs of the Reich after victory. Instead Belgrade was to be pounded into submission. High explosive and incendiary bombs were dropped and the city was soon ablaze. The bombing of Belgrade killed 17,000 people and reduced the city to ruins. Yugoslavia surrendered within a fortnight.

The next target was Greece where air and ground troops combined in an attempt to isolate and encircle the British troops fighting alongside the Greeks. The Royal Navy managed to extricate most of them safely but though the Greeks fought bravely the Germans were slowly winning.

At that point the Germans nearly over-reached themselves. On 20 May they dropped airborne troops on Crete but met with fierce resistance. On the first day they were nearly driven back with the paratroopers taking heavy casualties and in danger of being captured. Unfortunately this success was not followed up and soon an airbase was seized and reinforcements flown in. The Luftwaffe quickly established air supremacy and forced the Royal Navy to act purely defensively.

Although the Germans captured Crete they lost 4000 troops and of the 500 transport aircraft sent to the island 140 were destroyed and a further 150 damaged. By May 1941 7.5% of all aircraft had been lost and 12% of bombers. This rate of attrition against comparatively weak adversaries did not augur well for the next military operation planned by Hitler – the invasion of Russia. Halder declared after the war that he believed it had been the biggest single mistake of the whole conflict.[27]

The air war against the Soviet Union began with a bombing raid on the port of Sebastopol. Over 2000 aircraft were assembled for the invasion. After its preliminary strike on the naval base the Luftwaffe concentrated on the destruction of the Soviet air force. They eliminated 1200 aircraft with the majority being destroyed before they were able to take off. This success was followed up by a withering assault on tank brigades that smashed the units before they could even ready themselves for action. By the end of day two of the invasion the Luftwaffe had eliminated 2000 Soviet aircraft.[28]

By July the Soviets had lost over 6000 aircraft. This was the high point of the German offensive. Communications, transport and supplies became an increasing problem. The Germans had destroyed 95% of aircraft in European Russia and enjoyed complete air superiority.[28]

In spite of this success the Germans had grossly underestimated the strength and resilience of the Russians. The war was no longer being waged with a series of major confrontations but was becoming a battle of attrition. In such a conflict the vast land mass and greater population of Russia would inevitably win if it could withstand the fierce German pressure.

By October autumn rain and poor visibility dramatically reduced the offensive capability of the Luftwaffe. Then came November and the onset of one of the harshest winters in years. The effect of these horrific conditions was worse for the ground troops than for airmen. With the biting cold came frostbite and hypothermia. These conditions killed or maimed large numbers of the soldiers. Desertion and suicide became more common. Both Russians and Germans behaved with appalling callousness with Stalin demanding the destruction of homes and food in complete disregard of the fact that he was condemning his own people to death in the process. German troops behaved with equal cruelty by forcibly stripping clothes and boots from the Russians and turning them out naked into the snow.[29]

The Luftwaffe found the problem of supply increasingly difficult. Fuel and ammunition were running dangerously low. The further into

Russia the Germans advanced the more acute the difficulties became. Aircraft were increasingly shifted to a role supporting ground troops though raids on Moscow and Leningrad inflicted significant damage.[30]

By late autumn supplying the needs of the Luftwaffe was becoming a major problem. Aircraft were increasingly damaged but it was not possible to repair or even maintain them adequately.

The Luftwaffe virtually ceased flying for a time and suffered severe shortages of fuel and spare parts. They were compelled to operate from makeshift airfields and light fires beneath the engines of their planes to unfreeze them.

By contrast the Soviet Air Force had been waiting in aerodromes beyond Moscow and was ready for combat. December saw a dramatic turn in the aerial war and for the first time the Russians achieved air superiority.[31]

The Luftwaffe did not endure the same degree of hardship during the winter as the German soldiers. They were more able to take shelter and eat regularly though their transport and supply network was very variable. Essentially they waited out the winter and hoped that the coming of Spring would bring them fresh opportunities for victory.

That proved to be a phantasm. The Soviets had used the winter to replenish their fuel, repair and maintain their aircraft and train new crews to replace those lost in the first year of battle. The Germans had to make do with reduced resources, damaged or otherwise not wholly serviceable planes and with untrained or semi-trained aircrews. The effect was to make the Russian air force superior not only in quantity but in quality. Soon the air battle was to move decisively in their favour and the Luftwaffe lost its offensive capability. It was never again in a position of air superiority and the remainder of the campaign in Russia saw it become less and less effective.

The bleak winter left the Luftwaffe with only 15% of its aircraft capable of action. Shovels and sledges had to be used to clear snow away from the often improvised air strips. It was difficult to start planes and carrying out maintenance became a major problem. Tools had to be heated before work could begin and often reheated numerous times.

The army's desperate situation and the shortage of artillery forced bombers to be used to support ground troops. This was not a role for which they were suited and Russian fighters and anti-aircraft defences inflicted heavy casualties on the bombers.

Their difficulties were compounded by a crass blunder on Goering's part. Deciding that the Luftwaffe did not need a large component of technical staff led him to order them to fight as front line troops. This not only led to unnecessary loss of life but made it even harder to maintain and repair German aircraft.[32]

Further mistakes were made when Goering virtually shut down flying schools and sent their pilots, instructors and aircraft to the front. This meant that barely trained pilots were rushed into combat prematurely. It also affected the future training of pilots and the quality declined sharply as a result of this short-sighted measure.

Hitler then intervened in the already difficult conflict with a mistaken strategy of his own. Halder wanted German forces to adopt a defensive posture to rebuild its fighting capability. Hitler dismissed the idea and insisted that a new offensive would break Soviet resistance.

Hitler drew up new instructions in April. These required a small operation against Leningrad with the principal aim being to capture the oil fields in the Caucasus. At this stage the plan was risky and overly ambitious but not as bad as the revised version became. No mention was made of any role for the Luftwaffe beyond that of supporting ground troops. Hitler did not even consider using them to attack Soviet industrial targets which might have been a more effective use of air power.

A single concentrated thrust against the Caucasus might have achieved success but characteristically Hitler insisted on splitting his forces. This affected the Luftwaffe as well as the army and just over half of the air force took part in the south Russia campaign.

The aerial part of this phase of the war began with a series of devastating air raids on Sebastopol. At this stage on the southern front the Luftwaffe still enjoyed air superiority over the Russians and did considerable damage. Gradually the Soviets rebuilt and eventually the offensive on the ground became bogged down and the aerial campaign led to increasingly high losses of aircraft and crews. The Luftwaffe lost air supremacy and for the remainder of the war had to fight on the defensive. They continued to fight on bravely but increasingly hopelessly until their final defeat.[33]

Hitler's failure to prepare for a long conflict was a major strategic blunder. It was also at best naive of the Wehrmacht high command to underestimate Russian resources so badly in military and industrial terms and regard them as lacking resilience and even courage. In the case of Barbarossa even though Hitler began to meddle and made a series of strategic and tactical errors there is little doubt that the armed forces failed to produce an adequate and realistic plan for the invasion. They too readily assumed a quick victory partly because they realized that Germany did not have the resources to sustain a long war but principally because of their failure to recognize that conquering the Soviet Union was a far harder undertaking than the defeat of France. Perhaps the speed and relative ease of the German victories led them to become complacent and fail to make adequate provisions. Even in the earliest draft of Barbarossa there was no provision for equipping troops for, or preparing them to fight, in the conditions of a Russian winter.

It did not help that the Wehrmacht was principally concerned with the army. The result was that the Navy was neglected and the Luftwaffe, instead of working with the other armed forces, became Goering's personal project. If he had been a competent administrator or even willing to listen to advice from others who knew better that might not have been a problem, but except for Milch the Luftwaffe was staffed by people who were as incompetent as Goering. Milch tried to improve the quality of the service but not until 1943 – by which time the Luftwaffe was a shadow of its former self – were his views taken seriously. By then it was increasingly difficult for it to function effectively with the Allies destroying both aircraft and the factories and repair facilities they needed.[34]

Hitler's continual poor choice or priorities led him to make yet another mistaken decision. The Italians attempted to blast Malta into submission with the aim of adding it to their empire but without success. The German high command produced a plan for a co-ordinated assault on the island by aircraft, naval forces and ground troops. Hitler rejected the idea and instead ordered intensive aerial devastation.

Bombing began on 10 June 1940 without a declaration of war. It followed only hours after Mussolini's declaration of war on Britain and France. That day saw 55 bombers and 21 fighters attack the island.[35]

There were no aircraft units in Malta or any kind of air defences in place. The Royal Navy had left some Gloster Sea Gladiators in need of repair which were rushed into service and performed heroically against superior force. Towards the end of June four Hurricanes were sent to the island to reinforce the beleaguered inhabitants.[36]

Malta was crucial to both sides as ships transporting supplies to Axis forces in North Africa were subject to attack by the RAF and the Royal Navy. Until April 1941 nearly all their supplies reached Libya safely. Then the RAF in particular sank enormous quantities of material and the Germans were forced to respond. By November 77% of supplies destined for North Africa had been destroyed and the Luftwaffe established a presence in depth.[37]

The island of Malta was heavily bombed and its virtual lack of air defences made the battle one-sided for a long time. Stukas and Bf 109s based in Sicily caused death and destruction to the people of the island as well as inflicting heavy damage on shipping. July saw a tiny number of RAF planes facing 200 German aircraft. It is a tribute to the skill and bravery of the pilots that only one Gladiator and one Hurricane were lost. In August 12 Hurricanes and two Blackburn Skuas arrived to reinforce the defences.[38]

March and April 1942 saw the height of the aerial battle. Thousands of tons of bombs were dropped on Malta and the islanders were running low on fuel, ammunition and even food. It was almost impossible for ships to get through to deliver supplies as they faced relentless attacks by U-boats and from the air.[39]

So acute was the crisis that HMS Eagle made two hazardous journeys to deliver 25 Spitfires for the defence of the island. They were welcome but still insufficient to overcome the air superiority of the Luftwaffe.

The dire situation led to Churchill requesting assistance from the US. Roosevelt sent an aircraft carrier to ferry 48 Spitfires to Malta. This could have been a turning point in the battle but unfortunately the Germans knew of the operation and though the planes were delivered safely most were destroyed while still on the ground.

May 1942 was the darkest part of the battle for Malta. Britain again requested assistance from America. This time two aircraft carriers – one British and one American – ferried 64 Spitfires to the island. Only one plane was lost and as soon as the aircraft landed ground crews quickly refuelled them and they were rapidly in action against the Luftwaffe.

10 May saw a turning point in the battle. 100 German aircraft approached the island and 37 Spitfires and 13 Hurricanes were waiting to meet them. 63 German planes were destroyed or damaged – 57 by the RAF and 6 by anti-aircraft fire. This day is known in Malta as "The Glorious 10th of May." The RAF had no hangars for their aircraft and no petrol to transport the pilots which makes their achievement even more remarkable.[40]

Three convoys delivered a further 85 Spitfires to Malta between August and October 1942. Even though the island's defenders were gaining modern planes and gradually winning air superiority the bombardment of Malta continued. Slowly the RAF moved from a defensive role to attacking the enemy. Malta was saved and the route for transporting supplies to North Africa became once more a major headache for the Axis powers.[41]

The failure to subdue Malta showed once again Hitler's lack of appreciation of the crucial importance of the Mediterranean. He squandered large quantities of men and equipment in areas that were not significant yet failed to make available the relatively modest resources that would have enabled him to control the Mediterranean. The effect of Axis domination of that area would have hugely handicapped Britain and might have decisively affected the course of the war.

Hitler remained obsessed with bombers even though the success of RAF fighters against them ought to have made him recognize that both types of aircraft had a role to play and that fighter support for bombers was essential, both as protection and to assist them in carrying out their mission more effectively. As the war continued Milch and Speer attempted to streamline and improve aircraft production. The result was to produce fighters of exceptional quality – particularly the Me 262 – but Hitler remained unable to see the benefit of deploying these planes in their proper roles. On seeing the 262 his only response was to ask how effectively it could bomb the opposition forces. Goering's incompetence and his own blindness to any role for aircraft beyond that of pounding the enemy into submission were major negative factors in reducing the fighting capability of the Luftwaffe.

The last two years of the war saw a needless squandering of lives as Hitler's hubris led him to compel a weakened and thinly-spread Luftwaffe to operate on too wide a front and with inadequate fuel, insufficient spare parts and barely trained pilots. As the Allies gradually achieved total superiority in the air the futility of this approach rather than a targeted plan of campaign became evident but its obvious failure did not bring about any change in this mistaken strategy.

The campaign in the Soviet Union recommenced in 1943. As before it began with a German offensive but this time the Russians had learned from their previous mistakes and fierce fighting resulted between the Soviet air force and the Luftwaffe. Problems with transport and communications continued to dog the Germans and eventually the Soviets triumphed. For the remainder of the campaign on the "eastern front" the Luftwaffe, like the army, had to fight an increasingly hopeless defensive battle.[42]

The campaign in Italy was an extension of the North African disaster. Using bases on the continent the Allies launched a devastating assault on the Italians. There was comparatively little resistance on Sicily but the mainland was a different matter. The Italians tried to fight off the invasion but things went badly for them and the king of Italy dismissed Mussolini and appointed a new government. They promptly began secret negotiations for peace.

Hitler was enraged and insisted on sending paratroopers to rescue Mussolini and repel the Allied invaders. This was a futile waste of resources and lives and again tied down troops and aircraft in an unnecessary and unwinnable campaign rather than making best use of them to defend the frontiers.

He made the same mistake with the Balkans, insisting on using the Luftwaffe on what should in the circumstances have been a purely peripheral area of the war when it would have been more sensible to keep them tightly focused. Resources were thinly spread and both fighters and bombers became less effective than if they had been deployed on a narrower front.

Goering was as uninterested in the navy as Hitler and failed to appreciate how useful and effective air power could be in terms of attacking ships. The merchant navy in particular always enjoyed a measure of support from the RAF while the attacks on shipping were overwhelmingly conducted by U-boats without Luftwaffe assistance.

Air power was rarely employed against shipping but when it was used the effects were devastating. Perhaps the most dramatic demonstration of that was the destruction of PQ17 but several other lesser examples showed what could have been achieved. As it was the U-boats decimated merchant shipping and with sufficient air support it is highly probable that the Battle of the Atlantic – in any event a close run affair – might have resulted in a German victory.[43]

At the outset of war no real provision for air defence had been made. This was a major blunder and in spite of RAF bombing raids it took considerable time before Hitler and Goering saw the necessity of defensive measures against aerial bombing. In July 1940 the first steps towards providing adequate defences were put in place. Before long

Germany created one of the best aerial defensive networks in Europe. It became increasingly necessary for it to be used.

Again, Hitler and Goering with their obsession with offensive rather than defensive war hindered the adequate development of the systems. Provisions for air defence were largely based on anti-aircraft guns and searchlights.

General Josef Kammhuber commanded the 1st Night Fighter Division. He led his unit of Bf 109s and Do 17s in attacks on British bases. This was one of the most effective Luftwaffe operations and seriously hampered the RAF but in 1941 it was discontinued as the air force was required for the Soviet campaign.

Kammhuber created an extensive defensive network of searchlights assisted by Bf 109s. Radar units were also installed and by 1943 they made bombing raids on Germany extremely dangerous. This defensive air cover helped identify enemy aircraft rapidly. The consequence was that by 1944 these defences were at the peak of their performance and resulted in heavy casualties on Allied bombers.[44]

In spite of these achievements a combination of shortages of raw materials and difficulties in production made the task increasingly hopeless. The destruction of German factories and the lack of priority given by Hitler to the need for "defensive armaments" meant that they never received the resources that might have tilted the scale.[45]

From 1943 to 1945 the Allies continued with their "strategic bombing" campaign – a euphemism for blanket bombing without regard for casualties. In spite of the heavy toll on civilians inflicted by the bombers, their strategic errors and the high quality of German air defences meant that the price of these raids was excessive and led to unnecessary wastage of aircraft and pilots. The Allies continually failed to learn from their mistakes until very late in the war and as a result the campaign was partly responsible for prolonging the struggle.[46]

Major Hajo Herrmann proposed attacking bombers with a combination of searchlights and day fighters. In spite of strong support for the idea from Milch it was rejected by Goering.

After the Allied raid on Hamburg the Germans had to rethink their defensive strategy. Herrmann's proposal was adopted and his units increased in size. The value of this new approach was shown when an Allied raid on Peenemünde resulted in the destruction of forty bombers.

As the aerial war continued to deteriorate Goering made the mistake of using night fighters in daylight operations. The result was wholly unnecessary devastation and crews and aircraft were lost as a result. Herrmann and Milch were powerless to stop the mistaken strategy which accelerated the decline of the Luftwaffe from its former position of air superiority over Germany.[47]

Flak remained the main German anti-aircraft defence. A million men and women were involved in operating this weapon and by the end of the war they were responsible for bringing down over half of Allied aircraft.

As the Luftwaffe's effectiveness declined flak became the most important weapon in protecting the country from Allied bombing. From July 1944 onwards it claimed the majority of aircraft shot down.

The defensive network included concrete towers with heavy anti-aircraft guns above, air warning alerts, camouflaged streets and buildings and even dummy towns. Searchlight units also tried to give warning of the approach of Allied bombers. Barrage balloons were also used and during daylight smoke pots were used to hide the area from view.

Over a million people were involved in the air defence side of the struggle and a total of 15,000 searchlights to detect intruders were backed up by 30,000 light guns and 9000 heavy guns.

A "heavy" flak battery always had between four to six heavy guns. A "light" flak battery had around a dozen light guns. Some were mounted on top of buildings while others were placed in towers. Mobile guns were mounted on railway carriages to allow rapid changes of position.

Light guns were generally placed at strategic points like docks and factories. Sometimes they were sited on canals, roads or rivers. Heavy guns were often placed on the outskirts of cities.

Searchlights fulfilled a dual purpose – to illuminate bombers so that they could be attacked and to blind the pilots with their glare. This made it harder for the pilots to locate their targets and made the accuracy of their bombing poorer. On cloudy nights searchlights attempted to plot the course of the aircraft to help fighters or flak battalions locate and destroy it. On foggy nights the searchlights could not detect enemy aircraft so attempted to create a pool of light to make it harder for Allied bombers to locate potential targets.

Ironically the Allied bombing campaign was rarely as accurate as it pretended and the effects were less severe than they imagined. On the other hand the fact that it was intensive and caused heavy casualties compelled the Germans to invest more time and money and effort into their anti-aircraft defences than would otherwise have been necessary. To that extent the strategic bombing campaign assisted the Allies in winning the war in the air.

The Germans were as obsessed as the Allies with the mistaken idea that massive bombing would break the will of the civilian population and force the enemy to sue for peace. This mentality – particularly shared by Hitler and Goering – led to a disastrous preference for heavy bombers over fighter planes. Perhaps the most obvious example of this wastage of effort and neglect of fine aeronautical engineering was the story of the Messerschmitt Me 262. For its time this was the most advanced fighter in the world and could have done sterling service in attacking the Allied air forces. Instead both Hitler and Goering tried to divert it from its true purpose as a fighter into a bomber. The result was that it was not remotely as effective. When used in its proper role as a fighter the Me 262 proved devastating and its effect on Allied fighters and bombers showed what could have been achieved. Yet again Hitler's stubbornness and ignorance played a major part in losing the aerial war for the Luftwaffe.

Throughout its history the Luftwaffe was under-resourced, often misapplied in terms of its operations and badly led. It is a remarkable tribute to its pilots and German aeronautics that they came so close to victory in spite of these handicaps. As with many aspects of the war it could so easily have been different and Germany might have triumphed instead of tumbling headlong to total disaster.

Sea Wolves at Bay

Hitler had served as a Corporal during the First World War and remained obsessed with ground warfare. He saw the potential of tanks and heavy artillery to change the course of a conflict but was totally uninterested in naval warfare. During the early campaigning the bulk of the activity took place in the air or on the ground which made his inability to appreciate the role of the navy perhaps more understandable. Once France had fallen but Britain remained in a state of war he ought to have reconsidered his priorities.

At that time Britain not only retained its empire but was the largest naval power in the world. Germany was incapable of matching the British in terms of surface ships and yet again Hitler was poorly served by his advisers.

Admiral Erich Raeder was the head of the German navy and like Hitler obsessed with size. He saw the future of the navy as building a massive fleet of surface ships that would be able to challenge the British successfully. Raeder drew up an ambitious plan that was intended by 1948 to see the German navy supreme on the ocean.

However realistic Raeder's proposals may or may not have been, time was not on the side of Germany. The scale of the naval building programme he proposed would have taken years and required enormous expenditure. Far more practical was the advice given by Raeder's deputy Admiral Karl Dönitz who argued for a large flotilla of submarines – known as U-boats.

At the commencement of the war none of the combatants were equipped to strike a knockout blow against each other. Britain, France and Germany were all capable of fighting a purely defensive war at sea but none had the resources to defeat the other in naval conflict. All three had learned from the First World War that the day of great decisive battles on the ocean were over and naval warfare was now a slow process of attrition.

In such a war U-boats played a crucial role. That was one area of naval development in which the Germans led the world. The British retained an old-fashioned approach to submarines and favoured size over speed and manoeuvrability while the Germans had long adopted the opposite approach.

Naval war was no longer a question of big battleships facing each other with guns blazing till one emerged victorious and the other was sunk. The nature both of submarine warfare and of the importance of supply and communications network meant that merchant ships were now a prime target for attack. During the last two years of the First World War the German navy found that attacking merchant vessels brought Britain to the brink of starvation and almost forced it to surrender. Without the entry of the United States on the side of the Allies the Germans might well have won the war through their U-boat campaign.

Hitler had not learned that lesson and nor had Raeder who still thought in old-fashioned terms about battleships and destroyers. Dönitz – who had served as a U-boat commander during the First World War – had absorbed all the lessons of that campaign and was determined to put his knowledge to use.

Hitler's ignorance was compounded by his contempt for the Royal Navy. Dönitz knew how strong Britain was and feared and respected the navy. He was assisted by undue complacency on the British side. Numerically Britain was strong but many of its ships were obsolescent and the size of the British Empire forced it to disperse its resources. As a result the navy was spread too thinly which reduced its effectiveness.

The navy had seen the value of aircraft carriers early with the result that Britain had more of them than any other nation. Its possession of Gibraltar and Malta and control of the Suez Canal made the Mediterranean relatively secure.[1]

The widespread dispersal of British resources meant that the bulk of the navy was based in Asia or the Mediterranean with few ships located in the Atlantic. This became a major problem on the outbreak of war.[2]

Dönitz was aware of the relative absence of Royal Navy ships in the Atlantic and believed that this represented an Achilles heel in British power that he could exploit. For years he had been urging a flotilla of around 300 U-boats but Hitler's lack of interest in the navy and Raeder's obsession with surface ships meant that when his country went to war Dönitz had only 62 submarines at his disposal.[3]

In spite of the shortage of numbers the U-boats rapidly proved their worth in the Atlantic campaign. The Merchant Navy was not considered a fighting force and was essentially a rag-bag of ships of every type from tramp steamers to ocean liners. All carried goods and/or passengers across the sea but the U-boat threat was not taken seriously and no protection was afforded them by either the Royal Navy or the RAF.

The consequences of this neglect soon became apparent as German submarines took a heavy toll on shipping. Britain was hugely dependent on imports and the campaign resulted not only in loss of life but severe disruption to supplies of food, raw materials and even weapons. In spite of this the British continued to refuse to introduce the convoy system to protect merchant ships.

Opposition came from several quarters – the owners, the captains of the merchant ships and the Royal Navy. The owners were relatively indifferent to the fate of their crew as in the event of a ship being sunk they received full compensation and no longer had to pay the staff wages so had no real incentive to wish for protection. The captains of the ships felt it was somehow "unmanly" to require protection; they had often spent years battling rough seas and considered themselves tough and capable. The Royal Navy looked on the merchant ships as a lower form of life and their crew as not being "proper" sailors. They resented the idea that they should be protecting them rather than battling German navy vessels.[4]

This combination of attitudes led to needless loss of life as the U-boats were able to attack unprotected merchant ships more or less at will. Ship captains soon learned to take evasive action but its effectiveness was limited. German submarines hunted in "wolf packs" and single merchant vessels were easy prey. Even groups of ships were picked off by the U-boats.

The appalling toll on British merchant shipping forced the government to change its mind. Despite the opposition of the ship owners, Royal Navy and merchant ship captains they instituted the convoy system whereby naval vessels escorted merchant ships on their voyage across the Atlantic. The result was a dramatic fall in sinkings and it became harder for U-boats to achieve the same level of devastation.[5]

Hitler remained indifferent to the war at sea which in his eyes was nothing more than a side show to the main battles taking place. The fall of France made him master of Western Europe and with Spain neutral but sympathetic and Italy an active ally of Germany he felt that only stubbornness was preventing the British from making peace and leaving him in full possession of his spoils.

Britain's continuing refusal to surrender or sue for peace led him first to attempt to reduce them to submission through aerial bombardment and if that had been successful he planned an invasion with ships landing German troops on British soil. The failure of the Luftwaffe in the Battle of Britain and the incapacity of the German navy meant that suddenly Dönitz's plans for submarine warfare began to attract him.

Soon the U-boat fleet was expanded significantly. It remained well below the level that Dönitz had requested but it enabled German submarines to operate to devastating effect. If Hitler had given Dönitz the large fleet of U-boats he had asked for it is difficult to see how Britain could have survived the Battle of the Atlantic.

At the beginning of the war both the Germans and Allies still visualized the battleship as being the dominant force in naval warfare. The British had a large fleet of battleships but by the end of the war bitter experience had taught the Navy that using them as the main weapon in a naval conflict was an antiquated approach. Dönitz knew better but unfortunately for the Germans his voice was disregarded. Hitler always favoured size and Raeder's obsession with large battleships appealed to him more than Dönitz's championing of small, fast and manoeuvrable U-boats as the main weapon of attack. It was not until 1942 that Hitler finally came round to Dönitz's way of thinking.

Germany's area of naval control was restricted to part of the North Sea and the Baltic. All its exits to the Atlantic necessitated travelling through the English Channel and North Sea which were under British control. The Atlantic trade routes were essential to the survival of Britain while Germany was not dependent on them. This factor made Dönitz's strategy – in direct opposition to Raeder and other German naval leaders – focus on a campaign to use U-boats to sink merchantmen rather than naval vessels.

What Dönitz lacked was sufficient submarines to make his approach work. In spite of severe shortages the U-boats were the most effective weapon the Germans had and impacted sharply on British imports. The result was an approximate "balance of terror" where U-boats sank enough ships to cause alarm but not enough to decisively alter the amount of goods being transported to Britain.

Of course the surface naval war continued though with the imbalance of ships between the German and Royal Navy this was less important militarily. Germany entered the war with a number of battleships – the *Gneisenau*, *Scharnhorst*, *Bismarck* and *Tirpitz* being state of the art ships and the pride of the German navy.

On 8 November 1939 the *Gneisenau* was used as bait to draw the Royal Navy into range of U-boats and the Luftwaffe. The attempt failed but represented a growing awareness that the German navy was too weak to challenge the British fleet with its surface vessels alone. In a significant harbinger of the future the unsuccessful decoy operation took place off the coast of Norway.

The first casualty of the naval war was the passenger liner *Athenia*. This was sunk by U-30 to the north west of Ireland. The ship's captain steamed straight towards the submarine and at first the U-boat captain took evasive action, but the *Athenia* continued to steam directly towards the submarine. Imagining that they were under attack by an armed merchant cruiser, the U-boat loosed its torpedoes and sank the ship. Only when the captain saw women and children struggling and screaming did he realize his error.

This led the British to mistakenly believe that the Germans were engaging in unrestricted submarine warfare as they had during World War I. This incident alarmed the Admiralty and they began to soften their opposition to the convoy system.

Hitler was furious and reminded Dönitz that he wanted U-boats to follow international maritime law. The result was that crews took great care to ensure that passenger ships were not attacked.

On 4 September the RAF attacked German warships at Wilhelmshaven and Brunsbuttel. The only damage caused was to the cruiser *Emden* which was hit by a British plane that crashed. On 16 September U-32 sank one ship in the first convoy to be attacked. 30 September saw the battleship *Admiral Graf Spee* sink a ship off the coast of Brazil.

By the end of September U-boats had sunk 53 ships for the loss of 2 submarines. In October they sank 44 ships for the loss of 5 submarines. November saw 49 ships sunk for the loss of 7 U-boats.

Meanwhile the *Graf Spee* had sunk four vessels in the Atlantic and made its way to the Indian Ocean. It was pursued by Royal Navy vessels but eluded capture. The ship *Deutschland* also claimed a victim and returned to Germany where it was renamed *Lutzow*.

Attrition was affecting both sides but at least the British had a substantial number of vessels to replenish their stocks while the loss of U-boats represented a disproportionately high percentage of available submarines. This led Hitler and Raeder to agree to Dönitz's request for more U-boat construction although the level of submarines built remained well below the quantity required.

By March 1940 U-boats had sunk 222 British, Allied and neutral ships for the loss of 18 submarines. That was a horrific total of losses for the merchantmen but it represented a third of the U-boats available at the start of the war. Detection and counter-measures against the submarine threat remained poor but were slowly improving and the continuing shortage of replacement U-boats gave the Allies hope, particularly as at that stage France was still in the war.

Norway was considered crucial by both sides with the Germans receiving significant quantities of iron ore from Sweden and the Allies being anxious to stop or at least restrict the trade. The British drew up several plans for invading the country but hesitation by the government meant that none of them were put into practice. The Germans remained anxious about the possibility of British intervention which would have been quite effective given the strength of the Royal Navy in the area.

Hesitation on both sides about the prospects led to plans being postponed but eventually the British decided to invade. The plan they came up with was highly unlikely to have been successful but in any event the Germans finally made up their mind to invade and occupy Norway themselves.

The result was what is best described as a Pyrrhic victory – the Germans achieved their goal of conquering Norway but at such high cost that it was a military mistake. Germany invaded Norway with a pocket battleship, 14 destroyers and six cruisers together with thirty U-boats that were mainly engaged in patrol duties. The Norwegian campaign showed up major defects in the German navy, both technically and in terms of organization.

A day after the German invasion of Norway Britain sent ships into Ofotfjord to attack the German naval vessels occupying Narvik. The British lost two ships but sunk two German destroyers and several transport ships. A British submarine was also sunk by a U-boat.

Three days later nine destroyers and a battleship were sent into Narvik by the British to eliminate the remaining German vessels. A U-boat was sunk and eight German destroyers were either sunk or forced to scuttle themselves.

A combination of military hesitancy by British ground forces, lack of political will in the British government and the growing threat to France forced the British to withdraw from Norway. In spite of that the result of the German invasion was to write off nearly all the surface ships of the German navy and expose the serious deficiencies of U-boats used in inappropriate roles. The Norwegian fiasco also showed that the torpedoes available often malfunctioned and a rapid programme to update and improve torpedo efficiency was launched.

In addition to the catastrophic toll on the German navy the conquest of Norway was also a longer-term political and military error. It was a huge drain on German reserves and the conquest of France meant that other sources of raw materials became available and made the Norwegian invasion unnecessary. On every level it represented one of the most glaring mistakes made by Hitler in the naval war.

With the German surface fleet now barely in existence Hitler was forced to give greater priority to U-boat construction. The submarine flotilla represented his only effective naval weapon and at last he gave Dönitz his head. The numbers of U-boats remained below both what Dönitz asked for and the level at which they could have turned the tide in the naval war, but they began to be the biggest thorn in the side of Britain.

Dönitz and Raeder clashed over the most effective way of deploying U-boats with Raeder still thinking in terms of attacking the Royal Navy while Dönitz saw the key to a successful naval strategy being cutting off British trade. As a former submarine commander in the First World War he remembered how close the U-boats had come to forcing Britain to surrender as its trade routes were drastically hampered by German submarine attacks. He believed that the main priority for submarines should be attacking the Merchant Navy.

The term "Merchant Navy" was an invention of the press. It covered a rag-bag collection of vessels from tramp steamers to ocean liners. The core of it was the much despised tramps whose crews carried cargo all over the world. It was not even recognized as a fighting service until

1942 in spite of the crucial importance of its work in transporting essential supplies to and from Britain. Food, fuel, raw materials and weapons were ferried across the Atlantic, Arctic and Pacific Oceans with relentless attacks by aircraft, U-boats and occasionally surface ships adding to the normal hazards of stormy weather and unpleasant living conditions on board the ships.

Sailors on U-boats also endured privation. They had to face tempests and seasickness but also the constant danger of enemy attack. A standard U-boat had a crew of 40 who had to share two toilets (in practice only one as the other was generally used for storage of food and materials.) In addition to the difficulties this presented in terms of hygiene, whenever the waste matter was pumped out into the ocean it exposed the crew to danger as they became vulnerable to detection by enemy aircraft or surface ships.

The crew were unable to bathe or shave or change their clothes. Saltwater soap was supplied to the crew but this produced an unpleasant effect on the skin and was both disliked and not much used. They had no blankets or sheets but instead took their rest in sleeping bags that were only washed on the vessel's return to port. Deodorants were used to mask the inevitable smell of body odour. Conditions on board were cramped and there was no privacy for the crew. Bread had to be consumed immediately or it would become inedible. Smoking was only permitted on the deck when the submarine surfaced and even then there were severe restrictions. The crew of a U-boat would expect to spend an average of six months at sea and without being able to rest up in ports during that time. Being submerged at least avoided seasickness but brought with it further problems – claustrophobia, oxygen deprivation, boredom and a foetid atmosphere due to the closely confined conditions. As U-boats increasingly became the principal naval weapon for the Germans these factors added to the difficulties and stresses of fighting a war at sea.[6]

A bizarre use for condoms was as radio aerials which were filled with gas and raised up for transmission or reception. Condoms were also used to launch weather balloons. Harold Busch described life for a U-boat crew as follows:

> *"The most striking thing when one is at sea for the first time on a war-experienced submarine is the sober realization of the difficulty of everyday life on board: flight alarms, submarine traps, pursuing destroyers, even torpedoes, weeks of bitter cold temperatures, and ongoing high seas. So many extreme efforts have to be made before a brief and simple war report can be dispatched mentioning even the most modest of successes. It's difficult to conceive of the effort behind such a report."*[7]

Submarines were compelled to spend most of their time on the surface because of the limitations of speed and range underwater. This inevitably made them more vulnerable to attack and for that reason the majority of U-boat attacks took place at night and while the vessel was surfaced. They would dive only to avoid attack or on the rare occasions when they launched a torpedo assault in daylight. U-boats were faster and more stable on the surface than underwater though it was more difficult to detect them when they were submerged. This was particularly true during the early years of the naval war when British detection systems were poor and their complacency about the ability of the ASDIC method of discovering submarines led to numerous unnecessary losses at sea.

Fundamental problems for the Germans during the naval war were not only that they possessed too few U-boats to deliver the killer blow against the Allies but their flotilla was spread too thinly. The same was true of the British but with the largest navy in the world and the resources of the Empire to draw upon their shortages were less acute. In the light of thc small number of U-boats available it would have been better to confine their activities to the Atlantic. The small fleet of German submarines managed to inflict casualties out of all proportion to their numbers and Dönitz consistently argued for an "Atlantic" focus on their activities.

Events beyond his control meant that U-boats were compelled to operate over a wider area than practical. The failure of the Italians in their naval war led to Hitler ordering Dönitz to move U-boats away from the Atlantic and into the Mediterranean. This was a disastrous mistake as German submarines were enjoying considerable success in the Atlantic and their withdrawal reduced the effectiveness of the naval campaign. In the Mediterranean theatre German submarines performed poorly and the redeployment of these key weapons was an unnecessary diversion that assisted the Allies considerably. Very few U-boats could even enter the Mediterranean and in spite of isolated successes their effect on the naval war in that area was marginal.

Ironically the Mediterranean was one area where a concerted German and Italian offensive on a large scale could have made a difference. British naval resources were weak in that region and air cover was inadequate. They enjoyed three key factors giving them superiority but all of them were vulnerable to attack. The possession of Gibraltar made it difficult for German U-boats or surface ships to enter the Mediterranean. The control of the Suez Canal was of crucial strategic importance to the British. Malta was also a vital base for supplying British troops in North Africa. All these advantages could have been nullified by a bolder naval strategy but the Germans adopted a half-hearted approach that combined the drawbacks of two inconsistent approaches.

Hitler attempted to persuade Franco to either invade Gibraltar himself or allow German troops to pass through Spain to capture the rock. Franco's reluctance to co-operate made it impossible for the German navy to operate effectively in the Mediterranean. Hitler should either have ignored Franco and launched an assault on Gibraltar or called the bluff of the Spanish dictator and compelled him to attack the rock. Either course of action would have led to catastrophic consequences for the British. Instead Hitler simply accepted Franco's refusal and the result was that the British gradually achieved naval superiority in the region.

Italian submarines were large and slow and performed poorly against British ships. Their deficiencies added to Hitler's problems in the Mediterranean theatre. The failure to capture Gibraltar made the operations of U-boats in the area exceptionally difficult. In spite of these handicaps a small number of German submarines succeeded in destroying or incapacitating the bulk of the Royal Navy in both the eastern and western Mediterranean and this success demonstrated clearly how a major campaign in the region might have compelled the British to abandon North Africa altogether.

Malta was particularly vulnerable to attack and Mussolini's first assault on the island was devastating. It was protected by some ancient biplanes and little naval support was available for its defence. In spite of this early success the Italians did not follow up their attack and the result was that the British managed to send more advanced aircraft to the island and also began transporting supplies to it through the merchant ship convoys.

The Italians returned to the attack after the island's defences had been strengthened and a ferocious bombing campaign by them and the Germans nearly brought Malta to its knees. The unaccountable failure to follow up the aerial bombardment with ground troops and a naval assault enabled the beleaguered island to survive as convoys succeeded in bringing fresh supplies in the teeth of brutal assaults by the Luftwaffe and U-boats. The failure to conquer Malta was almost as big a mistake as the abandonment of plans to seize Gibraltar. With Malta in Axis hands the supply lines for the Italian and German troops in North Africa would have been reduced drastically and the British troops stationed there would have been unable to continue fighting. The Suez Canal would have been in Axis hands and the road to Asia would have lain open to German attack. Control of the Mediterranean would have enabled the Germans to concentrate on the destruction of shipping in the Atlantic and it is difficult to see how Britain could have survived in those circumstances.

This situation of needlessly using U-boats over too wide an area became more pronounced following the German invasion of the Soviet

Union. Raeder insisted that it was essential for them to secure the port of Murmansk but Hitler overruled him. This turned out to be a costly mistake as the British were able to use the port as a base for delivering supplies to the Russians.

Even without the possession of Murmansk German naval operations in the Arctic faced severe difficulties. In addition to the extreme weather there were technical problems in terms of the operational capability of the navy in the area. U-boats were particularly hampered by these difficulties and for long periods were completely ineffective against the Russians and the British convoys supplying the Soviet Union. There was also a shortage of air cover which made them vulnerable to Allied attack. The result was variable success with two large convoys being almost annihilated but ultimately there were too few of them to make the "Battle of the Arctic" winnable by U-boat activity alone.

Further pressure was put on scarce German resources by Hitler's reckless declaration of war on the United States. This not only made the Battle of the Atlantic infinitely harder but also led to precious U-boats being diverted to the Pacific Ocean. Their effect in this theatre of war was negligible and represented a wasteful use of manpower and resources that would have been better deployed in the crucial Atlantic naval campaign. They enjoyed early success against the too complacent South Africans but before long the Allies were able to take sufficient countermeasures to make U-boat activity relatively ineffective. Even there the western coast of Africa was attacked more successfully than the eastern areas. The collapse of the Italians in Ethiopia and Somalia deprived the Germans of bases that were formerly open to their submarines for repairs and refuelling. U-boats had to travel thousands of miles, generally without air cover, under constant attack by the Royal Navy and RAF. The proportion of "kills" by German submarines was not justified by the expenditure of fuel, manpower and effort for extremely limited rewards. Once again a failure to adequately determine naval priorities led inexorably towards the ultimate defeat of German forces at sea.

Dönitz had always been clear-sighted about the only naval strategy offering a chance of success but Hitler and Raeder consistently overruled him. Not until 1943 – by which time the naval war had been irretrievably lost – was he able to take full charge of the war at sea and in spite of his efforts it was too late to alter the final outcome.

During the 1930s Dönitz had demanded not simply a large flotilla of U-boats but that the submarine programme should be given maximum priority. In particular he wanted technical developments to improve speed, range and time spent submerged but this required considerable investment. The combination of Hitler's lack of interest in the navy and Raeder's preference for surface ships meant that Germany entered the war with only a fraction of the U-boats that Dönitz deemed necessary. Many were antiquated and had technical difficulties in terms of misfiring torpedoes, speed and range.

The outbreak of war inevitably led to greater emphasis being given to the submarine fleet but it remained underfunded and under-resourced until 1943 when Dönitz was finally able to devote maximum energy to developing advanced U-boats. By then the tide had turned and though some highly sophisticated and potentially deadly improvements to the fleet were made they came too late to be effective.

One of the most important examples of this was the *Elektroboot* – submarine Type XXI and Type XXIII. The original idea for the Super U-boat was put forward in 1942 at a time when German submarines were creating havoc on the seas and coming desperately close to winning the Battle of the Atlantic.

In spite of the timing for the project it was not until 1944 that construction of the new U-boats began. By the time it began to be developed the Germans had already lost the Battle of the Atlantic. 1943 was the crucial year in which the balance of the war at sea finally tipped in favour of the Allies. However effective the type XXI might have been a year or two earlier it came too late to alter the result of the naval conflict.

The type XXI Submarine represented a real advance in submarine technology. They were the first designed to spend most of their time submerged rather than on the surface. This made them harder to detect and able to travel faster under water. Had they been available in 1941 or 1942 the course of the naval war might have been entirely different.

Designs for the first type were laid down in January 1943 – at a time when the Battle of the Atlantic still hung in the balance – but production was not commenced until 1944, by which time the naval war had been lost. The Type XXI could achieve a speed of 17 knots underwater. However, production difficulties meant that by 1945 only five of the smaller and shorter-range Type XXIII were in service and only one of the Type XXI. The XXI carried out a single patrol and failed to make contact with the enemy; the XXIII carried out nine patrols and sank five ships.

On the debit side they were unreliable mechanically and slower when on the surface. It was also discovered that the engines were underpowered which meant that it took longer for the submarines to recharge their batteries. The hydraulic system was vulnerable both to damage in combat and to corrosion. The vessel's snorkel was badly designed and difficult to use.

Although 118 of these U-boats were constructed only six were ready to be put into service by the end of the war. The speed and sophistication of these submarines could have made them a potent weapon if introduced earlier and on a large scale. As so often it was a case of too little, too late.[8]

By contrast the Project Ursel rocket U-boat represented a wasteful and unnecessary use of scarce resources and even had it been successfully developed would have been unable to affect the course of the war. Project Ursel was a concept for a rocket U-boat that began in 1942. The background to its development was the devastating bombing raids on Germany which led the Nazis to examine any possible means of retaliating. Rocketry was a field where German scientists led the world and the V-1 and V-2 were being developed with the intention of launching them against both civilian and military targets.

The Navy became interested in the idea of using submarines as launching platforms for rockets. The U-boat U-511 was chosen as the test vessel and fired a number of rockets underwater but without success.

It was originally intended to use the rocket U-boat against convoys but without any adequate guidance system that was abandoned. It was impossible for it to be used against moving targets like ships and could only be an effective weapon if used as a method of bombardment from shore.

Later it was revived in the form of a proposed attack on New York City using V-2 rockets. They would be towed by a U-boat to within range of the target before being launched from a gyro-stabilized platform.

The Allies were aware of the research and while they were nervous the British felt that in spite of the potential for the proposed weapons German resources were so thin that they were unlikely to develop the project successfully.

In May 1945 American newspapers reported an attempt to attack New York using what they described as "a jet-propelled or rocket-propelled weapon" launched from U-boats. The US Navy immediately denied that any such attack had taken place.

In spite of an open threat by Albert Speer to launch rockets against New York it was an empty boast. The technical problems of using submarines to launch missiles were too great and dramatically reduced the seaworthiness of U-boats. Two German spies were arrested in December 1944 and one claimed that U-boats were being fitted with V-weapons designed to attack New York but after close analysis it was discovered that the spy's claims were untrue. In spite of this assessment the US Navy decided to sink any German U-boats sailing towards the Eastern Seaboard as a precaution and five submarines were sunk as a result although none carried missiles.

The concept was never tested and remained in the development stage and by the end of the war none of these proposed weapons had been employed. The time, money, resources and effort spent on this quixotic project would have been more effectively employed on building faster and more powerful conventional submarines.

A daring but worthwhile project that failed to be realized was the Manta hydrofoil. Even prior to the war Hans von Schertel had been working on hydrofoil projects, He wanted to create a vessel that was so fast it would be almost impossible to destroy.

Schertel tested a prototype in 1941 that was capable of laying mines. A rival designer, Oscar Tietjens, developed the Tietjens VS-7 that was faster than Schertel's prototype but had problems with manoeuvrability, was difficult to handle and slow to pick up speed.

Later Schertel developed a superior concept, the Untersee-Gleitflächen- Schnellboot Manta (USG Manta) which was one of the most radical projects entertained by Nazi military planners. Its name means "underwater sliding express boat" and it was a cross between an aircraft, a ship and a submarine.

It was primarily designed to be used as an underwater weapon and attempted to overcome one of the principal disadvantages of submarines, the drag upon the vessels while beneath the surface as a result of the torpedoes they carried.

Unlike conventional U-boats it needed only two crew members to operate. It was a superior type of "midget submarine" and would have been far safer for the crews than the normal type of that craft.

The Manta was configured like a trimaran with three cylindrical hulls and tanks that captured the air flow beneath the main wing when the craft was on the surface. The hulls were linked by a main wing and two vertical keels. They could carry both torpedoes and rockets. The keels were even fitted with aviation wheels so that they could roll over the waves which dramatically reduced drag on the vessel. It could carry 8 torpedoes or 12 mines.

This radical project was approved by the Kleinst-U-Bootwaffe (Miniature Submarine Weapons Command) but was never put into development. All blueprints and other research on it were destroyed as the war came to an end and only a model of the craft survived. From it the Allies were able to reconstruct this revolutionary idea.

Post-war analysis of the project shows that it could have made a significant difference to the naval war. In particular had Mantas been available in numbers the D-Day landings – hazardous enough as they were – would have been more difficult to accomplish and would certainly have resulted in huge casualties. It would have been extremely hard to detect and destroy the craft and at the very least would have prolonged the war considerably. It is entirely possible that if the Manta had been given a sufficiently high priority it could have made a difference to the naval battle. Its speed was so great that it was virtually impossible even for aircraft to destroy it. Yet again the failure to analyse and determine appropriate priorities cost the Germans dearly in the naval war.

U-boats remained the most effective weapon at Hitler's disposal but as the war widened they became increasingly vulnerable. The Luftwaffe did not have the same range as the RAF and once America entered the war control of the skies over the Atlantic was entirely in the hands of the Allies. In addition neither Hitler nor Goering recognized the importance of air cover for submarine operations which reduced their effectiveness and made them less able to avoid attack.[9]

Failures of Procurement

The structure of procurement for the armed forces in the Third Reich was dysfunctional to an extreme degree. Even in peacetime unnecessary overlapping of competing authorities resulted in obstruction by one group of projects favoured by another. Once armed conflict began these attitudes caused immense damage to the war effort.

Fundamental problems were also caused by the poor quality of most Nazi leaders. Goering was obsessed with heavy bombers but periodically slowed their development in favour of the cheaper fighter aircraft. His own defects were accentuated by a string of incompetent deputies who had as little idea as him of the proper priorities in research, development and production of aircraft. Instead of being able to evaluate projects on the basis of merit, decisions were too often made on the basis of personal contacts or often wildly futuristic ideas that were totally impractical given the constraints of war.

The tendency of most Nazi leaders to favour size over speed and power over performance led to a number of "vanity" projects such as the "Sun Gun," the supertanks, the V3 heavy gun and other wastes of time and effort. Millions of marks (billions in today's money) were consumed in fruitless endeavours that never saw the light of day or were never deployed in action. These wasted projects diverted resources away from developments with more practical military applications. To an extent even the V1 and V2 could be seen as "vanity" projects since the amount of time, money, raw materials and resources necessary for their production could more profitably have been spent on pressing military requirements. The V1 and V2, however impressive, were luxuries in the context of the war.

Further problems were created by the necessity of conforming everything to Nazi ideology. In some respects this was beneficial particularly in terms of programmes of research and development into what would now be called "alternative energy." In other ways it severely hampered progress and led to the pursuit of many dead ends.

In spite of the much vaunted *Gleichschaltung* (co-ordination) and *Wehrwirtschaft* (war economy) there was nothing resembling the co-ordinated approach taken by the British and Americans. Ministers, industrialists, designers, scientists and engineers competed for funding and development rather than being managed in a systematic fashion. Even more disastrous was the fact that these groups and/or individuals tended to attach themselves to the "star" of a particular Minister. The result was that, for example, those who had the ear of Ley were unable to persuade Speer and those whom Goering favoured would fail to impress Himmler. Projects were often approved or rejected solely on the basis of the personal relationship between a Nazi leader and the appellant rather than on merit.

Nor was the German economy being put on a war footing until 1943. Until that point Hitler continued to place as much emphasis on supplying the "Home Front" as funding his military ventures.

Even the manufacturers charged with supplying the armed forces lacked a sense of priorities. Heinkel for example worked on a dozen different aircraft projects and ended up discarding nearly all of them. Instead of concentrating on a single design that might have been effective he preferred to tinker and experiment needlessly which severely hampered the war effort.

Heinkel was responsible for the disastrously misconceived He 177. It was huge and unwieldy and originally designed as a long-range heavy bomber. Then Heinkel was abruptly ordered to modify it and turn it into a dive bomber. This involved remodelling the engines and redesigning the body of the plane.

None of these modifications improved the performance of the aircraft and test flights resulted in it either breaking up or catching fire. A handful saw action at Stalingrad but all were destroyed. What had been planned as the principal bombing weapon for the Luftwaffe was an abject failure.[1]

Another catastrophic mistake was the Messerschmitt Me 210. It was intended to be a long-range fighter but was dogged by a series of accidents, crashes and deaths. In 1939 it was unveiled as the bright new hope of the Luftwaffe but almost immediately serious faults were detected in the design of the plane. The wing platform and fuselage were unsatisfactory and pilots found it difficult and dangerous to fly. In spite of that a thousand orders were placed for the plane which represented a huge waste of finance and production. Even in level flight it was prone to unforced oscillation and stability in turns was poor. It was prone to spin wildly and stall unexpectedly.

None of these obvious defects led to either Messerschmitt or the Luftwaffe drawing the obvious conclusions and scrapping the project. Instead it was delivered for service to front line units though at the end of April 1942 production was abruptly terminated. Construction was then transferred to Hungary and continued until 1944. 267 of the aircraft were built but it saw limited action, principally in Sardinia and Tunisia.

By 1944 it had proved so unsuccessful that it was finally withdrawn from service. The cost of this failed plane was the equivalent of 600 serviceable aircraft. Goering remarked scornfully that the Me 210 should be engraved on his tombstone.[2]

Another handicap was the frequent initiation of production and then its equally abrupt cancellation. In August 1939 Goering took the astonishing decision to reduce aircraft production and the development of new planes. Instead he ordered the main effort in these fields to be devoted to the He 177 and Me 210. Both of them were dead ends and expensive mistakes. The failure to develop a new generation of fighters and bombers cost Germany dearly and not until the last year of the war was a different approach adopted.

Things improved when Milch took control of aircraft procurement and production after the suicide of the incompetent Udet. He immediately sidelined Willi Messerschmitt and Heinkel who had been far too cavalier both with public money and in terms of waste of resources under Udet's lax stewardship. Milch immediately saw the flaws in the He 177 and his first reaction was to cancel the project altogether but so many corrupt payments had been made to Udet and others that this proved impossible. He did at least force Messerschmitt and Heinkel to concentrate purely on aircraft development rather than being involved in the procurement process. He compelled Junkers to follow his strict instructions while Udet had allowed the firm to tender for contracts and be paid in advance for work that was then not delivered. Now that Milch was firmly in charge he made sure that waste and duplication were avoided and he instituted effective control and supervision of the aircraft companies.

The obsession with bombers meant that fighter production received a low priority until late 1944 when Speer managed to reverse the trend. By then it was too late for even the famous Messerschmitt Me 262 to turn the tide.

The story of the Me 262 is another classic example of incompetence and failure to focus development on projects offering the best chance of success. There were a variety of reasons why this cutting edge jet fighter was not rushed into mass production. Characteristically most of the blame rests with Hitler and Goering but even the plane's designer was culpable.

Willi Messerschmitt had favoured the Me 209 and its abrupt cancellation in favour of the Me 262 infuriated him. He had been feuding with Milch since 1942 over aircraft priorities and lacked enthusiasm for the new project.

The planning for this fighter had begun before the war and in 1941 Speer witnessed it being tested and was impressed. Production began in spite of Messerschmitt's lack of interest and then in September 1943 Hitler gave orders to abandon its production. Three months later he changed his mind with equal rapidity and demanded immediate mass production of the aircraft.

Matters became worse when Messerschmitt made a throwaway remark to Hitler, suggesting that the Me 262 could perhaps be used as a heavy bomber. Hitler seized on the idea and at first was supported by Goering. Robust opposition from Milch, Speer and Luftwaffe generals eventually led Goering to change his mind but even he failed to persuade Hitler. Not until late 1944 did Hitler finally approve the aircraft for its proper use as a jet fighter. By the time it entered service – still in nothing like the necessary numbers – it was too late to affect the outcome of the war. If it had been rushed into mass production much earlier it might have dramatically altered the balance of the war in the air. Instead the Germans contested the great aerial battles of 1943 and 1944 with aircraft that were essentially at the same level of development as the ones they used in the Polish campaign of 1939.[3]

The situation in terms of naval procurement was even worse. Hitler and Goering at least took an interest in armoury, gunnery and aircraft though their intervention was often misguided and counterproductive. Until 1943 neither showed any interest in naval affairs beyond Hitler's characteristic admiration for large surface ships.

Perhaps as major a blunder as the Me 262 fiasco was the failure – in spite of increasingly desperate pleas by Dönitz – for truly advanced submarine development and construction. It is true that Germany led the world in that field but that reflected more on the failure of the Allies to devote sufficient attention to their research and development than it did on the quality of the U-boats.

In April 1940 Helmut Walter launched the Walter V-80. This represented a quantum leap in submarine development and design. It could achieve a maximum speed of 23 knots underwater and could spend the majority of its time submerged. By contrast the existing U-boats had a top speed of 9 knots even when surfaced and spent as little time as possible submerged because of the short life of the submarine battery.

Dönitz was enthusiastic about the project and urged the navy to mass produce the V-80 but Raeder and the *Kriegsmarine* in general demurred. Not only was Raeder still fixated on large surface ships but the navy preferred to persevere with the existing Type VII U-boats. These were the workhorses of the submarine flotilla throughout the war but became increasingly unable to fulfil their primary purpose.[4]

The greater speed alone of the V-80 should have automatically recommended it to the navy. Its ability to remain submerged for long periods rather than a maximum of an hour – and in general much less – would also have been a crucial advantage. Yet again a weapon that would have transformed the naval war and almost certainly handed victory to the Germans in the Battle of the Atlantic was not introduced. Instead Dönitz was forced to continue with his effective but increasingly outdated flotilla with the result that eventually sheer numbers made his task impossible.[5]

Missed opportunities, unnecessary modifications, inappropriate uses for available weapons and a generally chaotic approach to the organization of the procurement side of the war were all handicaps that might have been overcome if it was a case of individual failures and mistakes. Far harder to excuse are the extraordinary amounts of money and the futile waste of resources on vanity projects.

One of the most bizarre and impractical examples was the "Sun Gun," also referred to as a "supergun." The idea was first proposed as early as the 16th century by the Scottish mathematician John Napier who suggested using a large mirror to collect the rays of the sun and direct them to burn enemy ships. In the early 20th century a modified version of the scheme was put forward by the German scientist Herrmann Oberth. He proposed erecting a giant concave mirror to harvest the sun's rays and reflect them back upon the Earth.

This idea attracted the attention of the Nazis and at Hillersleben scientists attempted to create the weapon. The project was based on the notion of a space station orbiting above the Earth. Their research focused on a reflector constructed of sodium and three million marks were wasted on this pointless endeavour. After the war when the plans fell into Allied hands they were astonished at the scale of the project and how detailed the planning for it had been.[6]

Less obviously crazy but certainly a misplaced procurement priority was the development of the V-3 "super cannon." It was based on a French design from the First World War that fell into German hands following the fall of France. The German engineer August Cönders who discovered the plans had already designed the Röchling artillery shell. Cönders believed that the French blueprints could be the basis of a long-range gun.

He built a 20mm prototype and test fired it. The results were good and in early 1943 Speer was approached with a view to using it as a super cannon to bombard London from Calais. Speer was always the most rational and realistic of the Nazi leaders but perhaps by 1943 he had become increasingly desperate at the worsening military situation.

Following Speer's recommendation Hitler approved the project. Construction began near Magdeburg but problems were quickly detected. The gun often failed to fire and its muzzle velocity was slower than expected. In spite of these teething troubles Speer approved building the gun on the Baltic island of Wolin. Construction also began on the intended launch site in France in September 1943. By March 1944 the German army took over the project and six companies were commissioned to produce projectiles. Between May and June 1944 tests were carried out at Wolin but results were inconsistent. On 4 July the gun even burst during test firing.

The main site for its construction was at Mimoyecques near Calais. Railway lines were built to supply it and shafts to house the gun were excavated. The intention was to create a total of 50 V-3s in underground facilities dug out of the hill. An underground railway would serve the site.

Work on the V-3 continued but eventually the British became suspicious. They imagined it was a launch site for V-2 rockets and 19 Lancaster bombers from the "Dam Busters" squadron dropped Barnes Wallis' experimental Tallboy bomb. 35 tons of explosive landed on the underground complex and rendered it unusable.

Speer and Hitler refused to admit defeat and moved the supergun into Germany. It saw service in the "Battle of the Bulge" in December 1944 but was hardly a decisive weapon. Between then and February 1945 a total of 190 rounds were fired from the gun. Only 140 hit their target and only ten people were killed and fifteen injured as a result.

Even without the technical difficulties the gun lacked the range to hit its intended target of London. A further problem was the lack of explosive power in the shells. A more fundamental objection is that the project consumed money, materials and resources that would have been better employed in more realistic military projects delivering immediate results. As so often the mirage of size and power blinded Hitler to practical considerations.[7]

Hitler's obsession with tanks became a double-edged sword. While he rightly favoured their use as highly successful weapons of war he became increasingly obsessed with the chimera of "supertanks." He failed to remember that it was their mobility that made them such effective weapons during the Blitzkrieg and instead became focused on the idea of larger, heavier and more powerful tanks.

The idea of "supertanks" arose from a 1941 study of Russian tank designs by Krupp. Following the analysis one of the directors of the firm recommended building a thousand ton tank. When this suggestion was put to Hitler he immediately approved it. The result was the Panzer VIII *Maus* (Mouse.) This tank was 10.2m long, 3.71m wide, 3.58m high and weighed 188 tons. It was equipped with a 128mm gun.

The plan was to introduce it in 1943 but in May of that year Hitler suddenly demanded an increase in its armament and weight. Over a year passed before the modified supertank was constructed but it was immediately discovered that its excessive weight made it incapable of crossing bridges. An attempt was then made to use it as an amphibious vehicle to ford rivers or even submerge before reaching land.

Further tests followed to determine its suitability for the new role but eventually only two *Maus* tanks were built. Neither saw active service and one was destroyed by German troops as the Russians advanced. Soviet forces captured the other example and it is now housed at a museum in Moscow.[8]

Even more impractical than the *Maus* was the Landkreuzer P-1000 *Ratte* (Land Cruiser P-1000 Rat.) This was another bad idea by Krupp first proposed in 1942.

The *Ratte* was monstrously large and heavy. It was armed with a 280mm gun protected by 24.4cm of heavy steel. The total weight of the tank would have been over 1000 tons and the gun alone weighed in at 100 tons. Its size would have made it an obvious target and its weight and width made it almost impossible to operate. After a series of tests Speer decided to cancel both grandiose projects. Not even a prototype was ever built. In spite of that considerable time, money, resources and effort were wasted on these futile vanity projects.[9]

Less of an absurdity was the *Jägdtiger* (Hunting Tiger) project. This was a tank destroyer and represented a Tiger II tank modified by the addition of a box-like superstructure. The front of the vehicle was protected by almost ten inches of armour and it was armed with a 128mm Pak 44 L/55 gun. This possessed more power and greater range than any Allied tank.

In spite of its power the gun could barely turn and its position could only be altered by moving the entire tank. It was also necessary for the projectile and explosive charges to be loaded separately.

The sheer weight of the vehicle at 71 tonnes made it extremely slow moving. It frequently broke down while being moved and it was necessary to permanently lock the gun into position to achieve accuracy in firing.

From the front its armour was almost impenetrable but the sides of the vehicle were thinner and vulnerable. 88 *Jägdtigers* were produced between July 1944 and March 1945. In action they were slow and ponderous and prone to mechanical failure but as long as the crew was able to present the front of the vehicle to the enemy it was almost impossible to defend against.

The *Jägdtiger* remains the heaviest armoured vehicle ever constructed. One of their commanders believed that this powerful weapon never realized its potential and could have been extremely effective if there had been more time to train crews and the technical problems had been overcome.[10]

Hitler's interference even reduced the effectiveness of conventional tanks. The Tiger tank was specifically designed for the campaign against the Soviet Union and was designed to weigh 50 tons. Hitler insisted on increasing its weight to 75 tons. After protests concerning the reduced mobility of the revised model a new 30 ton Panther tank was designed. Again Hitler raised the tank's weight to 48 tons. He appeared to have lost sight both of the necessity for tanks to be mobile and of the difficulties in delivering spares thousands of miles and in a war zone.

Until 1942 Dornberger, von Braun and the other scientists at Peenemünde had been developing rockets without interference. The only Nazi leader who showed interest in their work was Speer who encouraged their researches and left them alone. Then in 1942 Hitler heard about a successful rocket launch and immediately directed Himmler to take charge. Himmler visited the site and began stressing the need for their work to "conform" to Nazi ideology. The staff were then questioned on their political loyalties. His final acts were to inform the staff that they would be "assisted" by large numbers of slave labourers and to place SS General Kammler in charge of the project.

Even by Nazi standards Kammler was a brutal thug and had no scientific background. The result of his overseership was to create an atmosphere of permanent fear. The use of slave labour rather than the previous skilled workers reduced the quality of both research and production. Hitler approved of Himmler's actions and thereby directly hindered the formerly smooth development at the Peenemünde site.[11]

Procurement for the army was the responsibility of the HWA (Heereswaffenamt – Army Weapons Agency.) Until 1942 the process was dominated by army bureaucrats and businessmen. The result was delays, corruption, and overproduction and often misguided priorities.

The Luftwaffe was impeded in its procurement by the incompetence of Goering and Udet. Yet again this led to misconceived projects, waste and duplication.

1942 saw a radical improvement in procurement. Hitler placed Speer in overall charge of that side of military affairs. The results were immediate as Speer streamlined the procurement process, put scientists and engineers in charge and avoided duplication. He encouraged and directed funds towards rocket development and the German nuclear programme.

The same year saw Luftwaffe procurement pass out of the incompetent hands of Udet into Milch's control. Udet was responsible for the He 177 and Me 210 fiascos and his replacement by Milch was long overdue. Even Goering eventually recognized how incapable Udet had proved at managing procurement for the Luftwaffe.

Speer established a Central Planning Committee which he and Milch dominated. For the first time military procurement came under a centralized single authority and efficiency improved dramatically.[12]

No amount of greater efficiency could overcome the shortages of raw materials or over-extended supply lines but without the efforts of Speer and Milch Germany might have lost the war much earlier. By contrast if Speer and Milch had controlled procurement from 1939 onwards the situation might have been very different and led to a German victory. Yet again Hitler's failure to grasp the importance of procurement contributed to the ultimate defeat of his nation.

Unintelligent Intelligence

There were two fundamental reasons why German intelligence was inferior to its British counterparts. One was the pervasive fear generated by the Nazis which created a climate in which unfavourable news was too often ignored or dismissed. The second was the failure to co-ordinate intelligence activity.

British intelligence was far from perfect but overall was the most effective of all the combatants' agencies. MI5, MI6 and SOE did not always work together well but the central co-ordination meant that information was shared between them and resulted in a considerably more effective grasp of events.

In contrast Nazi Germany had a number of competing intelligence agencies who jealously guarded their empire. The navy had the B-Dienst (*Beobachtungsdienst* - observation service) which was effective and reasonably successful in its activity.[1]

The B-Dienst began life as the German Radio Monitoring Service during the First World War and came under the control of the navy. Before the war it was understaffed and lacked the resources to deal with the whole area of cryptography so instead laid its focus on the Royal Navy Administrative Code. By October 1939 there were 40 staff working on cracking the naval cipher and by the end of 1940 this number had risen to 150. Staff with foreign language skills and particularly English language ones were recruited and given a short training course.

By 1942 the "English desk" employed 275 staff. In that year as the war demanded ever more men to be called into the armed services B-Dienst was forced to begin recruiting women to aid in the process of decryption. By the time the war ended men and women worked in it in equal numbers.[2]

The Abwehr was the military intelligence service of the German High Command. It too enjoyed considerable success in gathering information. On the other hand they were less adept than B-Dienst in distinguishing fact from fiction and the paucity of spies available to them in Britain, America and Russia meant that they had to take the information they were given by their agents more or less on trust. The result of this was not simply that the British used these spies as channels of disinformation but that the agents themselves often made up stories simply to appear to be doing something or to please the Germans.[3]

In addition to these problems to which all intelligence agencies are prone the Abwehr leader until 1944 was Admiral Canaris. He was a complex character combining right-wing views and a fierce nationalism with contempt for Hitler and hatred of the Nazis. He was particularly repelled by the regime's anti-Semitism and often employed Jews as Abwehr agents abroad. From 1938 onwards he discussed with a small group of people the idea of assassinating Hitler. His deputy Hans Oster was heavily involved in the 1944 bomb plot and Canaris consistently refused to allow Nazis to join his team.[4]

Canaris played an enigmatic role from 1939 to his eventual arrest in 1944 and execution in 1945. When Hitler was considering the Gibraltar option he travelled to Spain and met with Franco. Canaris spoke fluent Spanish and urged him to resist Hitler.

His deputy Oster was not only heavily involved in the conservative German Resistance but was also a leading player in the "Lucy" spy ring. This routinely leaked sensitive military data including battle positions, battle strengths, dates and times. The principal beneficiaries of this flow of information were the Russians.

Initially the Soviets believed it to be disinformation but abruptly changed their minds. The material passed to the Allies by Lucy was of inestimable assistance in defeating the Germans.

The man behind the Lucy spy ring was a German émigré living in Switzerland. His name was Rudolf Rössler and he had published anti-Nazi literature for years. In 1939 the head of Swiss military intelligence approached him and asked him to work for them as a data analyst.

Rössler worked with a variety of intelligence networks including MI6, the GRU (Soviet military intelligence) and, crucially, anti-Nazi German officers. It was Rössler's GRU contact who gave the spy ring the code name "Lucy" because it was based in Lucerne. There were ten German members of Lucy with Oster being the most senior. They provided Rössler with a radio and an Enigma machine and asked him to pass on information to the Allies.

The information they provided was dynamite. Rössler approached his GRU contact and warned the Soviets of the imminent German invasion. He gave details of German code names, the order of battle, troop movements, equipment and even the time and direction of individual assaults. This information was passed on to Russia but dismissed. Only when the accuracy of Lucy had been demonstrated during Operation Barbarossa did they take it seriously. From then on any information coming from that source was given the highest priority by the Soviets.

Over the next two years Rössler forwarded classified military data that was hugely important to the war effort. In 1942 he gave precise details of the attack on Stalingrad and next year gave the Russians the detailed plans for the German assault on Kursk.

October 1943 saw his network shut down by the Swiss under pressure from Germany. In May 1944 Rössler was arrested on charges of espionage and spent a few months in prison. The failed July bomb plot led to the arrest of Oster and others and the Lucy spy ring fell silent at last. The espionage historian Ronald Seth declared that "Rössler must be ranked among the greatest spies of all time."[5]

Since Oster was Canaris' deputy and both were anti-Nazis who had discussed assassinating Hitler over some years it is possible that Canaris himself might have been responsible for channelling the Lucy material to the Allies. Certainly his consistent refusal to employ Nazis in the Abwehr and his use of Jews as agents abroad is at least curious. Himmler always distrusted Canaris and after his fall quickly absorbed the Abwehr into his own empire.[6]

Also effective was the *Forschungsamt* (Research Bureau) whose role was tapping telegrams and decoding radio and telephone conversations. This system came under Goering's control though characteristically Ribbentrop immediately established a rival decoding platform at the Foreign Ministry. Yet again unnecessary duplication, petty jealousy and a refusal to share information hampered Nazi intelligence.[7]

A further effective intelligence network was the Post Office whose staff unscrambled transatlantic telephone calls. As a result numerous phone conversations between Churchill and Roosevelt were reported back to Hitler.[8]

In addition to these agencies the SS employed its own intelligence network known as the *Reichssicherheitshauptamt* (Reich Security Head Office.) This was under the control of Schellenberg who reported directly to Himmler.[9]

To a lesser extent the Gestapo attempted to discover any possible internal threats to the regime. The quality of their personnel was poor and their methods anything but sophisticated. Compared with its British counterpart, Special Branch, it was completely ineffectual in a counter-intelligence role.

There were successes for German intelligence in spite of these problems. In 1939 before the outbreak of war a U-boat captain surveyed the defences at Scapa Flow. He passed on his information to B-Dienst and Dönitz used it to direct a U-boat to penetrate the base. A single U-boat entered Scapa Flow and sank the battleship *Royal Oak*. This sent shock waves throughout the British government who searched frantically for a non-existent German spy and dismissed the head of MI5 for failing to find him.

This success owed as much to British complacency and the skill of the U-boat captain as it did to any superiority of German intelligence. In some respects it gave the Germans a false sense that their intelligence service was more effective than it really was.[10]

Another success for the B-Dienst occurred when their cryptographers succeeded in breaking the British naval code. This provided huge assistance to U-boats which were able to track convoys with precision and take evasive action when air cover was available or merchant ships were too powerfully protected to be attacked with impunity.[11]

The Germans were severely handicapped by the arrest of every agent in Britain on the outbreak of war. Some were executed as spies but others became double agents. Incredibly their reports back to the Abwehr were never questioned and as a result the British were able to make extensive use of them to provide disinformation which on several crucial occasions wrongfooted the Germans completely.[12]

The unwillingness – even the inability – of the various intelligence agencies in Germany to co-operate not only meant that valuable information was often missed but that it was impossible to cross check or evaluate properly. Rather than a co-ordinated network operating towards a common goal German intelligence agencies became groups competing for the favour of Goering, Himmler, Canaris, Ribbentrop and other leaders. The lack of knowledge by one agency of information held by another but concealed from it was senseless and gravely handicapped the services involved. Even without the other factors predisposing intelligence chiefs to refrain from presenting Hitler with unpleasant realities the disorganized methods employed by them would have made it difficult for him to arrive at a proper evaluation even without this concealment.

Of course by the nature of their work every intelligence agency has to keep secrets. In Britain a handful of people possessed or had access to top secret information. Only six members of Churchill's Cabinet were regularly advised on sensitive matters. The British government was even more reticent with the people and kept the news of the V-2 rockets from them for some time. Instead they initially blamed the death and destruction they caused on gas explosions. In spite of this culture of secrecy Bletchley Park, MI5, MI6, SOE and other agencies shared information and collaborated.

If such a level of organization and co-operation could be achieved in a democracy while retaining secrecy it *ought* to have been even easier in a dictatorship. Once more the chaotic administrative structure of Nazi Germany and Hitler's preference for divide and rule over centralized organization cost his country dearly.

The Germans set great store by their Enigma code which they considered unbreakable. Even B-Dienst shared that mistaken view. A combination of good fortune with skill and persistence eventually led to Bletchley Park breaking the code.

The first fortuitous circumstance was the capture of Enigma rotors when a U-boat was sunk. The second was the capture of another submarine containing the boat's codes and ciphers. A third U-boat foundered near Egypt and again crucial information was retrieved. The skill of the Bletchley Park cryptographers enabled them to use these as keys to decipher German transmissions which drastically reduced the effectiveness of U-boats.

Only Dönitz queried whether the code might have been cracked. No one else entertained the idea and German arrogance and complacency meant that the British were fully aware of their plans.

Technically Bletchley Park's operations came under the control of MI6 but in practice it was afforded considerable freedom. Its staff worked together as a team and neither concealed nor distorted the information they received. Hitler could have achieved the same degree of co-ordination of his intelligence networks. Instead he allowed them to compete against each other in the mistaken belief that such an approach strengthened him against possible rivals. Churchill and Roosevelt both had authoritarian tendencies but were always receptive to dissenting voices and never shirked unpleasant facts. This attitude enabled their spies, cryptographers and other intelligence staff to act effectively without fear or favour.

The desperate shortage for Germany of hard information in the Allied countries allowed the British in particular to mislead and misinform them. Not only did the double agents play their part to perfection but networks of entirely fictitious spies were – so the pretence ran – "recruited" by those people. As the British took good care to include confirmable facts along with the fiction the Germans swallowed the bait.

One of the most famous examples of British deception was "The Man Who Never Was." His true identity is still disputed but the probability is that he was a Welsh tramp. Whoever he was his corpse was used to devastating effect.

The man's dead body was carefully prepared. He was fitted with a uniform and given a few classified items including a fake letter to Mountbatten. His corpse was then delivered to the coast of Spain and allowed to wash up on the shore.

The Spanish authorities allowed the Abwehr to examine the body and its "documents." They included a humorous reference to a proposed invasion of Sardinia by Allied forces. The Germans swallowed the idea and moved troops and planes to the island.

The real target was of course Sicily and Churchill was convinced that the Germans could hardly mistake the intentions of the Anglo-American forces. It was not entirely down to "Operation Mincemeat" as the planting of the dead body was code named. Additional disinformation was spread suggesting an imminent attack upon Greece. Hitler's paranoia about the Balkans led him to believe that so German forces were diverted to that region as well as Sardinia. The deception was completely successful and as a result the invasion of Sicily went more smoothly than might have been the case. Yet again the ineptitude of the Nazi intelligence network led to disaster.[13]

By contrast a rare German success in terms of disinformation occurred in 1940. Just as the British were assisted by some good luck in decoding Enigma so too the German success arose as the result of an accident.

What became known as the "Mechelen affair" took place on 10 January1940. It represented a rare example of successful disinformation by the Germans. The incident itself came about by chance when a German plane crashed in Belgium. The pilot was not significant but his passenger Helmut Reinberger was carrying military documents of the highest importance. He carried with him the German plans for the invasion of Holland and Belgium. At the time of the crash the invasion was scheduled for 17 January.

The passenger became agitated and started to burn the papers. This attracted the attention of Belgian border guards and both men were quickly arrested. They were interrogated by an officer from Belgian military intelligence and Reinberger again tried to destroy the documents. He failed to burn them completely and enough remained for the authorities to be able to grasp the gist of them. The two men were then taken away for further questioning.

The news reached Berlin later that evening and produced panic in the German High Command. Hitler was furious and dismissed two army officers immediately. Two days later Jodl told Hitler that if the plans had been discovered the military position was "catastrophic."

A game of bluff and double bluff ensued with the Belgians pretending that Reinberger had succeeded in destroying the documents. Reinberger then told the German military attaché that he had been able to burn the plans. The French and Belgians considered the documents genuine though the Dutch were sceptical.

Jodl advised Hitler to postpone the invasion and reluctantly he agreed. Hitler had always been doubtful about the original strategy which was essentially a rerun of the Schlieffen Plan that had failed in World War One. He considered it too predictable and lacking in dynamism.

Manstein had always been sceptical about the plans for the invasion and proposed a new strategy involving attack further to the south in the region of Sedan. Hitler preferred his ideas and gave his approval.

At this point a policy of disinformation was adopted and the Germans encouraged the Allies to believe that an assault through Holland and Belgium remained their strategy. This smokescreen continued even when the German invasion occurred with German troops luring the French and British forces into a trap while directing their main military thrust towards Sedan. It was an espionage triumph for Germany and one of their few throughout the war.

Even during the invasion the Germans used deception successfully. A sergeant who spoke French broadcast messages over the radio for French troops to withdraw from the field. They obeyed and of course the Germans advanced without opposition.

Bottom of Form

Other successes were in communications where they established listening posts in Spain and were able to share information about ciphers with the Italians, Japanese, Hungarians and Finns. Their cryptographic team was also an effective weapon and the only nation whose codes they never managed to break was the Soviet Union. During the North Africa campaign Rommel was able to read the encrypted reports of the American military attaché about British forces and positions. Another key weapon for Rommel was the 621st radio interception company. They were able to predict when the British would attack and gave him important information on their order of battle. Eventually it was such an effective tool that Australian tanks and infantry destroyed it.

Traffic analysis was another area where German intelligence worked well. They engaged in detailed analysis of intercepted messages and also liaised with other intelligence agencies (though regrettably from a German point of view that was truer of their allies than it was of their domestic agencies.) The results of their traffic analysis yielded a success rate of 90%.

Aerial reconnaissance was another area where the Germans achieved success. They flew regularly over targets and this provided them with valuable information until the Allies achieved aerial supremacy and the reconnaissance flights had to be abandoned.

In 1942 a Ju-88 flew right over Alexandria at a height that was beyond the reach of the British fighters in Egypt. It photographed British merchant ships that were attempting to resupply Malta. Armed with their aerial photographs the Germans were able to attack the ships and 90% of them were destroyed. Aerial reconnaissance enabled them to detect Soviet attempts to build a dam across the Sea of Azov and German bombers destroyed the dam. This delayed the planned Russian offensive by several months.

In the field Manstein and Rommel were the outstanding examples of generals using intelligence productively. They were both able to take advantage of the information they had gathered to launch successful attacks or guard against forthcoming assaults.

In spite of their ability to use intelligence Manstein and Rommel were the exceptions among army officers. Too often commanders simply discounted news they disliked or preferred to listen to sources confirming what they wished to hear.[14]

After the intelligence fiasco of Operation Mincemeat and the Germans being caught off balance when the Allies invaded Sicily it might have been imagined they would be more cautious about the information they received. Instead they continued to fall for misleading British ploys designed to put them off the track.

Throughout the war Britain operated one of the most successful "dirty tricks" campaigns ever mounted. Perhaps the most important area of this work was "strategic deception." Operation Mincemeat is one of the most famous examples but there were many others. Often they acted in response to information received about the enemy. For instance soon after the discovery of the V-2 rocket programme the British heard that Goering was concerned about a runway extension at an RAF base. Immediately the strategic deception team contacted one of their double agents and through him created an entirely fictitious RAF project. To add credibility to the story a dummy control tower was erected on the airfield. The agent claimed that it was either a long-range rocket or a pilotless plane. His message was believed and Goering ordered the Luftwaffe to prepare for possible attacks by British pilotless planes.

Strategic deception was key to the success of the D-Day landings. They came close to disaster as it was but without the deliberate misleading of the Germans into imagining that the invasion of France would occur via Calais rather than Normandy it would have been even harder for it to succeed.

It is remarkable that the Germans did not learn from the successful deception over the Allied invasion of Sicily. Operation Overlord – the plans for the D-Day landings – took a year to prepare and during that time a disinformation campaign code named Operation Fortitude was launched to mislead them about the plans and the objective. Hitler realized that the Allies would attempt to invade France sooner or later but was confident that his "Atlantic Wall" was impregnable.

On the British side plans were considered for a number of invasion points between Cherbourg and Dunkirk. The obvious place to strike was Calais which was the shortest route for an invading force to use to cross the English Channel. It also possessed two large deep-water ports and its capture would leave the road to Paris open. On the other hand the port was heavily defended and the Allies decided that a more promising line of assault would be to land troops in Normandy.

It was considered essential to deceive the Germans about the intended target and as a result an extensive campaign of disinformation was launched. There were five double agents working for MI6 and all of them, amazingly, were completely trusted by German intelligence. Through these agents the Germans were provided with a plethora of false information. One of them sent a number of fictitious messages to Germany via radio. These "messages" were read by them and believed and consequently mistaken decisions were taken on the basis of this false information.

The star performer among the British spies was Dushan Popov. In 1944 he provided the Germans with an astonishingly detailed but of course utterly fictitious account of the Allied plans for invasion. On the basis of his "reports" his Abwehr controller told Berlin "the landing in Western Europe will not take place until next Spring."

Further diversionary tactics were employed by instructing these double agents to feed German intelligence with the idea that an attack on Norway and Denmark by British forces was imminent. That persuaded the Germans to tie down forces in those areas that would otherwise have been available for the defence of France. The agents also stressed that Calais was definitely the invasion point for any attack on the French coast.

In addition to these deceptions by British spies an entirely fictitious American army group led by Patton was set up and carried out phantom manoeuvres. An equally imaginary British 4th Army unit was created and the spies let it be known that it was making preparations to invade Denmark and Norway. Dummy tanks and aircraft and similar non-existent military paraphernalia were put into place and German reconnaissance aircraft fooled into believing they were readying themselves for the forthcoming invasions of Denmark, Norway and possibly Calais.

In spite of the elaborate deceptions carried out by the Allies it is still surprising that the Germans learned nothing from the Operation Mincemeat fiasco. They were fooled completely about the true date and location of the D-Day landings. Calais was the obvious point of attack but the German failure to at least consider alternative landing sites is extraordinary. These intelligence failings were compounded by a German overestimation of the strength of the Atlantic Wall.

Even when the Allies landed in Normandy the Germans continued to regard it as a purely diversionary attack and still anticipated the major thrust to come via Calais. They were encouraged in this false belief by the British spies who continued to feed them false information. It was several weeks before the Germans finally recognized the truth and by then the Allies had overcome the initial difficulties and were established firmly in northern France and on the road to winning the war in that country.[15]

German intelligence achieved two final successes. The first followed the deposition of Mussolini. He was originally held prisoner on an island but was then moved to a mountain fortress. The Germans discovered his location and a team led by Otto Skorzeny were charged with his rescue.

In what was codenamed Operation Eich (Oak) Skorzeny led his team to the mountain and landed there on gliders. The guards were taken completely by surprise and Mussolini was rescued. He spent the remainder of the war as the puppet leader of the Republic of Salo in Northern Italy.[16]

The Ardennes offensive also caught the Allies off guard. It was not only a brilliant military plan that with greater resources might well have succeeded but represented the last successful example of German disinformation.

Allied complacency played a huge part in the failure of their intelligence agencies to focus on the coming attack. Captured German prisoners of war were heard mentioning a new offensive but this was put down to optimistic bluster or even disinformation. The Allies refused to believe that the Germans would commit so many troops to a Western attack rather than fight in a defensive campaign.

The Allies also believed that fuel and ammunition shortages made any substantial attack impossible. Even German troop movements were observed but as they quickly moved on the assumption was made that Bitburg was simply a transit point. Bad weather meant that few reconnaissance flights over the Ardennes were possible. The Germans deliberately moved troops around to mislead the Allies.

Total radio silence was observed by the Germans and Ultra was unable to detect or intercept any signals. Instead of regarding this as suspicious Allied command simply assumed that some minor engagement was being planned. When a US intelligence officer expressed his suspicions of an imminent German assault via the Ardennes his concerns were dismissed and he was sent on leave. Even information from Bletchley Park about Luftwaffe activity and news of "impending special operations" and "operations in the West" was not taken seriously by Allied commanders. Allied complacency played into German hands.

An additional advantage for the Germans was that their signals intelligence had a thorough knowledge of the US order of battle. As the head of MI6 commented "out of thirty-odd US divisions in the West, the Germans have constantly known the locations, and often the intentions, of all but two or three."[17]

Of course the German offensive failed but from an intelligence point of view it was a triumph. The Ardennes campaign represented the last success for Germany in this field.

That fact that the Germans enjoyed considerable if spasmodic success shows clearly that they had the potential to run an effective intelligence service. Of course they were fundamentally handicapped by their failure to place agents in the three countries that mattered – Britain, America and the Soviet Union. In spite of that they achieved some notable coups and if their agencies had been as organized and co-ordinated as the British or Russians the outcome of the "Secret War" might have been very different.

The War of the Boffins

Until the Nazis came to power in 1933 Germany was home to some of the finest scientific minds in the world. Then everything changed as science and technology had to "conform" to National Socialist "philosophy."

Most Nazi Party members were working class or lower middle class. They were largely ignorant of science and shared with the regime's leadership a distrust of intellectuals and scientists in general. Their attitude towards it was at best suspicious and at worst openly hostile.[1]

The scientific community at large simply wished to be left alone and allowed to continue its long tradition of research without interference. German scientists routinely corresponded and met with others from abroad. There was no culture of secrecy and on the whole the pursuit of research for its own sake unfettered by restrictions was the norm.

Many of the leading scientists were Jewish and on the accession of Hitler to power they were understandably concerned about their future under an openly anti-Semitic regime. It did not help that Rosenberg was the official ideologist for the Nazi Party and his knowledge and understanding of science was far less than he boastfully imagined.[2]

Hitler immediately began a programme of rearmament – with its inevitable accompaniment of secrecy – that alarmed many scientists. It was not only Jewish scientists who were concerned but all those scientists who valued the free critical intelligence and the freedom to pursue scientific research unhindered.

In 1934 Bernhard Rust was made Minister of Science, Education and Culture. Among his responsibilities were leading science along the guidelines laid down by Nazi ideology and directing scientists and engineers to direct most of their efforts towards military priorities.[3]

In spite of the heavy hand laid on both science and engineering there were numerous new inventions and discoveries. 1933 saw the invention of the first electron microscope, the first quartz clock and the development of diesel-electric transmission. In 1934 the industrial production of the artificial fibre Rein was commenced along with the first public broadcasts and the construction of a giant ship lift. The following year saw the introduction of sulfamide drugs into medical practice. In 1936 the nerve agent tabun was invented and Buna began producing synthetic rubber. That year saw the development of technological methods of purifying iron ore, manufacturing multi-layer chromogenic photography, early experiments with cinema featuring both sound and colour, a telecast carried out by telephone and, most significant of all, setting up the Peenemünde research and development centre for rocketry.

1937 saw the invention of the artificial fibre perlon, while 1938 saw a major scientific breakthrough when Otto Hahn discovered the decay of the nucleus of the atom. Later that year he also discovered the process of nuclear fission. His results were confirmed by the exiled Jewish scientist Lise Meitner who was a close personal friend of Hahn's and whose enforced exile was a huge loss to German science.[4]

1939 saw the invention of DDT, the beginning of manufacturing artificial fats, early research into radar, the first flights of jet aircraft and the invention of sarin.

The outbreak of war saw an acceleration of scientific and technical development though its purpose was now to aid the war effort. Any scientific work that did not produce an immediate result was sidelined and only areas that were of military importance were focused on.

In addition to his general contempt for science Hitler also demanded impossibly rapid results. This attitude made him incapable of long-term planning and resulted in projects being rushed. Naturally this meant that new weapons or other technological plans were often defective and as a result either had to be modified or abandoned altogether.

An additional problem was that Hitler blew hot and cold on individual projects. Periodically research and development were initiated and then abruptly cancelled or suspended. This impacted particularly strongly on the development of the atom bomb, rocketry and even aircraft.

Further unnecessary difficulties were created by Hitler's divide and rule approach. The result was fragmentation of resources and organization which hampered progress. Instead of the various institutes, companies, research facilities and similar bodies working together in a co-ordinated fashion with a common aim there was competition, duplication, waste and an unwillingness to share research or pool resources.

Even in basic areas such as tank production the unnecessary diversification of resources created problems. By 1942 there were seventeen different tank models all requiring different processes and modes of operation and all consuming vast quantities of steel and fuel. Rather than concentrating on two or three types of tank the constant attempt to devise more effective models was in itself counter-productive.

In spite of these handicaps and the pervasive terror of Himmler's expanding empire the success of German science and technology was extraordinary. Speer, Milch and to a lesser extent Dönitz were particularly adept at harnessing their potential in the service of the war effort.

One area where German technology was supreme was the development of the 8.8 cm Flak 18/36/37/41. Its muzzle velocity was 1000 m/s and it was so powerful that it compelled enemy aircraft to fly at extremely high altitude. It was also an effective anti-tank weapon.[5]

Throughout the war development on aircraft, tanks, artillery and other areas that benefited military operations proceeded rapidly. "Pure" science was effectively driven to the margins as everything was directed towards the goal of helping Germany win the war.

The exodus of Jewish scientists over the years 1933-1939 was a catastrophe for Germany. The quality of those lost to the nation is impossible to calculate but certainly represented a huge "brain drain." Einstein, Meitner and numerous other great names fled abroad and in most cases began working for the Allies. The effect of their loss was inestimable and perhaps most marked in the Nazi nuclear programme.[6] Contrary to popular belief German scientists were not far behind the Allies in the development of an atomic bomb and if they had been able to draw on the full panoply of talent available to them before 1933 there is no doubt they would have been the first to produce a successful nuclear weapon.

The sheer folly – leaving aside its utter immorality - of Hitler's anti-Semitism was demonstrated most clearly in terms of its baleful effect upon science. When Max Planck protested to Hitler about the dismissal of Jewish professors and the exiling of Jewish scientists and told him that it would have a disastrous effect on German science the response was incredible. "Very well, we shall have to do without science for a few years," Hitler remarked.[7] The idea that somehow he could "do without science" and at the same time fight an effective military campaign – let alone a world war – shows how little grip upon reality he had. As Speer remarked some years later Hitler seemed incapable of grasping new ideas or adapting his views to changed situations.[8] The First World War had shown in dramatic fashion the crucial role science and technology played in achieving victory in a conflict and Hitler's refusal to see that was one of his most fundamental errors.

In complete contrast to Hitler's attitude both Churchill and Roosevelt – in spite of their relative ignorance of science and their authoritarian tendencies – were always willing to listen to scientists and be guided by their advice even if it felt counter-intuitive to them. Hitler's combination of ignorance and dogmatism was a toxic combination that almost inevitably led to a failure to make the best use of the scientific resources available to him.

In one of the bitterest ironies of history the Jewish scientist Fritz Haber who had served his nation during the First World War and developed poison gas as a weapon was excluded from his scientific institute. He went into exile and died the following year. One of his lasting legacies was the invention of Zyklon B gas, the very method used by the Nazis to kill their victims in the gas chambers.[9]

The absence of Jewish scientists was a severe loss in itself but the sudden lack of free exchange of scientific information between German scientists and those abroad also handicapped them. Instead of corresponding with or meeting their fellow researchers and developing their work on the basis of the widest possible source material they were forced to work in isolation with little input from the world outside.

The obsession with making science "conform" to Nazi ideology was a further brake on progress. It led to a tolerance of very strange ideas most of which were dead ends but in spite of their frequently irrational basis managed to receive considerable government funding. On the part of some scientists it led to a rejection of the theory of relativity and quantum physics and the proposal of a new theoretical approach known as "Aryan physics."[10]

The leading exponents of Aryan physics were Phillip Lenard and Johannes Stark. Both men were serious scientists who had won Nobel Prizes. Unfortunately both were also anti-Semitic and as the Nazi Party began to grow in strength in the 1920s they became members. When Hitler became Chancellor in 1933 they hoped to be able to direct and dominate science in Germany but were unable to do so. They attached themselves to Rosenberg's wing of the Nazis and hoped that he would use his influence to put them in charge of German science.

Their failure to achieve their ambitions was not because of any views on science held by Hitler but more that he had no intention of allowing any other dictators in Germany – in the field of science or anywhere else. Their attacks on relativity and quantum physics were only partially successful. Both subjects continued to be taught in Nazi institutions but the names of any Jewish contributors to that field were excised and "Aryan" ones substituted.

When they attacked Heisenberg as a "white Jew" they stirred up a hornet's nest. Himmler and Heisenberg had attended school together and the result of their attacks was to isolate Stark and Lenard. Himmler took Heisenberg's side and told him that after the war he would make him the supremo of German science.[11]

The German Chemical Society (DChG) soon directed its main research efforts into military projects. They worked on ersatz products and polymers but their principal focus was researching and developing chemical weapons for use by the military. They not only researched tabun and sarin but invented a new poison gas known as soman. Their researches were published in the *Reich Berichte* (Reich Reports) which were secret journals on the military applications of chemistry. During the war its members went into the occupied countries and stole journals and scientific equipment. They even forced scientists to join them in their researches into military projects. Among their "researches" were the use of metal carbonyls to disable gas mask filters and a device to spray enemy combatants with poison gas. Although chemical warfare was not used during the conflict it was extensively researched and its use periodically considered.[12]

Members of the German Chemical Society were placed in an awkward position following Hitler's appointment as Chancellor. Four out of the six German Nobel Laureates in Chemistry were Jewish and both the President and Vice-President of the Society were Jewish. In spite of that the Society quickly adapted itself to the new situation. Even before the Nazis had introduced a raft of anti-Semitic laws it asked its most prominent Jewish members to resign. By 1935 it was asking all Jewish members to leave and by 1938 the Society had become completely "Aryanized."

Between 1933 and 1938 a staggering 25% of all chemists in academic institutes were dismissed. 90% of them were removed from their posts on purely racial grounds – being Jewish, having Jewish ancestry or being married to a Jew. The other 10% were dismissed for political reasons.[13]

In spite of this willingness to go along with Nazi policy and "Aryan ideals" the Society attempted to disguise this fact from the international community. They recognized not only that the policy itself would be unpopular but that it would affect both the standing and the finances of the Society. A historian of the period describes their attitude as being "to Aryanize in an opaque way to avoid showing it in public."[14]

A problem for the Society was that 40% of its members came from outside Germany and their membership fees and journal subscriptions were crucial sources of revenue. The regime wanted to present a picture of German scientific excellence and even the Nazis knew that the loss of international members from a leading scientific organization would represent a severe blow to the country's prestige.

Another historian of the period points out the silence – amounting to complicity – by German scientists concerning the purely racial dismissals of Jewish workers and researchers in the field. Only one German scientist refused to take up a position because the vacancy had occurred through removing a Jewish scientist from his post. Others eagerly grabbed the new opportunities, particularly young scientists who would otherwise have been compelled to wait years for career advancement.[15]

Chemistry was a crucial necessity but the Nazi attitudes hampered its effective development. The need for fuel and food led to a huge investment in efforts to create ersatz products and to find alternative methods of turning coal and other substances into petrol and oil. This process began as soon as Hitler became Chancellor and by 1937 attracted the attention of the world press.[16]

For all the effort put into these substitutes for fuel, food and clothing the results fell short of the demands of the nation even in peacetime. Once Germany was at war the need for these items to be produced on a massive scale became acute and it was impossible for production to keep up with demand.[17]

In spite of the difficulties Germany led the world in this field of research. Only the Soviet Union also made use of ersatz products on a large scale. Germany's lack of natural resources other than coal forced it to rely heavily on imports and the ersatz policy was an attempt to reduce this dependence – particularly given the shortage of foreign exchange or gold reserves. Even Hitler recognized this problem and from the moment he became Chancellor promoted a policy of driving towards self-sufficiency.

For some years the conversion of coal into oil was successful as was the use of wood as an alternative fuel rather than petrol. The process continued throughout the war but from 1941 onwards the demand for the substitute fuels or even coal in its natural state could no longer be provided from domestic resources.[18] Two methods of conversion were used – one known as the Bergius process which produced liquid hydrocarbons by hydrogenating bituminous coal at high temperature and high pressures and the Fischer-Tropsch process which converted a mixture of carbon monoxide and hydrogen into liquid hydrocarbon. These processes were able to convert 97% of the coal into fuel.[19]

I G Farben employed the Bergius process while the Fischer-Tropsch process was used by the Braunkohle Benzin AG (BRABAG) group of companies.[20] During the war both processes were used to extract oil from coal or water gas.

Allied bombing severely affected production and by 1944 the situation was so acute that construction of underground factories began. The work remained unfinished when the war ended.[21]

Greater foresight and less complacency about Allied air power ought to have led the Germans to begin constructing underground facilities in 1942 or 1943. These locations would have been harder to damage and production might have been maintained. Once more the failure of forward planning and the arrogant assumption that German air supremacy would continue indefinitely cost Hitler dearly.

A strike that year by Belgian miners – quickly followed by another in France – led to a dramatic fall in coal supplies. The Belgian strike began on 10 May 1941 and lasted until 18 May. It was led by the head of the Belgian Communists and the strikers demanded increased wages though political issues also played a part. The strike began at the Cockerill steel works in eastern Belgium. Quickly other workers came out in solidarity and before long 70,000 workers were on strike. The Belgian Resistance was completely supportive of the strikers and even conservative Belgians sympathized with them. The Germans had become desperate for coal to continue fuelling their military and were compelled to agree to raise the wages of the workers. They received an 8% increase in pay.[22]

After the strike was over the Germans arrested 400 workers and tried to root out dissident elements. The action was a triumph for the strikers and a severe defeat for the Nazis.

The success of the Belgian strikers led French miners to down tools on 27 May. Their strike lasted until 9 June and 17,000 miners came out to demand improvements in pay and better food. Women were particularly active in supporting the strike and formed picket lines to prevent tanks entering the mines. The women also encouraged the miners to continue their strike action. German troops began dispersing crowds by using live ammunition which of course inflamed the situation. Arrests were quickly made but this failed to halt the gathering momentum of the strike and troops were called in to try and intimidate the people.

When these measures failed German troops occupied the pits. Distribution of ration cards stopped abruptly and wages were no longer paid. The strikes continued in spite of these steps and hundreds more were arrested.270 miners were deported to Germany and others were shot. Eventually the miners called off the strike on 10 June having denied the Germans 500,000 tonnes of coal.

In spite of the brutality of the means used to bring the strike to an end it forced the Germans to make concessions to the miners. They were granted additional food and higher wages on 17 June. Both the French and Belgian strikes resulted in limited success for the strikers.[23]

In spite of these setbacks there was little alternative to continuing the development and processing of synthetic fuels and other ersatz substances. By 1936 the Buna Company was producing synthetic rubber on an industrial scale and continued its work throughout the war. In a sinister sideline to its activities it ran the Monowitz-Buna factory section at Auschwitz where the production of synthetic oil and rubber was carried out by slave labourers working under appalling conditions and where life expectancy was only a few months.[24]

The shortage of coal was one of the clearest demonstrations of the counter productiveness and futility of slave labour. Miners – except German nationals – received inadequate rations and worked under exceptionally poor conditions. Hitler suggested importing miners from the Ukraine and Poland. Pleiger, head of the German coal industry, told Hitler that the plan was probably impossible and that even if the men could be transferred to Germany there needed to be radical improvements in working conditions or their work would be inadequate.[25]

In spite of Pleiger's concerns and his protests being a rare example of someone daring to disagree with Hitler the policy of forced labour was imposed on the Ukrainians.[26]

It made little difference to the production difficulties and the desperate labour shortages compounded the situation. Fuel supplies became a major problem and the lack of adequate quantities of oil and petrol made it inevitable that the war effort would fail.[27]

No amount of ingenuity could overcome the difficulties created by the war. Over-extended lines meant that most German surface ships were compelled to remain in harbour as precious fuel was prioritized for the troops on the Russian front. The treatment of the occupied countries made the situation worse as they had been so ruthlessly stripped of food, natural resources and even manpower that it was impossible to use them to replace German shortages. Factories in many conquered nations were compelled to close as many of their workers had been deported to Germany to serve as forced labour.

By 1942 the situation was so serious that even rations were not being fully taken up because of decreasing purchasing power. Once again the inability of Germany to sustain a long war on multiple fronts was exposed. The country was only equipped to win short campaigns and the perpetual drain on dwindling resources made victory all but impossible.

Chemistry became completely subordinated to Nazi attitudes and policies in spite of rare cases of individual resistance by a handful of scientists. The same was true of biology where some of the darkest episodes in history were carried out by biologists in support of Nazi racism and genetic "philosophy." Their betrayal of scientific ethics was particularly extreme and resulted in death or permanent damage to millions of people.[28]

Biologists subscribed to Nazi views on eugenics and were actively involved in medical experiments, enforced sterilization and the euthanasia programme. They failed to protest about the dismissal of Jewish scientists or to refuse involvement in Nazi "racial hygiene" policies. Their complicity in genocide was the most active of any scientific community.

Der Biologe (The Biologist) was the journal of the German Biological Society. It was a platform for Nazi views and biologists were among the worst collaborators with the regime. 57% of biologists joined the Nazi Party which was a higher proportion than any other group of scientists. The Society advocated the doctrines of racial superiority and inferiority as well as a generally "Social Darwinist" philosophy. Its members had no compunction about the consequences of their attitudes and behaviour in spite of their attempts to pretend after the war that they were "non-political scientists" who were ignorant of the excesses committed by the regime. These claims are flatly contradicted by their public pronouncements and even more so by their actions in being actively involved in sterilization and medical experiments.[29]

Ernst Rüdin was the director of the Kaiser Wilhelm Institute for Psychiatry in Munich and he advised senior Nazis on "racial" and "hygiene" policies. Other guilty men included the two men heading the KWI for Anthropology in Berlin, Ernst Fischer and Otmar von Verschuer. All had regular contact with Nazi leaders and Rüdin and his fellow worker Fritz Lenz were members of a committee advising the government on population and racial policies.

Rüdin received direct funding from Hitler's office and his role was to provide a scientific basis for the German racial laws. He chaired a committee focusing on "racial hygiene and racial policies." It advocated the "scientific basis" on which criminals were castrated and "inferior women" sterilized. Rüdin even asked the Nazis to allow him to widen the range of his "criteria." This allowed sterilization not merely on genetic or medical grounds but on purely racial ones. It was Rüdin who persuaded the Nazis to sterilize 600 children born to black French soldiers and German women during the French occupation of the Rhineland in 1923 (known contemptuously as the "Rhineland bastards.")[30]

Von Verschuer was declared an "expert" by the Research Department on Jewish Questions of the Reich Institute for the History of the New Germany. Its role was to "research" what it called "world Jewry." He wrote to Fischer and declared that it was "important that our race policies, including the Jewish question, develop an objective scientific background that is broadly accepted".[31]

Huge sums of money were spent on this pseudo-scientific "research" to say nothing of the appalling sterilization and castration programmes. There was not the slightest scientific basis for the policies let alone any moral justification for them. A fraction of the millions of Marks spent on these projects could have been more profitably employed for beneficial purposes or even the more effective prosecution of the war.

The complicity of the medical profession in some of the worst aspects of the Nazi regime is well known. Twenty doctors were put on trial at Nuremberg for war crimes and though seven were acquitted the rest were found guilty. Some were executed while most received prison sentences.[32]

Compared with their colleagues in other disciplines the record of German physicists was comparatively good. Physicists did not exclude Jews from membership until 1938–1939 and even then only after sustained pressure by the Nazis. The German Physical Society also refused to join the Nazi umbrella association for scientists and engineers. This however owed as much to snobbery as moral considerations since scientists resented the fact that the majority of members of the NSBDT (National Socialist German Technical Association) were engineers.[33]

The role of science before the war was dubious at best with biologists promoting Nazi eugenics and racial policy, chemists working on poison gas, physicians engaged in sterilization and euthanasia. Physicists at the time were regarded as less crucial to the *Wehrwirtschaft* (war economy) and so received less funding but suffered less interference from the authorities.

The war accelerated the decline of science across the Reich as biologists and doctors carried out medical experiments, chemists worked on military projects with the use of slave labour and physicists concentrated on developing missiles and the atom bomb. Their complicity in Nazi crimes grew greater as the unfavourable course of the war led the regime to increase the genocide programme and use slave labour as the mainstay of the work force.

Technology was completely subordinated to the needs of the military from 1939 onwards and particularly from 1942. Engineers might have been expected to focus on the simple and practical rather than the complex and aesthetically appealing aspects of design and production but in reality the opposite was true.

As was often the case with the Nazis there were conflicting approaches and attitudes towards engineering and technology. Feder and his supporters urged a *völkisch* technocracy but that failed to find favour with the regime in the teeth of fierce opposition from industrialists and the military. Todt argued for the notion of man, machine and nature all working together in harmony and he was able on the whole to make his view prevail until his death. After his demise Speer ruthlessly dismissed both Todt's approach and Feder's and instead geared every aspect of technology and engineering to the war effort. Todt has often been described as the champion of "reactionary modernism" while Speer was a technocrat pure and simple. In the context of a world war it is easy to understand how his pragmatic view triumphed over those of his rivals.[34]

By December 1941 General Georg Thomas was so furious at the over-elaboration of engineers that he wrote a blistering memorandum on the subject which Hitler also signed. He demanded "simplification and increase in performance of our arms production." Thomas added: "the usefulness and ability to be produced easily and the savings of materials is to be given priority over aesthetics and other exaggerated demands that are not necessary for the use of war and that are irresponsible."[35]

The German obsession with detail and aesthetics meant that it took three times longer to produce a machine gun for the *Wehrmacht* than the equivalent British weapon. In the same way Messerschmitt, Heinkel and Junkers were commencing new projects rather than concentrating on mass production of existing fighters and bombers.[36]

As was generally the case under the Nazis the army suffered less than the other services. On the whole the civilian providers of equipment for the *Wehrmacht* were able to produce good models though again until the change of direction in 1942 often wastefully.

The car industry was quickly commandeered to produce military vehicles. As early as 1938 Colonel Adolf von Schell was appointed to develop a plan to restrict the proliferating types of motor vehicle. This project became known as the Schell Plan and was formally introduced in January 1940. Only four basic types of lorries were allowed to be produced – those of 1.5 tons, 3 tons, 4.5 tons and 6.5 tons. Manufacturers were only allowed to produce two types at most. The 114 types of lorries were reduced to 19 and the 52 models of passenger cars were reduced to 30. That was the plan but characteristically it was not consistently followed particularly in the occupied countries.[37]

Armoured vehicles were particularly needed during the war and the Gaggenau plant run by Daimler-Benz became the main production hub for them. The Mercedes-Benz Types L1500, L1500A and L1550S were 4x4 vehicles built for the German army. Their principal use was for transporting troops. The Type L3000 A and S were three-ton supply trucks. Heavier Mercedes trucks were also built but Allied bombing and Speer's rationalization of the production process forced most of the heavy trucks out of operation by 1943.

On the outset of the war the Wehrmacht commandeered Mercedes buses and used them as troop transporters. All privately owned cars with engines over 1000cc were expropriated by the government. The majority of Mercedes cabriolets were turned into staff cars for officers or Nazi Party members.[38]

When the war expanded to include Russia and America it made success immeasurably harder. The already stretched resources were now spread so thinly that they were inevitably less effective.

In spite of these problems which in most cases were avoidable Hitler continually failed to appreciate the crucial importance of science and technology. Throughout his life he had nothing but contempt for scientists and any other group or individual that he considered an "intellectual." He used them purely because even he realized that military success increasingly depended on scientific and technical progress. The technocrats raised no objections to being used for his nefarious purposes.

As David Irving wrote, "the greatest hindrance to the pace of German research was the attitudes of the government to science."[39]

Yet again Hitler's failure as a leader to grasp the importance of science and technology and understand the need to prioritize research and development in the simplest, most rapid and effective manner was a fundamental flaw that contributed enormously to ultimate defeat.

Perhaps the most obvious area of this is the German atomic programme. As early as 1940 Hitler's attention had been drawn to its potential for military victory but characteristically he dismissed it out of hand. He did not understand the science behind it and he was surrounded by people who referred to it as "Jewish physics." Above all his obsession with immediate results rather than forward planning meant that he took no interest in the project until the latter stages of the war.

By contrast Speer was keenly interested and liaised with the atomic scientists throughout the war. Unfortunately for them as the war lurched towards ultimate defeat Hitler finally became interested in the project with predictably negative consequences.

There are many misconceptions and myths surrounding the Nazi nuclear programme. At the beginning of the twentieth century they were at the forefront of atomic research. Many of the leading scientists in the field were Jewish and consequently became excluded from the scientific community once Hitler came to power. Their previous research remained available to "Aryan" nuclear scientists and the émigrés also wrote scientific papers in exile. These were immediately used by German scientists to further their research projects.

In April 1939 a group of nuclear physicists founded the Uranium Club. It met to discuss developing nuclear weapons for military purposes. Two of its founding members approached the authorities and received guarded approval for the idea.

Work swiftly began at the Georg-August University in Stuttgart but the outbreak of war halted its progress. With characteristic lack of foresight or priorities many of the scientists were called up for military service.

In spite of this setback others joined the project including the leading physicist Heisenberg. He rapidly became the dominant force in the Uranium Club and was the prime mover in its research.[40]

The *Wehrmacht* swiftly laid down guidelines for the project. They demanded research focused on development of a nuclear reactor, production of uranium and heavy water and on the separation of isotopes. Seventy scientists worked in these areas and research was progressing well. Short-term considerations then intervened and the status (and funding) of the project was downgraded. The fact that it could not be developed soon enough to be used in the near future made the *Wehrmacht* lose interest. Many of the scientists were transferred to other military projects. Even more disastrous for progress in the field was the decentralization of its control and its division between nine institutions all working on separate aspects of nuclear physics.[41]

Surprisingly Speer's involvement in June 1942 also hampered the project as he directed the scientist to work on nuclear physics as an alternative energy source rather than a weapon of war.[42] This sudden change in approach also delayed unnecessarily the early development of an atomic bomb.

How crucial these delays in the process were is shown by the fact that in 1942 the Germans were *ahead* of the Allies in terms of developing a viable nuclear bomb. In April 1942 Heisenberg and Döpel achieved a significant increase in neutrons during their attempts to create nuclear fission. The Americans only accomplished that feat in July of that year and in war an advantage of months can be decisive.

1943 saw two major setbacks for the nuclear programme. One was the destruction by Norwegian saboteurs of the heavy water facility in Norway.[43] The second was a chemical explosion that destroyed Döpel's nuclear reactor.[44]

It has been assumed too readily that these two events marked the effective end of the Nazi nuclear programme. Evidence from both German and Allied sources shows that work on the project continued in spite of these handicaps.

No attempt was made to construct another reactor of the type used by Döpel and the Americans. Instead cold nuclear reactors were used by German scientists. One employed dry ice to cool the reactor and the result was the production of large numbers of isotopes. Another member of the Uranium Club used methane for the same purpose and with the same results. Both types of reactor were cheaper than the conventional type and equally effective.[45]

Further support for the idea of a Nazi atom bomb comes both from eyewitness testimony and the evidence of radiation. In October 1944 a German pilot was flying over Lübeck when he observed "a cloud shaped like a mushroom." His report was later submitted to American intelligence which concluded that it was "highly probable" that the Germans had successfully tested a nuclear bomb.[46]

An Italian correspondent also observed a nuclear test on the island of Rügen and reported the results to Mussolini. Most striking of all these claims for Nazi tests of nuclear weapons are those made for the town of Ohrdruf in Thuringia. It is claimed that on 4 and 12 March 1945 two nuclear devices were detonated and killed over 700 prisoners in the Oranienburg concentration camp. German and Soviet witnesses testify to the explosions and details were forwarded to Russia of the "new secret weapon." Examination of the site at Ohrdruf shows clear evidence of a large explosion and the area also possesses the highest level of background radiation in Germany.[47]

Successful testing of a nuclear bomb is highly probable but the Germans faced he problem of "delivery." The V-2 rockets were capable of carrying the necessary payload but restricted in range. Some German aircraft possessed the necessary range to fly to the United States but could not support the weight of the bomb.

These twin problems were never successfully overcome but it is possible that they might have been if the war had continued even a few months longer. There is strong evidence that German scientists were working on a "fizzle" bomb – a semi-fission atomic device.

The advantage of a fizzle bomb is that it creates an atomic explosion but requires a much smaller mass. Surviving blueprints of German nuclear research demonstrate clearly that Heisenberg and his team were working on a fizzle bomb rather than the larger fission bomb. This would not only have created the destruction caused by an ordinary bombing raid but also disperse radioactivity over a large area.

Further evidence of this work comes from a German physicist given to British intelligence after the war. He told them that the Messerschmitt P-1073 jet fighter was in the planning stages and was designed to be powered by three different types of engine. One of them was said to be an "atomic engine." According to the physicist a single prototype was manufactured but then destroyed by the SS as the Allies advanced.[48]

All these and other factors point to an uncomfortable truth – that Nazi scientists were almost as far forward as the Allies in developing a successful nuclear bomb. A rambling comment by Hitler to his doctor in February 1945 mentions Germany's possession of an "atom bomb" that would change the course of the war. Finally there is the curious remark by Heisenberg after the dropping of the atomic bomb on Hiroshima. He said to his colleagues "they have it too"[49] which can only mean that the Germans also possessed a nuclear bomb.

The failure of the Germans to launch an atomic attack against America or Britain was not due to incompetence, moral considerations, anti-Nazi attitudes or even impossible technical problems. Characteristically the nuclear programme failed because of administrative chaos, an inability to grasp the importance of the project and the lack of adequate resources to hasten its development. All these problems were self-inflicted and yet again Hitler's shortcomings as a leader resulted in the defeat of his country.

The Myth of the Master Race

There were many strands to Nazi ideology but the most pervasive and destructive was its racial mythology and in particular the party's anti-Semitism. Ever since Hitler became the party leader he made "Aryan superiority" and the Jewish "conspiracy against the world" central planks of its political programme.

The notion of the supremacy of the white race was deeply embedded in Western culture and the triumph of the theory of evolution increased this belief. Darwin, Haeckel, Galton and other leading evolutionists were convinced that the white races represented a higher stage of evolution than others.

The idea of an Aryan race was based on linguistic confusion. In the late eighteenth and early nineteenth century comparative studies of languages identified a group known as Indo-European. This classification was often known by the alternative name of Aryan.

Aryan languages were regarded as superior to those of other groups including "Semitic" languages such as Hebrew and Arabic. The next step was taken by racists of confusing speakers of particular languages with ethnic groups. This elementary fallacy can be readily falsified by considering the millions of people who speak English, French or Spanish and yet have not a drop of English, French or Spanish blood.

Nevertheless the Aryan myth took hold and was particularly influential in Germany, Britain and America. It was rapidly taken up by the growing eugenics movement and Hitler and other Nazis were well aware of their ideas. When Hitler became Chancellor one of the first foreign books to be translated into German was Madison Grant's *The Passing of the Great Race*. Grant was an American eugenicist and Hitler wrote to him praising his work.

Nietzsche's idea of the übermensch – the superman – was adopted by the Nazis and given a racial interpretation that was certainly not the intention of its originator. Ideas about "selective breeding" and the "elimination of inferior types" were borrowed from the eugenicists and became part of Nazi racial thinking.

An elaborate mythology was created claiming that a lost Aryan civilization was the foundation of all subsequent human advancement. It was variously regarded as having been Atlantis, Thule – a "lost land" in the region of the North Pole – or even the entirely fictitious Atland, a nineteenth-century invention. All civilization was increasingly attributed to Germans and Himmler and Rosenberg spent large sums of money on "proving" the existence of this lost civilization.

For centuries Germany had been a geographical expression rather than a nation state. Bismarck's unification of the country led to a new sense of national pride which quickly expressed itself in extreme nationalism and imperialism. The defeat of Germany in 1918 left the nation bruised and uncertain. The Kaiser abdicated and Germany became a republic. Far left and far right groups attempted revolutions but all were suppressed.

In this climate the attraction of extreme ideas offering easy solutions and scapegoating others for the defeat of Germany grew stronger. Hitler identified the Jews as the principal cause of the nation's misfortunes and this attitude became a fixed dogma for Nazi supporters. It partly explains (in so far as *anything* can "explain") the particular cruelty with which the Jews were treated.

Anti-Semitism had a long history in Germany and Europe but German Jews had assimilated more rapidly than most European countries. There were none of the pogroms that periodically shamed Tsarist Russia. Of course there was prejudice and even petty discrimination but there was nothing in the political climate of Germany to suggest that the nation's leader would embark on a policy of genocide.

Jews had served Germany and the states that preceded it for two hundred years. They had fought and died for the nation in the First World War. The Jewish spy Julius Silber was the only effective German agent throughout that conflict. The Jewish scientist Haber had devised a way of feeding the people that enabled them to survive the Allied blockade as well as developing the poison gas used against Allied troops.

There was a willingness to serve the nation among German Jews and the overwhelming majority were assimilated and patriotic. In Germany they constituted 1% of the population but exerted an influence far in excess of their numbers. The fields of science, medicine, music, literature, cinema, media, business and the retail sector were disproportionately represented by Jews or people with Jewish ancestry. Gertrud Kolmar was one of the greatest German poets but that did not save her from being murdered in the camps in 1943.

This range of talent was readily available to Germany and even at lower levels of society they could have provided a crucial boost to manpower both in terms of military service and the German economy. Instead this important human resource was wantonly destroyed. From a moral point of view their treatment is indefensible but even on the practical level the exclusion of Jews from the life of the nation – let alone the barbarity of genocide – made no sense.

Ironically in 1932 the League of Jewish Veterans campaigned on behalf of Hitler against Hindenburg in the Presidential election that year. In spite of the Nazi leader's open anti-Semitism the group still chose to fight for his victory. Of course they had no idea that he would embark on a campaign of extermination against them but at that stage even Hitler had probably not yet decided to go down that path.

Hitler's myriad contradictions were even mirrored to an extent in his anti-Semitic policies. There were special categories of "privileged Jews" who were exempt from the worst excesses of the regime's racism. The historian Gordon Craig writes:

> *"These included war veterans, Jews over sixty-five, holders of the Iron Cross First Class, senior civil servants, Jews with foreign connections or an international reputation, and others who still had the means to bribe thepolice"*[1]

Further "exceptions" concerned the status of *Mischlings* – people with some Jewish blood in them. Their "fitness" to be considered Germans was hotly debated and while many perished or were subjected to discrimination and persecution most managed to survive. Even in the SS, whose members were required to provide a "Jew-free" family tree showing no Jewish blood and dating back to their great-grandparents, it was quickly discovered that the rule could not be enforced. Too many applicants had some Jewish ancestry and Himmler was compelled to allow them to join to swell the numbers of the SS.

Throughout his career Hitler showed a readiness to abandon his stated principles in the interests of expediency. Perhaps one of the most obvious and public examples of this came when he allowed two Jews to represent Germany in the Berlin Olympics in 1936. Another example is the Nazi-Soviet Pact and the strange treatment of Herschel Grynszpan. Grynszpan shot and killed a staff member of the German Embassy in France and although arrested and held prisoner he was allowed to live a life of luxury compared with most prisoners of the Reich and was never executed or murdered. In spite of his favourable treatment he died during the course of the war. After the fall of France the former Prime Minister Leon Blum was also a "privileged" prisoner.

Hitler continually reversed policies and although anti-Semitism was a principal plank in his platform so was anti-Communism. The treatment of the Poles is a classic example where as late as 1938 – even the beginning of 1939 - they were trusted allies yet in the space of a few months became bitter enemies.

Hitler had the popularity and the audacity to pull off such a major reversal in policy. If he had done so he would have carried the German people with him. The ideal moment for him to adopt such an about-face was in 1934 after the "Night of the Long Knives."

Most Germans disliked Röhm and regarded the SA that he led until his murder as brutal thugs. Hitler could easily have blamed him and the SA for the vitriolic anti-Semitism and at least reduced the level and intensity of it to a degree with which the Jews were familiar. They might still be "inferior" to the "Aryan" Germans but they would have been regarded as Germans and as capable as any other citizen of serving their country and rewarded for that service.

Such a course of action would have transformed the political, economic, scientific and even military situation. The pool of Jewish talent would have been available to Germany and have immensely strengthened the nation.

Hitler preferred not simply to discard the willing service of German Jews but instead to increase their persecution and eventually institute the genocide programme. Its utter immorality is beyond question but the purposelessness of it also defies belief. Resources were devoted to exterminating people that could easily have been diverted to military projects or other areas that would have benefited the nation.

Inhumane and irrational as the demonization of the Jews undoubtedly was Nazi racial mythology also targeted other groups as "subhuman." The fate of the Roma and Sinti – the gypsies – is almost impossible to understand. The Jews were at least alleged to be all-powerful and engaged in a conspiracy to rule the world and in particular to destroy the German "race." This belief was a paranoid fantasy but at least the Jews were imagined to be deadly and dangerous enemies.

It is hard to see any similar basis for the treatment of gypsies. Even Nazi propagandists could hardly present them as a threat to the survival of Germany and its people. The most they could offer was that they were "asocial" and "criminal."

Ironically the persecution of the gypsies was largely based on even more bizarre "principles" than Nazi anti-Semitism. The main architects of the campaign against Romanies were Dr Robert Ritter, the nurse Eva Justin and the anthropologists Sophie Erhardt[3] and Ruth Kellermann.[4] All four of them had the strange idea that "pure blooded gypsies" were "Aryan" and could therefore be assimilated into the German Reich. By contrast they regarded those gypsies who had intermarried into the non-Romany community as being "half breeds" and "racially degenerate." According to their theories the *Mischling* Roma and Sinti were "hereditary criminals" and "born degenerate." Quite how racially mixed Romanies could be more "criminal" or "degenerate" than those with "pure blood" was never clarified.

They conducted extensive research on the Romanies and Justin even spoke their language and used her knowledge of it to gain their trust. None of this research prevented them from declaring that they were genetically inferior, born criminals and fit only for exclusion from the Aryan community. All four of them were involved in the forced deportation of gypsies to concentration camps and Justin and Erhardt in particular visited them and were privy to the genocide against them.

In spite of the "classifications" of Romanies as being pure blooded Roma and Sinti rather than Mischlings, the Nazi death machine made no distinction between them and both groups of gypsies were indiscriminately sent to the camps and murdered. 80% of the population in Europe perished in the gypsy Holocaust.

None of the four faced justice after the war though attempts were made to put them on trial but all failed. Kellermann remained unrepentant about her activities as did Ritter who died not long after the end of the war. Justin and Erhardt attempted to plead ignorance but their visits to the camps and knowledge of the genocide programme are indisputable and their excuses implausible.

Apart from the obvious humanitarian objection to the policy it is difficult to see any purpose that it served. Gypsies were no threat to the regime – not even an imaginary one like the portrait painted of the Jews. Their murder was pointless as well as savage.

The Slavs were also identified as belonging to the "subhuman" group. Unlike anti-Semitism, "anti-Slavism" was a relatively recent prejudice, dating back only two hundred years or so.

The earliest example of anti-Slavism was formulated by the eighteenth century writer Christoph Meiners. When the Nazis came to power he was hailed as the "founder of the racial theory." Meiners believed that the differing races on earth had separate origins rather than all stemming from a common ancestor. He was also a strong supporter of slavery and the slave trade and coined the term "Caucasian" to describe the white races.

Meiners placed blacks at the bottom among human races and gradually moved upwards until he arrived at the Germans. Strangely he classified the Slavs in a bewilderingly wide category that included not simply the generally accepted ethnic groups but also Arabs, Jews and Indians. The Slavs were far below the Germans and he declared that they were so inferior that their "German masters were obliged to treat their Wendic [Slav]serfs much more harshly than other serfs, since experience showed that it was only by the strictest supervision and indispensable punishments that they could be induced to be good and avoid evil".[4]

In the mid nineteenth century Gustav Klemm declared that there were "active" and "passive" races and that the Slavs belonged to the "passive" group. The Germans of course were seen as an "active" race. Klemm's *General History of Civilization* was considered a standard work in Germany.[5]

The late nineteenth century saw another anti-Slav work that prefigured the imperial and racist fantasies of Hitler. Josef Reimer wrote *Ein Pangermanistisches Deutschland* (A Pan-German Germany) and in it demanded that the Germans should conquer the whole of Europe and Russia even including Siberia. He declared that Jews and Slavs were subhuman and called for their "exclusion from the community of procreation." His ideas were coupled with a fierce anti-capitalism, advocacy of *lebensraum* and the demand for "German socialism" to dominate the new empire. All these elements clearly foreshadow the Nazis even down to Reimer's demand for "racial commissars" to monitor breeding.[6]

Pan-Germanism in general was overwhelmingly anti-Slavic and its popularity grew from the 1890s onwards. It became increasingly strident and racist and it is impossible when studying the politics, speeches and writing of the time not to see dark shadows presaging the horrors of the Nazi era.[7]

At the end of the First World War when the Austro-Hungarian Empire broke up the Austrians wished to be united with Germany but the Allies refused to allow their union. They created the new states of Hungary, Czechoslovakia and Yugoslavia, mainly out of the former Austrian territories and their very existence infuriated Austrians and Germans particularly those who subscribed to the Pan-German view of the world.

Hitler's Austrian origins played a part in predisposing him towards accepting these ideas and he grew up when the Habsburgs ruled over Hungarians, Czechs, Slovaks and Poles and the German element of the empire was very much dominant. By contrast the Germans only ruled over Polish subjects so there was less resentment between the nationalities, His Austrian roots undoubtedly explain why he was more concerned about the Sudeten Germans, whose fate was of little concern to most Germans, whereas he waited until the last year of peace before raising the issue of Danzig which was of passionate concern to them. Even as Chancellor of Germany Hitler still tended to see the world from an Austrian viewpoint.

In *Mein Kampf* Hitler was openly contemptuous about the Slavs and saw them as fit only for slavery or extermination. His "Eastern policy," though primarily focused on the Soviet Union, also included the other Slavonic people who were referred to in Party literature as *slawische Untermenschen* – Slav subhumans.[8]

This racial arrogance was not simply immoral but had practical downsides for the regime. When the Germans invaded Russia they were welcomed as liberators from Stalin's tyranny but it swiftly became clear that the Nazis saw them as inferior and fit only for exploitation or death. The result was to turn them against Germany while if they had adopted a different policy – as Rosenberg vainly urged upon the regime – the result might have been entirely different.

Nazi ideology and Hitler's prejudices were time and again directly responsible for the failure of his regime. With greater subtlety of approach it is beyond doubt that the results of the war could easily have led to German victory. Yet again an entirely avoidable defeat was snatched from the jaws of possible triumph.

The Brutal Dictatorship

The four years of the First World War saw death and destruction on an unprecedented scale. After Germany's defeat the country was plunged into political and economic chaos that was not overcome for some years. In this climate of perpetual fear, resentment and poverty many people turned to extreme politics. Far left and far right paramilitary groups clashed with each other and roamed the streets like private armies.[1]

It was five years after the end of the First World War that the last of several abortive revolutions occurred. Hitler's failed *putsch* in Munich marked the end of attempts to seize power by force. This did not lead to any decrease in political violence as the Nazis, Communists and Social Democrats all possessed paramilitary contingents that operated virtually beyond control. All three fought one another on a regular basis and the result was a number of fatalities and substantial damage to property.[2]

In addition to the militia groups directly associated with political parties there were also unattached bodies of ex-soldiers who tended to be extreme nationalists and many of whom subsequently joined the Nazis. The *Freikorps* (Free Corps) and *Stahlhelm* (Steel Helmets) were the most active and numerous of these movements.[3]

The violence continued unabated and individual cases became notorious. Horst Wessel was an unsavoury character who belonged to the SA and was murdered by the Communists. Goebbels' skilful propaganda turned him into a martyr.

A series of political assassinations also rocked the country with Eisner, the first leader of "Soviet Bavaria" being murdered as he was about to tender his resignation. Other notable assassinations included Matthias Erzberger (the man who signed the Armistice in 1918)[4] and

Walther Rathenau the Foreign Minister.[5] Eisner was a hero to the young Hitler who had fought on his behalf during the brief period of Soviet Bavaria. He attended Eisner's funeral and one of his first acts as Chancellor was to arrest the man who had murdered him.

Hitler condemned these assassinations and believed that individual terrorism achieved nothing and only revolution could bring about the transformation he sought. He remained committed to seizing power by violence until the failure of the Munich putsch and his subsequent imprisonment but opposed "propaganda by the deed."

After his release from prison Hitler abandoned the idea of revolution but continued to use the SA to intimidate opposition and create a climate of fear. His Brownshirts not only fought political opponents in bloody clashes but also engaged in assaults on Jews. There is no doubt that the thuggish behaviour of the SA alienated many Germans and partly explains the lack of widespread support for the Nazis between 1924 and 1928.[6]

When the world economy crashed in 1929 Germany suffered more severely than most countries. Its unemployment rate rose to 30% and in the changed economic situation support for the Nazis and Communists increased dramatically. Both groups began to consider the possibility of power and the result was an escalation in violence.[7]

One of the slogans of the SA was "possession of the streets is the key to power in the state" and the continual street fighting between them and their opponents brought increasing terror to the towns and cities of Germany. Communists began shooting police officers as well as clashing with Nazis and the violence on both sides ratcheted up an already tense situation.

Hitler skilfully employed both the use of violence and its threat to promote his views. He knew he had to tread carefully with the SA and his intention was to frighten conservatives into supporting the Nazis through fear of an imminent revolution. Many, perhaps most, SA leaders hoped for a revolutionary outcome and Hitler employed this desire to motivate them into following him and terrifying the establishment.[8]

Hitler directly encouraged the SA in their campaign of terror but equally Stalin directed the Communists to employ violence and murder. Walter Ulbricht – later the leader of East Germany – was directly responsible for the shooting of police officers on instructions from Moscow.[9]

In a brief flurry of revolt in 1930–1931 the SA overreached themselves. They had always been more radical than many of the party leaders and increasingly demanded that the socialist aspects of the programme should be implemented if the Nazis formed a government. Their leader in Berlin, Walter Stennes, was bitterly opposed to the policy of gaining power by constitutional means which he saw as impossible under the Weimar electoral system. He had lost faith in Hitler's revolutionary credentials and christened him "Adolf Legalité" as a derisory comment on his commitment to achieving power through the ballot box.

Goebbels, as Nazi leader in Berlin, was initially asked to quell the revolt but partly as a result of his insensitive treatment of the rebels the Berlin branch mutinied and vandalized the Party's headquarters in the city. Hitler went to Berlin and managed to calm down the situation but decided to recall Röhm and place him in charge of the SA.[10]

In the short term this move was successful and Hitler's authority over the turbulent Brownshirts was restored. The Nazis fared well in the 1930 elections and were now the second largest party in the Reichstag. Violence on the streets did not appear to have affected the party's share of the vote. This was equally true of the Communists who also increased their votes.

In the longer term Röhm's return stored up problems for the future. He was genuinely committed to the revolutionary and socialist parts of the National Socialist agenda and also harboured the aim of creating a "people's army" in which the SA would be the dominant element. This ambition inevitably led him into conflict with the Army and is the principal reason why he was murdered during the "Night of the Long Knives."

It is easy to condemn Hitler for his cynical use of violence but from 1918 onwards Germany had been one of the most violent countries in

Europe. It had seen abortive revolutions, political assassinations, the murder of police officers, turmoil on the streets and a high crime rate. Hitler and the Communists saw the economic crash as an opportunity to gain power and both used violence as a tool to further their ends.

Whether or not the Nazis could have come to power without the omnipresent background of violence is difficult to determine. The evidence is contradictory and while there is no doubt that in the early years of the movement it assisted their cause it is at least arguable that the 1930 elections offered an opportunity for Hitler to abandon its use as a weapon. It is probable that such a course of action would have aided rather than reduced the appeal of his movement. There is no doubt that the murder of a Communist by the SA in front of his family shocked the nation. Hitler's open defence of their actions cost him support in the 1932 elections when the Nazi vote fell by 5%. The German people were certainly attracted by his promises to end unemployment and restore national pride through military strength. Defending murder by thugs under his control was a different matter and made many of them decide to vote against the Nazis. Perhaps Hitler believed that without at least the implicit threat of revolution he would never be able to come to power. Given the state of German politics at the time he was probably mistaken in that belief.

Once he became Chancellor Hitler continued to use violence and terror to silence opposition. Initially he allowed the SA to run riot and a string of murders, brutal beatings, vandalism and robbery ensued. Before long it was found necessary to "control" this unbridled aggression and the result was the institution of concentration camps. Initially the camps held political prisoners but as the regime's anti-Semitism grew Jews also found themselves incarcerated in them.[11]

Another example of "controlled" violence was the Gestapo. During the first year of its existence it was subject to the relatively lax direction of Goering but in 1934 was transferred to Himmler's expanding empire. It became notorious for its routine use of brutality and torture and struck fear into the heart of German dissidents.[12]

Was this degree of repression necessary and in particular would it have been possible for Hitler to have survived without the barbarity of the camps and Gestapo? There is little doubt that Hitler could have retained power without the excessive brutality that quickly came to characterize the regime. Even Germans who were sympathetic to the Nazis were at least uneasy about the Gestapo and the camps. It would have been possible for him to continue with his popular policies of economic growth and rearmament and it is doubtful that he would have faced much serious opposition on either of those issues. Perhaps the Communists and Social Democrats might have continued to stir up trouble but the chances are that they would have failed to dislodge him from power. He could almost certainly have continued in office even in a democratic regime without the camps and the Gestapo to enforce obedience to his will.

By contrast the murders of Röhm and other political opponents in 1934 were broadly welcomed by public opinion in spite of their violence. The SA was deeply unpopular with most German people and following the murders street violence in Germany ended for the next four years.

In 1938 the assassination of a member of staff at the German Embassy in Paris led to the appalling *Kristallnacht* – Night of Glass – pogrom. Jewish shops and businesses were looted, vandalized and destroyed. Many Jews were murdered and a far greater number arrested and placed in concentration camps.

Kristallnacht led to widespread revulsion abroad and was not simply brutal but unnecessary on any rational analysis. Once more Hitler's obsessional anti-Semitism led him to make a major error of judgement. The pogrom played a considerable part in hardening British and French attitudes against Hitler and also led Roosevelt to become concerned. It even sickened Rudolf Hess and was a disastrous mistake on every level.

The outbreak of war saw an escalation of violence both on the field of battle where numerous atrocities were committed and with the beginning of the extermination programme. It was so brutal that the violence turned potential supporters into enemies. The genocide programme wasted resources both human and otherwise. It is impossible to rationalize the policies even in practical terms and it was of course morally indefensible.

Perhaps the sad truth is that Hitler was incapable of reining in the brutality and in particular abandoning the policy of mass murder. For most of his life he lived in an atmosphere of violence and his lack of empathy made him unable to recognize or recoil from the suffering and death he needlessly inflicted upon millions. Yet again his personal defects contributed directly to his ultimate failure.

Endgame

There were several key moments in the war which in hindsight at least were clear turning points. The failure to capture Allied troops at Dunkirk, the loss of the Battle of Britain, the inability to grasp the crucial importance of the Mediterranean theatre and the insistence on maintaining the offensive against Russia when retrenchment might have led to a different result are clear examples of a pattern of errors.

1943 was the year when it became clear to everyone except Hitler that the war was irretrievably lost. The Allies were victorious on every front from the Battle of the Atlantic to Germany's defeat in North Africa. Italy was on the brink of collapse and the last German offensive in Kursk failed.

At this point several options remained open to Germany. The most promising initiative came from Stalin who offered to conclude a separate peace. Naturally his terms would have been harsh but if the Germans had been able to concentrate on defending against Britain and America without facing a Soviet advance from the east it might have been possible to salvage the situation in the West.[1] Ribbentrop and others urged Hitler to accept Stalin's offer but he refused. After the agreement at Yalta between Roosevelt, Churchill and Stalin to insist on the unconditional surrender of Germany the chance was lost.

Hitler would certainly have found conceding defeat in Russia a bitter pill to swallow but it would have resulted in less devastation for Germany and enabled him to transfer precious resources in men, equipment and materials to the western front. There are two questions around this intriguing possibility. One is whether Hitler's reputation and authority could have survived such a capitulation. Would army officers, Goering or (most likely of all) Himmler have mounted a coup to unseat him? The other is the possible reaction of the British and Americans. Would they have been so enraged by Stalin's treachery that, for example, they launched D-Day prematurely and with less success?

By 1943 Hitler had become so detached from reality that he was probably incapable of weighing up the advantages and disadvantages of such a course of action. It would have compelled him to at least reduce the scale of his extermination programme which became a greater and more overriding obsession with him as the military situation worsened. Most of all his vanity and egotism would not allow him to relinquish his grasp on the territory he had acquired.

Having refused the opportunity, Hitler found himself facing the unpalatable truth that an offensive strategy no longer made sense. The only sane course of action was to concentrate his resources. On the one hand he needed to hold off the forthcoming Russian advance while preparing to meet the Allied invasion of France. After the loss of the Battle of the Atlantic it was inevitable that the British and Americans would attack and this meant defending strong but narrow frontiers against the invasion.

It would have been better to abandon Italy to the Allies rather than squander lives, equipment and resources in a doomed attempt to turn back the invaders. Hitler's best paratroopers were lost in this futile and bloody campaign.

His best tank regiments were far from the scene of action when the Allies landed in Normandy. The Luftwaffe wasted its diminishing strength in peripheral theatres of war rather than focusing on strategically important areas.

Most costly of all was Hitler's persistent refusal to retreat and regroup rather than holding fast and squandering lives needlessly. He could not accept that in his situation it was essential to trade space for time and fight a defensive war rather than launching futile attacks against superior Allied forces.

There were still opportunities for limited success. The D-Day landings were bungled and nearly failed and if Rommel's advice had been followed the liberation of France would at the very least have been delayed considerably. The Allies might have been compelled to abandon the idea of an invasion via northern France and instead advanced from Italy through the south of the country.

Equally a resolute defence could have held Soviet forces at bay much longer. In a war of attrition time is as important as space and concentrating effort on key positions rather than dispersal of resources would have been the best strategy.

Hitler's policy of divide and rule worked against the defence of Normandy. Authority was split between Rundstedt, the SS divisions that answered to Himmler and the anti-aircraft paratroops and anti-tank divisions that answered to Goering. Guderian also had effective responsibility for tank divisions. Military reserves were under the command of Fromm and in Paris the military governor von Stülpnagel was in charge. The only theoretical commander of these disparate units was Hitler who was of course far removed from the conflict. Even Ribbentrop enjoyed a certain amount of control over the troops. This degree of dispersal of command hampered every aspect of the defence of France.

The result of this chaotic structure was laid bare immediately. Rommel demanded tanks and armoured vehicles at the front to repel the invaders as they landed on the beaches. Rundstedt and Guderian preferred to hold them back further inland. Hindsight quickly showed that Rommel was correct. If his advice had been taken it might have led to the D-Day landings failing as disastrously as the attempted raid on Dieppe two years previously.

An additional problem was the poor quality of many German troops. Some divisions in France were not only below strength but overwhelmingly made up of old, ill or young men. Transport was in short supply and armament provision inadequate. Infantry units increasingly contained large numbers of Russians, Romanians, Hungarians, Dutch, Yugoslavs, Czechs and Poles rather than Germans. There were 60,000 soldiers from the Soviet Union alone serving in France.[2]

The initial mistakes made in response to the D-Day landings were compounded by Hitler's refusal to countenance retreat. Rommel and Rundstedt pleaded with Hitler to be allowed to withdraw behind the Seine but he refused. The Falaise gap doomed thousands of German troops as a result.

The Battle of the Bulge might have been a brilliant idea earlier in the war but at this stage it simply accelerated defeat. Hitler's continuing failure to accept that sometimes retreat was necessary cost him dearly. He lost 120,000 men in the battle and accomplished nothing.[3]

By January 1945 the Russians advanced westwards and captured Warsaw.[4] Still refusing to face reality Hitler raged against the armed forces and the German people. He still hoped vainly for a split between the British and Americans. Though there were tensions between them – particularly in the case of Eisenhower and Montgomery who disliked each other intensely – there was never any prospect of the Alliance fracturing with victory clearly within their grasp.

Goebbels knew in 1943 that the war was lost though like Hitler he clung to the mirage of hope. He succeeded in raising a million extra men to fight but they were nearly all too old or too young to be of military assistance.

His most desperate plan was the creation of the *Werwolf* (Werewolves) who were intended to be a German guerrilla movement slowing down the Allied advance and committing acts of sabotage. They began operating in 1944 and continued until at least 1946 and possibly as late as 1949.[5] They were few in numbers but skilful propaganda by Goebbels magnified the threat they posed. In reality they were relatively ineffective and some of their actions were counterproductive. An attack by them in Czechoslovakia led to the death of 27 people but the new Communist-dominated government reacted with harsh reprisals and ultimately the expulsion of the Sudeten Germans. Many of their victims were Germans who were prepared to work for the Allies rather than fight on in a hopeless struggle. The plan was born out of desperation and the *Werwolf* increasingly turned to criminality rather than guerrilla warfare. Their resistance fizzled out and accomplished nothing significant.[6]

While Goebbels pinned his hopes on raw conscripts and the *Werwolf* plan the Russian advance continued. As they occupied Auschwitz the world became fully aware of the horrors within the camp and across the Reich.[7]

The Russian advance led to a refugee crisis as Germans ran from the Red Army. Thousands of people fled before the invaders and straggled into Germany cold, hungry, dispirited and fearful. Local leaders forced to receive the refugees were anything but welcoming and saw them as a further drain on already limited resources. This human tide also created a crisis in fuel supplies and overwhelmed the transport network.

Characteristically Hitler compounded the problem by deporting some of the refugees to Czechoslovakia. An official explained his thinking as being "if the Czechs see the misery, they will not be tilted into a resistance movement." It had the opposite effect as when the Czechs saw German weakness they immediately began planning to defeat the Nazis.[8]

Even in the West the Allies were beginning to liberate the camps. The horrors were similar but at least the treatment of the inmates by the British and Americans was better. In the East many survivors were raped by the Red Army while in the West at least they escaped that fate.[9]

Guards who had not been able to escape attempted to present themselves as inmates or as forced labour but the inmates quickly denounced them to the troops and they were arrested.[10]

A further bizarre mistake came on 24 January when Hitler appointed Himmler as commander of German troops in East Prussia and Silesia. Himmler's headquarters was equipped with an out of date map, no transport or supply network and no signalling facility.[11]

The result was chaos as Himmler ordered a futile attack that was easily repulsed. Reinforcements were sent to his post but came under heavy fire from the Soviets and promptly retreated.

On 22 January the Russians captured the mines and steelworks of Silesia. This dramatically affected Germany's productive capacity and led Speer to conclude that the war could not continue much longer. The German army in the area was forced to retreat westwards.

Hitler's response to the news that Soviet forces were coming closer to Berlin was to create a new "division." This consisted of Hitler Youth members on bicycles carrying the *Panzerfaust* anti-tank weapon. It demonstrated another instance of his detachment from reality.

Of his Ministers only Speer and Goebbels seemed able to face up to the disastrous situation. Hitler, Himmler and Goering were all in denial and even Bormann appeared more concerned with the succession to Hitler than with the utter ruin his country faced.[12]

The course of the war in both east and west continued to unravel for German forces. Military commanders began to complain about the impossible orders they were given. The retreat continued as the Allies pressed onwards.

In February 1945 Speer despaired and finally recognized that Hitler was the problem. He concluded that the only possible solution was assassination. He knew that Hitler regularly met in the Chancellery with Goebbels, Bormann, Ley and Burgdorf and Speer knew that the bunker was ventilated by an air-conditioning facility. His plan was to pump poison gas inside and kill the leadership in a matter of minutes. Speer visited the Chancellery prior to putting his plan into action and discovered that a chimney had been built around the funnel to protect it and his plan would no longer succeed.[13]

By March Speer told Hitler openly that the war was lost and that from now on the country should concentrate on salvaging as much as possible for the future. Hitler reacted furiously and not only accused Speer of defeatism and treason but declared that if he failed then Germany must also be destroyed.

Meanwhile Himmler had lost faith in Hitler and was cautiously considering a coup to remove his leader from power. By now he was the only person in Germany with sufficient military resources to carry out such an audacious plan. Himmler remained blind to the possibility that Hitler might regard his machinations as treason which of course he did.

Inch by inch the Allied advance continued relentlessly. Hitler remained defiant and persisted in imagining that the dwindling number of German troops could somehow miraculously turn the tide.[14]

He continued to move increasingly phantom armies on the map room in his bunker. Still unwilling to countenance defeat, he began consulting horoscopes and reading Carlyle's biography of Frederick the Great. The death of Roosevelt filled him with sudden hope but Truman had no intention of withdrawing America from the war. As the Russians closed in on Berlin it slowly dawned on Hitler that all was lost.

On hearing the news of Mussolini's death Hitler finally conceded defeat. The once proud empire which he had boasted would last a thousand years had crumbled away. Hitler had risen to supreme power and ruled over most of Europe but now had to face reality for the first time in years. Characteristically he took no responsibility or blame for the unfolding catastrophe. Years of uncritical adulation made the destruction of his dream almost unbearable.[2]

Hitler was urged to make his escape as Russian forces closed in on Berlin. He offered Eva Braun the opportunity to leave but she refused. Hitler spoke scornfully of the Kaiser's flight at the end of the First World War which he regarded as abandoning his country. He would rather die in the ruins than try to escape. Eva begged him to let her share his fate and the two of them married at last. Her brief happiness was ended with their mutual suicide.

Hitler named Goebbels as his successor as Chancellor and appointed Dönitz as President. Shortly after his appointment Goebbels and his family committed suicide and Dönitz became the effective holder of both positions. A few days later he surrendered to the Allies.

It is characteristic of Hitler's shambolic government that it collapsed in chaos and ruin. There was not only no orderly transition of power but his numerous errors over the twelve years of his rule meant that there was scarcely a country for his successors to rebuild.

Hitler's anti-Semitism facilitated the creation of the state of Israel while his anti-Communism resulted in its control of Eastern Europe and the eastern half of Germany for over forty years. The man who once enjoyed spectacular power and success saw his "career" end in abject failure and achieving the exact opposite of his intentions.

Notes

Introduction

1. August Kubizek, Young Hitler, The Story of Our Friendship, Allen Wingate, 1954.

The Dark Dreamer

1. Krysia Diver, "Journal reveals Hitler's dysfunctional family," *The Guardian*, 4 August 2005.
2. Adolf Hitler, Hitler's Secret Conversations, Signet, 1961.
3. Testimony of Helene Hanfstaengl. A relative, Johanna Mayrhofer, confirms the story of the family's unsuccessful attempt to apprentice Hitler to a bakery.
4. Helene Hanfstaengl's testimony.
5. Heinz A Heinz, Germany's Hitler, Hurst and Blackett, 1934. Also the testimony of Josef Keplinger.
6. Hitler's Secret Conversations.
7. Testimony of Paula Hitler.
8. Kubizek, op. cit.
9. Ibid.
10. Ibid.
11. Hitler, Mein Kampf, Hijezglobal 2017. (First published 1924–1928).
12. Kubizek, op. cit.
13. Testimony of Karl Honisch.
14. Kubizek, op. cit.
15. Reinhold Hanisch, "I Was Hitler's Buddy," *New Republic*, April 5, 12, 19, 1939.
16. Ibid.
17. Wilfrid Daim, Der Mann, die Hitler die Ideen gab, Dietz Verlag, 1993. The standard work on Adolf Lanz and his influence on Hitler.

18. Hanisch, op. cit.
19. Testimony of Karl Honisch.
20. Ibid.
21. Heinz, op. cit.
22. Ibid.
23. Wilfred Owen, Futility.
24. Hitler, Mein Kampf.
25. Ernst Deurlein, Hitler, List, 1969.
26. Rudolph Binion, Hitler Among the Germans, Elsevier, 1976.
27. Dr. Eduard Bloch, "My Patient Hitler," *Colliers,* 15 & 22 May 1941.
28. Bernhard Grau, Kurt Eisner: 1867-1919, Beck, 2017.
29. Volker Ullrich, Hitler: Ascent 1889-1939, Vintage, 2016.
30. Ian Kershaw, Hitler: 1889-1936 Hubris, Penguin, 2001.
31. Richard Dove, He Was a German: A Biography of Ernst Toller, London Libris, 1990.
32. Paul Frölich, Eugen Leviné, Vereinigunginternationaler Verlagsanstalten, 1922.
33. Kershaw, op. cit.
34. Balthasar Brandmayer, Zwei Meldegänger, Bruckmühl, 1932.
35. Karl Alexander von Müller, Mars und Venus, Klipper Verlag, 1954.
36. Captain Karl Mayr, "I Was Hitler's Boss," *Current History*, November 1941.
37. Otto Strasser, Mein Kampf, Heinrich Heine, 1969.
38. Ernst Deurlein, Der Aufstieg der NSDAP in Augenzeugenberichten. Karl Rauch Verlag, 1969.
39. Charles Hamilton, Leaders & Personalities of the Third Reich, Vol. 1, James Bender Publishing, 1984.
40. Strasser, op. cit.
41. Philipp Bouhler, Kampf um Deutschland, Eher, 1938.
42. Randal Bytwerk, Julius Streicher: Nazi Editor of the Notorious Anti-Semitic Newspaper *Der Sturmer*, Cooper Square Press, 2001.
43. Hitler, Secret Conversations.
44. Ronald Smelser, Robert Ley: Hitler's Labour Front Leader, Berg, 1988.
45. Hans Frank, Im Angesicht des Galgens, Beck, 1953.

46. Jochen von Lang, The Secretary, Martin Bormann: The Man Who Manipulated Hitler, Random House, 1979.

Unstable State

1. Martin Broszat, The Hitler State, Longmans, 1981.
2. Karl Dietrich Bracher, The German Dictatorship, Penguin, 1970.
3. Claudia Koonz, The Nazi Conscience, Belknap Press, 2003.
4. Ronald Lewin, Hitler's Mistakes, Morrow, 1984.
5. C Essner and E Conte, ""Fernehe", "Leichentrauung" und "Totenscheidung". Metamorphosen des Eherechts im Dritten Reich," *Vierteljahreshefte für Zeitgeschichte* 44(2) (1996).
6. Stephen H Roberts, The House that Hitler Built. Methuen, 1937.
7. Alan E Steinweis, Law in Nazi Germany: The Ideology, Opportunism and the Perversion of Justice, Berghahn Books, 2013.
8. Ibid.
9. Anthony McElligott and Tim Kerk, Working Towards the Führer: Essays in Honour of Sir Ian Kershaw, Manchester University Press, 2003.
10. Albert Speer, Inside the Third Reich, Weidenfeld and Nicolson, 1970.
11. David Schoenbaum, Hitler's Social Revolution: Class and Status in Nazi Germany 1933-1939, Norton, 1997.
12. Ibid.
13. Ibid.
14. Jane Caplan, Government without Administration: State and Civil Service in Weimar and Nazi Germany, Clarendon Press, 1989.
15. *Deutsche Mitteilungen,* No 48, 2 June 1938.
16. *Frankfurter Zeitung,* 1 March 1936.
17. Ibid.
18. Schoenbaum, op. cit.
19. Lewin, op. cit.
20. James Webb, The Flight from Reason, Macdonald, 1971.
21. Edvard Westermarck, Ethical Relativity, Littlefield, Adams, 1932.
22. James Webb, The Occult Establishment: The Dawn of the New Age and the Occult Establishment, Open Court, 1984.
23. Ibid.
24. Hitler speaking to the foreign press, November 1938.

25. Richard Grunberger, A Social History of the Third Reich, Weidenfeld and Nicolson, 2005.
26. Ibid.
27. Lewin, op. cit.
28. Martin Bormann, public statement in 1941. Citied in William L. Shirer; The Rise and Fall of the Third Reich, Secker & Warburg, 1960.
29. Goebbels, cited in Kershaw, op. cit.
30. https://www.vatican.va/content/pius-xi/de/encyclicals/documents/hf_p-xi_enc_14031937_mit-brennender-sorge.html
31. Friedrich Heer, God's First Love: Christians and Jews Over Two Thousand Years, Phoenix Giants, 1999.
32. Guenter Lewy, The Catholic Church and Nazi Germany, Da Capo Press, 2000.
33. Ibid.
34. John Cornwell, Hitler's Pope: The Secret History of Pius XII, Penguin, 1999.
35. Dietrich Bronder, Bevor Hitler Kam, Eine Historische Studie, Marva 2, 1975.
36. Ibid.
37. Lewy, op. cit.
38. Max Geiger, Kirche, Staat, Widerstand: Historische Durchgänge und aktuelle Standortbestimmung (Theologische Studien; 124), Theologische Verlag, 1978.
39. Bronder, op. cit.
40. Richard Gutteridge, Open Thy Mouth for the Dumb: German Evangelical Church and the Jews, 1879-1950, Wiley-Blackwell, 1976.
41. H D Leuner, When Compassion Was A Crime, Oswald Wolff, 1964.
42. Lewy, op. cit.
43. Ibid.
44. Martin Niemöller, Here Stand I, Willett, Clark & Co, 1937.
45. Kirklicher Jahrbuch für die Evangelische Kirche in Deutschland, 1933-1944, C Bertelsmanns Verlag, 1948.
46. Ernst Klee, 'Euthanasie" im NS-Staat. Die Vernichtung lebensunwerten Lebens". S. Fischer Verlag, 1983.

47. Hans-Walter Schmuhl, Rassenhygiene, Nationalsozialismus, Euthanasie: Von der Verhütung zur Vernichtung "lebensunwerten Lebens", 1890–1945, Vandenhoeck & Ruprecht, 1983.
48. Beth A Griech-Polelle, Bishop von Galen: German Catholicism and National Socialism, Yale University Press, 2002.
49. Bernhard Vollmer, Volksopposition im Polizeistaat, Stuttgart Deutsche Verlags-Anstalt 1957.
50. Lewy, op. cit.
51. Heinrich Hermelink, Kircheim Kampf, Wunderlich, 1950.
52. Ibid. Other sources worth reading on the Nazi-Christian conflict are: Richard Steigmann-Gall, Christianity and the Nazi Movement: A Response, Journal of Contemporary History, 42 (2), 2007.
    Derek Hastings, Catholicism and the Roots of Nazism: Religious Identity and National Socialism, Oxford University Press, 2012.
    I Hexham, The mythic foundation of National Socialism and the contemporary claim that the Nazis were Christians, *Koers, 76(1)* 2011.

The Twists and Turns of Foreign Policy

1. Anthony Nicholls and Eric Matthias (eds.), German Democracy and the Triumph of Hitler, Allen & Unwin, 1971.
2. F L Carsten, The Reichswehr and Politics: 1918-1933, University of California Press, 1974.
3. Gerald Freund, Unholy Alliance: Russian-German Relations from the Treaty of Brest-Litovsk to the Treaty of Berlin, Gerald Freund, 1957.
4. Carol Fink, Axel Frohn, and Jurgen Heideking, eds., Genoa, Rapallo, and European Reconstruction in 1922, Cambridge University Press. 1991.
5. G Post, The Civil-Military Fabric of Weimar Foreign Policy, Princeton University Press, 1973.
6. Carsten, op.cit.
7. Piotr Stefan Wandycz, The twilight of French eastern alliances. 1926–1936. French-Czecho-Slovak-Polish relations from Locarno to the remilitarization of the Rheinland, Princeton University Press, 1988.
8. C A Macartney and A W Palmer, Independent Eastern Europe, Macmillan, 1962.
9. Anthony Polonsky, The Little Dictators, Routledge & Kegan Paul, 1975.

10. E H Carr, A History of Soviet Russia: The Interregnum, 1923-4, Penguin, 1960.
11. Wandycz, op. cit.
12. William Evans Scott, Alliance Against Hitler: The Origins of the Franco-Soviet Pact, Forgotten Books, 2018.
13. Gerhard L Weinberg, The Foreign Policy of Hitler's Germany: Diplomatic Revolution in Europe, 1933-36, Chicago University Press, 1970.
14. Scott, op. cit.
15. Luigi Villari, Italian Foreign Policy Under Mussolini, Devin-Adair, 1956.
16. David Nicolle, The Italian Invasion of Abyssinia 1935-36, Osprey Publishing, 1997.
17. Weinberg, op. cit.
18. Richard Overy, The Origins of the Second World War, Routledge, 2022.
19. Michael Brecher, The World of Protracted Conflicts, Lexington Books, 2016.
20. Aristotle A Kallis, Fascist Ideology: Territory and Expansionism in Italy and Germany, 1922-1945, Routledge, 2000.
21. J T Emmerson, The Rhineland Crisis 7 March 1936: A Study in Multinational Diplomacy, Iowa State University Press, 1977.
22. Judith M Hughes, To the Maginot Line: The Politics of French Military Preparation in the 1920's, Harvard University Press, 2006.
23. Weinberg, op. cit.
24. Hugh Thomas, The Spanish Civil War, Eyre and Spottiswoode, 1961.
25. Anthony Beevor, The Battle for Spain: The Spanish Civil War 1936-1939, Penguin, 2006.
26. Thomas, op. cit.
27. Ibid.
28. George Orwell, Homage to Catalonia, Penguin, 2003, (First edition 1938).
29. Ian Westwell, Condor Legion: The Wehrmacht's Training Ground. Spearhead. Vol. 15, Ian Allan, 2004.
30. Norman Ridley, Hitler's Air War in Spain: The Rise of the Luftwaffe, Pen & Sword, 2022.
31. Peter Padfield, War Beneath The Sea, Lume Books, 2020.

32. Weinberg, op. cit.
33. A J P Taylor, The Origins of the Second World War, Penguin, 1964.
34. Documents on German Foreign Policy 1918-1945, US Government Printing Office, 1949-1983.
35. *Morning Telegraph*, January 5, 1938.
36. Franz von Papen, Memoirs, *Dutton,* 1953.
37. Schuschnigg's highly partisan version is given in: Kurt von Schuschnigg, Austrian Requiem, Putnam, 1946. More measured appraisals of Schuschnigg are given in John Gunther, Inside Europe, Harper, 1936 and a review of Schuschnigg's book by Kurt List in *Commentary*, October 1947. List's review is particularly damning showing how entirely self-serving and evasive Schuschnigg's account was and how little difference there was between his own political position and that of Hitler.
38. Documents on German Foreign Policy, op. cit.
39. Galeazzo Ciano, Ciano's Diary: 1937-1943, Phoenix, 2002.
40. Taylor, op. cit.
41. Jiirgen Gehl, Austria, Germany and the Anschluss, 1931-1938, Oxford University Press, 1963.
42. Johann Wolfgang Bruegel, Czechoslovakia Before Munich: The German Minority Problem and British Appeasement Policy, Cambridge University Press, 1973.
43. Soviet Peace Efforts on the Eve of World War II, Novosti Press Agency, 1973.
44. Esmonde M Robertson, Hitler's Pre-War Policy and Military Plans, 1933-9, Citadel Press, 1967.
45. Ministere des Affaires Etrangers, Documents Diplomatiques Français 1932-1939, 2E Séries (1936-1939), Imprimerie Nationale, 1963.
46. Jozef Lipski, Diplomat in Berlin 1933-1939: Papers and Memoirs of Jozef Lipski, Ambassador of Poland, Columbia, 1968.
47. James Franklin Baker, The United States and the Czechoslovak Crisis 1938-1939, Tulane University, 1971.
48. Ibid.
49. Ronald L Smelser, The Sudeten Problem, 1933-1938, Wesleyan University Press, 1975.

50. Ministerstwo Spraw Zagranicznych, Official documents concerning Polish-German and Polish-Soviet relations, 1933-1939, Hutchinson, 1940.
51. Anna M Cienciala, Poland and the Western Powers 1938-1939, University of Toronto Press, 1968.
52. William Carr, Arms, Autarky and Aggression: Study in German Foreign Policy 1933-9, Hodder Arnold, 1972.
53. Documents on German Foreign Policy, op. cit.
54. Ciano's Diary, op. cit.
55. Documents on German Foreign Policy, op. cit.
56. Joseph Goebbels, The Goebbels Diaries, op. cit.

Economy in Crisis

1. Frieda Wunderlich, Farm Labour in Germany 1810-1945, Princeton University Press, 1969.
2. Schoenbaum, op. cit.
3. Wunderlich, op. cit.
4. *Völkischer Beobachter*, 4 July 1933.
5. *Völkischer Beobachter*, 23 June 1933.
6. *Völkischer Beobachter,* 20 July 1934.
7. *Völkischer Beobachter,* 14 November 1935.
8. Heinrich Uhlig, Die Warenhäuser im Dritten Reich, VS Verlag für Sozialwissenschaften, 1956.
9. Craig, op. cit.
10. Williamson Murray, Strategy for Defeat: The Luftwaffe 1933-1945, Eagle Editions, 2000.
11. Schoenbaum, op. cit.
12. Burton Klein, Germany's Economic Preparations for War, Harvard University Press, 1959.
13. Roberts, op. cit.
14. Germa Bel, "Against the Mainstream: Nazi Privatization in 1930s Germany," *Economic History Review*, 63 (1), 2010.
15. Peter Hayes, "Corporate Freedom of Action in Nazi Germany," Lecture at the German Historical Institute, October 16, 2008.
16. Ibid. See also: Hans-Joachim Braun, The German Economy in the Twentieth Century, Routledge, 2010.

17. Caleb Yoken, Cartel Practices and Policies in the World War II Era, Honor Thesis, Union College, 2019.
18. Nick James Mariani, The International Ramifications of Germany's Cartel System, 1920-1955, Thesis, University of the Pacific, 1956.
19. *Völkischer Beobachter,* 5 April 1933.
20. Schoenbaum, op. cit.
21. Avraham Barkai, Nazi Economics: Ideology, Theory and Policy, Yale University, 1990.
22. Ibid.
23. Rebecca Harvey, "Hitler's Hit List: Co-operatives and Co-operators During War Time," https://www.thenews.coop/98666/sector/hitlers-hit-list-co-operatives-co-operators-wartime/, 22 October 2015;
    See also Co-operative Union Ltd, Co-operation under the Nazis, Co-operative Union Ltd., 1939 and Jana Stoklasa, The Transformation of German Consumer Cooperatives after the Second World War, Acta Universitatis Carolinae Studia Territoralia 1, 2020.
24. Schoenbaum, op. cit.
25. Robert Koehl, "Feudal Aspects of National Socialism," *American Political Science Review*, 54 (4), December 1960.
26. Adalheid von Saldern, "The Old Mittelstand 1890-1939: How Backward Were The Artisans?" *Central European History*, 25 (1), March 1992.
27. Frederick L Mcitrick, "An Unexpected Path to Modernization; The Case of German Artisans During the Second World War," *Contemporary European History,* 5 (3), November 1996.
28. Richard Overy, The Nazi Economic Recovery 1932-38, Cambridge University Press, 1996.
29. Schoenbaum, op. cit.
30. Louis P Lochner, Tycoons and Tyrant: German Industry from Hitler to Adenauer, Henry Regnery, 1954.
31. Roberts, op. cit.
32. Ibid.
33. T. W. Mason, Social Policy in the Third Reich: The Working Class and the "National Community", 1918-1939, Berg Publishers, 1993.
34. On the women who combined feminism with Nazism, see:

Lydia Gottschewski, Männerbund und Frauenfrage: Die Frau im Neuen Staat, J F Lehmanns Verlag, 1934;
Guida Diehl, Die deutsche Frau und die Nationalsozialismus, Neulandverlag, 1932;
Silvia Lange, Protestantische Frauen auf dem Weg in den Nationalsozialismus. Guida Diehls Neulandbewegung 1916 bis 1935, Metzler, 1998;
Sophie Rogge- Börner, Zurück zum Mutterrecht? Studie zu Professor Ernst Bergmann: 'Erkenntnisgeist und Muttergeist, Adolf Klein, 1932; Von nordischen Frauen, Königen und Bauern - Erzählung aus der Überlieferung der Sagas, Union Deutsche Verlagsgesellschaft, 1935; Die innere Gestalt der nordischen Frau. Eine seelenkundliche Untersuchung, Bott, 1938.
Sadly, there is very little on them in English. Some books have sections on women in the Third Reich and a few have been written on that subject but they are either focused on the social aspects of women's lives or are too slanted in a particular direction. The best available sources in English are:
Clifford Kirkpatrick, Nazi Germany: Its Women and Family Life, AMS Press, 1979;
Claudia Koontz, Mothers in the Fatherland, St Martin's, 1987;
Jill Stephenson, Women in Nazi Society, Croom Helm, 1975; The Nazi Organisation of Women, Croom Helm, 1981.

35. Leila J Rupp, Mobilizing Women for War: German and American Propaganda, 1939-1945, Princeton University, 2016.
36. Two of the best books on the forced labour programmes are:
Alexander von Plato, Almut Leh and Christoph Thonfeld (editors), Hitler's Slaves: Life Stories in Forced Labourers in Nazi-Occupied Europe, Berghahn Books, 2010;
Memorial International, Ost: An Untold History of Nazi Germany's Forced Labour Camps, Granta, 2021.

From the Blitzkrieg to the Battle of the Bulge

1. This will be examined in the section on the war at sea.
2. The Battle of Britain will be examined in the section on war in the air.
3. Christopher Buckley, Greece and Crete 1941, P Efstathiadis& Sons, 1984.

4. Gerhard Weinberg, The World at War, Cambridge University Press, 2005.
5. Leni Riefenstahl, Leni Riefenstahl: A Memoir, Picador, 1987.
6. Anthony Beevor, Crete: The Battle and the Resistance, *Westview Press,* 1994.
7. Jozo Tomasevich, “Yugoslavia during the Second World War,” in Wayne B Vucinich (ed.), Contemporary Yugoslavia: Twenty Years of Socialist Experiment, University of California Press, 1969.
8. Franz Halder, Kriegstagebuch: Tägliche Aufzeichnungen des Chefs des Generalstaabs des Heeres, 1939-1945, Kohlhammer, 1962-1964.
9. Albert Seaton, The German Army, 1933-1945, Weidenfeld & Nicholson, 1982.
10. On the North African campaign, see: George Forty, The Armies of Rommel, Arms and Armour Press, 1998;
    Rick Anderson, An Army at Dawn: The War in North Africa, 1942-1943, Abacus, 2004;
    Thomas L Jentz, Tank Combat in North Africa: The Opening Rounds, Operation Sonneblume, Brevity, Skorpion and Battleaxe, February 1941, Schiffer Publishing, 1998;
    Ronald Lewin, Rommel as Military Commander, B & N Books, 1998.
11. Sir Basil Liddell Hart, History of the Second World War, Cassell, 1970.

The Fall of Eagles

1. Murray, op. cit.
2. David Irving, The Rise and Fall of the Luftwaffe, Weidenfeld & Nicolson, 1977.
3. Bartolomiej Nelcarz and Robert Peczkowski, White Eagles: The Aircraft, Men and Operations of the Polish Air Force 1918-1939, Hikoki Publications, 2002.
4. Denis Richards, The Fight At Odds: Royal Air Force 1939-1945, HMSO, 1953.
5. Henrik O Lunde, Hitler’s Pre-emptive War: The Battle for Norway, 1940, Casemate Publishers, 2009.
6. Jerry Murland, Allied Air Operations 1939-1940: The War Over France and the Low Countries, Pen and Sword, 2022.

7. Ryan K Noppen, Holland 1940: The Luftwaffe's first setback in the West, Osprey, 2021.
8. Murray, op. cit.
9. Brian Cull, Twelve Days in May, Grub Street Publishing, 1999.
10. Norman Franks, The Air Battle of Dunkirk, William Kimber, 1983.
11. Robert Jackson, Air War Over France, May-June 1940, Allan, 1974. For a general overview of the whole aerial campaign in the West in 1940, see: Edward Hooton, Luftwaffe at War: Blitzkrieg in the West, Midland Publishing, 2007.
12. Murray, op. cit.
13. Len Deighton, Fighter: The True Story of the Battle of Britain, Jonathan Cape, 1977.
14. Stephen Bungay, The Most Dangerous Enemy: A History of the Battle of Britain, Aurum Press, 2002.
15. Ibid.
16. Ibid.
17. Wilhelm Keitel, Memoirs, William Kimber, 1965.
18. Francis K Mason, Battle Over Britain: A History of the German Air Assaults on Great Britain, 1917-18 and July-December 1940, and of the Development of Britain's Air Defences Between the World Wars, McWhirter Twins, 1969.
19. Winston S Churchill, The Second World War: Their Finest Hour, volume 2, Reprint Society, 1956.
20. Peter Stansky, The First Day of the Blitz, Yale University Press, 2007.
21. Hooton, op. cit.
22. John Ray, The Night Blitz: 1940-1941, Cassell Military, 1996.
23. Angus Calder, The Myth of the Blitz, *Pimlico.* 2003.
24. Christopher Shores, Giovanni Massimello, Russell Guest, A History of the Mediterranean Air War, 1940-1945, Volume One: North Africa, Grubstreet Publishing, 2012.
25. Ibid.
26. Keitel, op. cit.
27. Alan Clark, Barbarossa: The Russian-German Conflict 1941-45, Weidenfeld and Nicolson, 1995.
28. Ibid.

29. Anthony Beevor, Stalingrad, Penguin, 2007.
30. Ibid.
31. Ibid.
32. Murray, op. cit.
33. Mike Guardia, Air War on the Eastern Front, Casemate Publishers, 2020.
34. Irving, op. cit.
35. Ernle Bradford, Siege: Malta 1940-1943, Pen & Sword, 2003.
36. Anthony Rogers, Battle Over Malta: Aircraft Losses and Crash Sites, 1940-42, Sutton, 2000.
37. James Holland, Fortress Malta: An Island Under Siege, 1940-1943, Miramax Books, 2003.
38. George Hogan, Malta: The Triumphant Years, 1940-1943, Robert Hale, 1978.
39. Holland, op. cit.
40. Rogers, op. cit.
41. Bradford, op. cit.
42. Murray, op. cit.
43. Ibid.
44. Horst Boog, Gerhard Krebs and Detlef Vogel, Germany and the Second World War: The Strategic Air War in Europe and the War in the West and East Asia, 1943-1944/45, Clarendon Press, 2001.
45. Cargill Hall, Case Studies In Strategic Bombardment, Air Force History and Museums Program, 1998.
46. Boog et al, op. cit.
47. Murray, op. cit.

Sea Wolves at Bay

1. Kev Darling, Fleet Air Arm Carrier War: The History of British Naval Aviation, Pen and Sword, 2009.
2. David K Brown, Atlantic Escorts: Ships, Weapons and Tactics in World War II, Navy Institute Press, 2007.
3. Michael FitzGerald, Hitler's War Beneath the Waves: The Menace of the U-boats, Arcturus Publishing, 2020.
4. Ibid.
5. Ibid.

6. Ibid.
7. Harold Busch, Jagd im Atlantik, C. Bertelsmann, 1943.
8. FitzGerald, War Beneath the Waves.
9. Gordon Smith, The War at Sea: Royal and Dominion Navy Actions in World War 2, Ian Allan, 1989.

Failures of Procurement

1. Manfred Griehl and Joachim Dressel, Heinkel He 177-277-274, Airlife Publishing, 1998.
2. Lewin, op, cit.; also Murray, op. cit. On the aircraft itself, the standard work is:
   George Punka, Messerschmitt Me 210/410 in action, Carrollton TX: Squadron/Signal Publications, 1994.
3. Lewin, op. cit.
4. Dönitz op. cit.
5. Ibid.
6. "Science: Sun Gun," *Time Magazine*, 9 July 1945; also "The German Space Mirror," *Life Magazine*, 23 July 1945.
7. Peter Thompson, The V-3 Pump Gun, ISO Publications, 1999.
8. Thomas L Jentz and Hilary Louis Doyle, Panzer Tracts 6-3 Schwerer Panzerkampfwagen Maus and E-20 Development and Production from 1942 to 1945, Panzer Tracts Publications, 2008.
9. David Porter, Hitler's Secret Weapons, 1933-1945: The Essential Facts and Figures for Germany's Secret Weapon Programme, Amber Books, 2000.
10. Otto Carius, Tigers in the Mud, Stackpole Books, 2003.
11. Walter Dornberger, V-2, Hurst and Blackett, 1954.
12. FitzGerald, Hitler's Secret Weapons of Mass Destruction.

Unintelligent Intelligence

1. Lewin, op. cit.
2. Jak P. Mallmann-Showell, German Naval Codebreakers, Naval Institute Press, 2003.
3. Ibid.
4. FitzGerald, Hitler's War Beneath the Waves.

5. Michael FitzGerald, Unsolved Mysteries of World War Two, Arcturus, 2019.
6. Ibid.
7. Lewin, op. cit.
8. Ibid.
9. Walter Schellenberg, The Schellenberg Memoirs, Andre Deutsch, 1956.
10. FitzGerald, War Beneath the Waves.
11. Ibid.
12. Lewin, op. cit.
13. FitzGerald, Unsolved Mysteries.
14. United States War Department General Staff, German Military Intelligence, 1939-1945, University Publications of America, 1984.
15. Anthony C Brown, Bodyguard of Lies: The Extraordinary True Story Behind D-Day, Harper and Row, 1975.
16. Greg Annussek, Hitler's Raid to Save Mussolini, Da Capo, 2005.
17. Anthony Beevor, Arnhem: The Battle for the Bridges, 1944, Penguin, 2018.

The War of the Boffins

1. Margit Szöllösi-Janze (Editor), Science in the Third Reich: v. 13 (German Historical Perspectives), Berg, 2001.
2. Ibid.
3. Monika Renneberg and Mark Walker (Editors), Science, Technology, and National Socialism: 23-24 (Econometric Society Monographs,) Cambridge University Press, 1993.
4. Otto Hahn, My Life, Herder and Herder, 1970.
5. Terry Gander, German 88: The Most Famous Gun of the Second World War, Pen and Sword Books, 2009.
6. David Irving, The Virus House, William Kimber, 1967.
7. Kristie Macrakis, "Harnessing science for Hitler," *Nature*, vol.25, 23 October 2003.
8. Albert Speer, Inside the Third Reich, Weidenfeld and Nicholson, 1979.
9. Chris Bowlby, "The Chemist of Life and Death," *BBC Radio 4*, 12 April 2011.
10. Alan Beyerchen, Scientists under Hitler: Politics and the physics community in the Third Reich, Yale University, 1977.

11. Thomas Powers, Heisenberg's War: The Secret History of the German Bomb, Knopf, 1993.
12. Sarah Everts, 'Chemistry in Nazi Germany,' *Chemical and Engineering News*, 16 September 2013, vol. 91, issue 37.
13. Ibid.
14. Helmut Maier, Chemiker im "Dritten Reich" – Die Deutsche Chemische Gesellschaft und der Verein Deutscher Chemiker im NS-Herrschaftsapparat, Wiley-VCH, 2015.
15. Ute Deichmann, Biologists under Hitler, Harvard University Press, 1999.
16. "German Ersatz," *The Literary Digest*, 9 October 1937.
17. Raymond G. Stokes, "The Oil Industry in Nazi Germany, 1936-1945" *Business History Review*, 59. Summer 1985.
18. Anthony N Stranges, Germany's Synthetic Fuel Industry 1927-1945, Paper 80a, presented at the AIChE Spring National Meeting, 2003.
19. Anthony N Stranges, "Friedrich Bergius and the Rise of the German Synthetic Fuel Industry," *Isis, The History of Science Society*, 75 (4), 1984.
20. Stranges, Germany's Synthetic Fuel Industry.
21. Major Gene Gurney, The War in the Air: A Pictorial History of World War II Air Forces in Combat, Bonanza Books, 1962.
22. José Gotovitch, La grève des 100,000 (Mai 1941), *Jours de Guerre*, No 7, 1992.
23. https://www.cheminsdememoire.gouv.fr/fr/la-greve-des-mineurs-du-nord-pas-de-calais/
24. Frank A Howard, Buna Rubber: The Birth of an Industry, D. van Nostrand Company, Inc., 1947.
25. Adam Tooze, The Wages of Destruction: The Making and Breaking of the Nazi Economy, Penguin, 2007.
26. Andrew Gregorovich, "World War II in Ukraine: *Ostarbeiter* Slave Labor," Forum *Ukrainian Review*, No 92, Spring 1995.
27. Shawn P Keller, Turning Point: A History of German Petroleum in World War II and its lessons for the role of oil in modern air warfare, Air Command and Staff College Air University, 2011.
28. Alison Abbott and Quirin Schiermeier, "Deep roots of Nazi science revealed," *Nature*, volume 407, 19 October 2000.
29. Deichmann, op. cit.

Also Katrin Weigmann, "In the name of science: The role of biologists in Nazi atrocities: lessons for today's scientists," *Embo Reports,* Volume 2, Issue 10, 1 October 2001.

30. Abbott and Schiermeier, art. cit.
31. Ibid. See also:
George J. Stein, "Biological Science and the Roots of Nazism," *American Scientist*, Vol. 76, No. 1, January-February 1988.
32. See:
Professor Volker Roelcke, "Nazi medicine and research on human beings," *The Lancet*, December 2004;
George J Annas, The Nazi Doctors and the Nuremberg Code: Human Rights in Human Experimentation, Oxford University Press, 1992;
Naomi Baumslag, Murderous Medicine: Nazi Doctors, Human Experimentation, and Typhus, Praeger, 2005.
33. Klaus Hentschel, The Mental Aftermath: On the Mentality of German Physicists 1945-1949, Oxford University Press, 2007.
34. John C Guse, "Nazi Technical Thought Revisited," *History and Technology*, volume 26, issue 1, 19 March 2010. See also:
Jeffrey Herf, Reactionary Modernism: Technology, culture, and politics in Weimar and the Third Reich, Cambridge University Press, 1985.
35. Bundesarchiv-Militärchiv, Freiburg, RW 19/2178.
36. James Holland, The War in the West: A New History, Volume 2: The Allies Fight Back 1941-1943, Corgi, 2017.
37. Peter Kirchberg, Heeresmotorisierung, Schell-Programm und die Auto-Union. In: Peter Kirchberg (Editor): Vom Horch zum Munga: Militärfahrzeuge der Auto-Union. Delius Klasing, 2010.
38. Neil Gregor, Daimler-Benz in the Third Reich, Yale University Press, 1998.
39. Jeremy Bernstein, Hitler's Uranium Club: The Secret Recordings at Farm Hall, Copernicus, 2001.
40. Klaus Hentschel and Ann M Hentschel, Chemistry, Physics and National Socialism: An Anthology of Primary Sources, Birkenau, 1996.
41. Dan van der Vat, The Good Nazi: The Life and Lies of Albert Speer, Houghton Mifflin, 1997.
42. Ray Mears, The Real Heroes of Telemark: The True Story of the Secret Mission to Stop Hitler's Atomic Bomb, Hodder and Stoughton, 2003.

43. Irving, The Virus House.
44. Ibid.
45. Allan Hall, "Did Hitler Have A Nuclear Bomb?" *Mail Online*, 23 February 2017; file APO 696 in the National Archives, Washington.
46. Klaus Wiegrefe, "How Close Was Hitler to the A-Bomb?" *Der Spiegel*, 14 March 2005.
47. Mark Walker, Nazi Science: Myth, Truth and the German Atomic Bomb, Basic Books, 2001.
48. Joseph P Farrell, The SS Brotherhood of the Bell: The Nazi's Incredible Secret Technology, Adventures Unlimited, 2006.
49. Bernstein, op. cit.

The Myth of the Master Race

1. Gordon Craig, Germany 1866-1945, Oxford University Press, 1978.
2. Sophie Erhardt, Bruno Kurt Schultz: Wandtafeln für den rassen- und vererbungskundlichen Unterricht, J. F. Lehmann, 1940.
3. Paul Behrens, Prozeß, Vollzigeuner und Mischlinger, Die ehemalige Rassenforscherin Ruth Kellermann verteidigt ihren Ruf, *Die Zeit,* 7 February 1986, No 7.
4. Meiners, quoted in: Leon Poliakov, The Aryan Myth: A History of Racist and Nationalist Ideas in Europe, New American Library, 1974.
5. Poliakov, op, cit.
6. George W Stocking (ed), Volksgeist as Method and Ethic: Essays on Boasian Ethnography and the German Anthropological Tradition, Vol. 8, University of Wisconsin Press, 1996.
7. Sylvia Jaworska, "Anti-Slavic imagery in German radical nationalist discourse at the turn of the twentieth century: A prelude to Nazi ideology?" *Patterns of Prejudice*. 45 (5), 2011.
   See also:
   Yura Konstantinova, The Slavic and Anti-Slavic Idea in the Context of the East-West Dilemma. Slovenians, Bulgarians, and Greeks in Late 19th and Early 20th Centuries, Études balkaniques, (3), 2015;
   Christian Promitzer, "The South Slavs in the Austrian Imagination: Serbs and Slovenes in the Changing View from German Nationalism to

National Socialism". Creating the Other: Ethnic Conflict & Nationalism in Habsburg Central Europe, Berghahn Books, 2003.

8. John Connelly, "Nazis and Slavs: From Racial Theory to Racist Practice". *Central European History*. 32 (1), 1989.
   See also: John Connelly, "Gypsies, Homosexuals, and Slavs". The Oxford Handbook of Holocaust Studies, Oxford University Press, 2010; Donald Kenrick and Grattan Puxon, Gypsies Under the Swastika, University of Hertfordshire Press, 2009.

The Brutal Dictatorship

1. Dirk Schumann, Political Violence in the Weimar Republic, 1918-1933: Fight for the Streets and Fear of Civil War, Berghahn, 2009.
2. Timothy S Brown, Weimar Radicals: Nazis and Communists Between Authenticity and Performance, Berghahn, 2009. See also:
   Enzo Traverso, The Origins of Nazi Violence, The New Press, 2003.
3. Robert G L Waite, Vanguard of Nazism: The Free Corps Movement in Post-War Germany, 1918-1923, W W Norton, 1969;
   See also:
   Rolf Volker, Der Stahlhelm: Bund der Frontsoldaten 1918-1935, Berghahn, 1966.
4. Klaus Epstein, Matthias Erzberger and the dilemma of German democracy, Princeton University Press, 1959.
5. Harry Kessler, Walther Rathenau: His Life and Work, Fertig, 1969.
6. Richard Bessel, Political Violence and The Rise of Nazism: The Storm Troopers in Eastern Germany, 1925–1934, Yale University Press, 1984.
   It is however fair to say that while public support for the Nazis remained low its membership grew slowly but steadily particularly in northern Germany where Gregor Strasser was highly successful in attracting working class members to abandon the Social Democrats and Communists and join the Nazis.
7. Brown, op. cit.
8. David Littlejohn, The Sturmabteiling: Hitler's Stormtroopers 1921-1945, Osprey Publishing, 1990.
9. Brown, op. cit.

10. The revolt in Berlin became known as the "Stennes *putsch*" as Stennes was the ringleader. The best account of it is found in Ernst Hanfstaengl, Hitler: The Missing Years, Eyre and Spottiswoode, 1957.
11. Friedrich Schlotterbeck, The Darker the Night, the Brighter the Stars: A German Worker Remembers, 1933-1945, Left Book Club, 1947.
12. Edward Crankshaw, Gestapo: Instrument of Tyranny, Viking Press, 1956.

Endgame

1. Peter Kleist, European Tragedy, Gibbs and Phillips, 1965.
2. Matthew Cooper, The German Army 1933-1945, Macdonald and Jane's, 1978.
3. Lewin, op. cit.
4. Anthony Beevor, Berlin: The Downfall 1945, Penguin, 2002.
5. Alexander Perry Biddiscombe, Werwolf: The History of the National Socialist Guerrilla Movement, 1944-1946, University of Toronto Press, 1998;
   Alexander Perry Biddiscombe, The Last Nazis: SS Werewolf Guerrilla Resistance in Europe 1944-1947, Tempus, 2004.
6. Ibid.
7. Beevor, Berlin.
8. Ibid.
9. Ibid
10. Frank E Manuel, Scenes from the End: The Last Days of World War II, Profile Books, 2000.
11. Beevor, Berlin
11. Hugh Trevor-Roper, The Last Days of Hitler, Macmillan, 1947.
12. Ibid.
13. Ibid.

Index